AF412188

Bounded rationality in decision-making

Manchester University Press

Issues in Environmental Politics

series editors Mikael Skou Andersen and Duncan Liefferink

At the start of the twenty-first century, the environment has come to stay as a central concern of global politics. This series takes key problems for environmental policy and examines the politics behind their cause and possible resolution. Accessible and eloquent, the books make available for a non-specialist readership some of the best research and most provocative thinking on humanity's relationship with the planet.

already published in the series

Science and politics in international environmental regimes *Steinar Andresen, Tora Skodvin, Arild Underdal and Jørgen Wettestad*

Animals, politics and morality (2nd edn) *Robert Garner*

Implementing international environmental agreements in Russia *Geir Hønneland and Anne-Kristin Jørgensen*

Implementing EU environmental policy *Christoph Knill and Andrea Lenschow (eds)*

Environmental politics in the European Union: policy-making, implementation and patterns of multi-level governanc *Christoph Knill and Duncan Liefferink*

Sweden and ecological governance: straddling the fence *Lennart J. Lundqvist*

Global warming policy in Japan and Britain: interactions between institutions and issue characteristics *Shizuka Oshitani*

North Sea cooperation: linking international and domestic pollution control *Jon Birger Skjærseth*

Climate change and the oil industry: common problem, varying strategies *Jon Birger Skjærseth and Tora Skodvin*

Environmental policy-making in Britain, Germany and the European Union *Rüdiger K. W. Wurzel*

Bounded rationality in decision-making

How cognitive shortcuts and professional values may interfere with market-based regulation

Helle Nielsen

Manchester University Press

Manchester and New York

distributed in the United States exclusively by Palgrave Macmillan

Published by Manchester University Press
Oxford Road, Manchester M13 9NR, UK
and Room 400, 175 Fifth Avenue, New York, NY 10010, USA
www.manchesteruniversitypress.co.uk

Distributed in the United States exclusively by
Palgrave Macmillan, 175 Fifth Avenue, New York,
NY 10010, USA

Distributed in Canada exclusively by
UBC Press, University of British Columbia, 2029 West Mall,
Vancouver, BC, Canada V6T 1Z2

British Library Cataloguing-in-Publication Data
A catalogue record for this book is available from the British Library

Library of Congress Cataloging-in-Publication Data applied for

ISBN   978 0 7190 7992 4 *hardback*

First published 2009

18 17 16 15 14 13 12 11 10 09   10 9 8 7 6 5 4 3 2 1

Typeset
by Action Publishing Technology Ltd, Gloucester
Printed in Great Britain
by CPI Antony Rowe, Chippenham, Wiltshire

Contents

List of tables

List of boxes

List of figures

Preface

This book builds on research I did for my PhD dissertation. For this work I benefited from the help of many. First and foremost, I want to thank my supervisors Professor Jens Blom-Hansen, Department of Political Science, University of Aarhus, and Professor Mikael Skou Andersen, The National Environmental Research Institute of Denmark (NERI). Their knowledgeable suggestions, challenging questions, and general encouragement provided a most inspiring setting.

The farmers who agreed to participate in interviews and who shared their time, their knowledge and their experiences, also uniquely contributed to this study for which I am grateful.

My colleagues at the Department of Political Science, University of Aarhus, and NERI's Department of Policy Analysis provided insightful comments on various parts of the project, which contributed to improvements along the way. Thank you in particular to Søren Serritzlew for his accessible explanations on finer statistical points, to Vibeke Lehmann Nielsen for ongoing inspiration through direct input and by her good example, and to Jytte Seested for many stimulating discussions about economic theory and methodology. I appreciate also the help of Gitte Blicher-Mathiesen of NERI's Department of Freshwater Ecology, in providing data and in answering my many, many questions.

During the course of my PhD study I spent a semester at Duke University; I would like to thank Professors Mike Munger and John Aldrich of the Political Science Department for providing this opportunity and for their theoretical and methodological input.

I am also most grateful to Carey Smith, NERI, for her careful reading of and perceptive linguistic suggestions for multiple versions of this manuscript.

Lastly, I want to thank Paul, Emmy, and Tobias for great companionship, patience, and for helping me to keep things in perspective.

1

Introduction

The rational paradigm has long dominated the theoretical discourse within the economic and political sciences. Fundamentally, the paradigm revolves around the notion that individual and collective actors strive to maximise their self-interest and, furthermore, that actors are able to assess which among several alternatives best serves their interest. This model of man mimics the consumer, and self-interest is typically viewed in material terms, but in the political realm this could also extend to power. In any case, the rational actor is generally described by the abstraction 'economic man', reflecting both the economic and the material aspects of the model.

This book examines rational models of behaviour as well as their implications for incentive-based public policies, particularly in the field of environmental regulation.

Incentive-based public reforms

The paradigm has provided the behavioural template for the public reforms which have swept the western world over the last decades, encouraged by the the Organisation for Economic Co-operation and Development (OECD), the EU, and other agenda-setting international institutions (Hood, 1991; OECD, 1995; Kettl, 1997; Christensen, 2003a: 98–99). These reforms, often referred to under the well-known, but ill-defined heading of New Public Management, aim to increase the use of markets and economic incentives in the public sector and in public policy. They have addressed the internal workings of government, provision of public services, and regulation in the environmental as well as other arenas.

Market-based reforms of the public sector were introduced in response to concern about growing and inefficient government, poor public management, and unresponsive public institutions (Hood, 1991; Walsh, 1995; Bruun, 1997; Boyne *et al.*, 2003). Public choice theory explains these problems with a lack of competition in public service provision, as public organisations are not pressured by the threat of economic failure to produce efficiently and in accordance with the preferences of users. Furthermore, public sector managers and employees whose employment is by tenure and therefore does not depend on performance, have little incentive to pay attention to costs or to the users of public services (Christensen, 2003c). A less benign version of the theory, perhaps, holds that public employees actively pursue independent policy preferences and work less efficiently than possible; they shirk (Niskanen, 1971; Wilson, 1989: 155; see also Christensen, 2003a). These explanations rest on the notion of information asymmetry, which derives from principal-agency theory and holds that public employees have an informational advantage over their political principals, because their work cannot easily be observed or measured. When the principal does not know the true cost of services, they may not be able to determine the optimal level of public production.

Public choice reform prescription follows two overall tracks. One has been to increase the competitive pressure on the public sector by creating market-like structures in public service provision. The idea is that competition increases transparency with regard to cost and quality of public services and thus ensures both efficient production and responsiveness. This has involved outright privatisation, tendering procedures where private companies bid on public service contracts in competition with public agencies or in private competition alone, and internal markets which seek to create markets inside the confines of public service provision by separating the purchase and provision of services and setting up contractual relationships (Walsh, 1995; Boyne *et al.*, 2003). Many countries have sought to create consumer-like markets by opening up free choice among service providers, for instance in elderly care, healthcare, and education (Pallesen, 1997; Boyne *et al.*, 2003).

The other track has focused on changing the incentive structures facing public managers and employees so as to align the goals and interests of individual employees or organisational units with the overall goals of the organisations within which they operate (Walsh, 1995; Boyne *et al.*, 2003). Incentives may also be designed so as to reward economic efficiency. Contract management within public administration is expected to ensure a higher degree of goal achievement, because the pay or career opportunities of managers are tied to achievement of specified goals reflecting the political will or the purpose of the organisation (Gregory and Christensen, 2004). Contract management also typically includes regular performance reviews, as the contract specifies achievement targets. These measures are often aimed at executives or other managers (Gregory and Christensen, 2004, describe the development of such reforms in New Zealand and Denmark). But new merit-based wage systems aiming at the lower echelons of government have also been introduced to spur public employees to give their best. At least two-thirds of the OECD countries have introduced some measure of performance-related pay, and this includes also increasing the use of pay incentives to non-managerial staff (OECD, 2005).

In the area of environmental regulation, which is of particular interest here, policy-makers have also increasingly favoured market-based policy instruments over command-and-control regulation (Tietenberg, 1990; Sprenger, 2000; OECD, 2001). Recent and noteworthy examples are the European Union's adoption of an emission trading scheme for CO_2 emissions (European Environment Agency (EEA), 2005; Speck *et al.*, 2006) and the EU directive on taxation of energy products in 2003). The United States have used emission trading systems for some years (Miljøstyrelsen, 2004; EEA, 2005). Environmental taxes have been widely adopted, but new instruments such as the above-mentioned tradable emission schemes, as well as liability and compensation, are also increasingly used (EEA, 2005). Furthermore, economic instruments are applied to a diverse range of policy areas, from air and water pollution to waste reduction, traffic congestion in large cities, and cost recovery for environmental services (EEA, 2005). In Denmark, a 2003 government policy paper entitled 'A Green Market Economy' mapped out a strategy for how to achieve a market-based and cost-effective environmental policy (Miljøstyrelsen, 2003). Current waste strategy, for instance, puts increased focus on economic instruments (Speck *et al.*, 2006: 72). These efforts follow on the heels of environmental tax reform of the 1990s when revenues from environmental taxes to some degree replaced income tax revenues (EEA, 2002). Hence, Denmark employs a wide range of environmental tax schemes, including fuel taxes, waste taxes, and a pesticide tax. Emission trading schemes for greenhouse gases and subsidies for renewable energies are other market-based instruments in place in Denmark (see Speck *et al.*, 2006, for a complete overview of the use of economic instruments in environmental policy in the Nordic and Baltic countries).

Such environmental policy has been driven by the objective of designing policy that is both effective and cost-effective. Economic policy instruments affect the relative prices of raw materials, pollution, or products. Such price changes provide incentives for producers or consumers to change behaviour, whether towards reduction of emissions or other pollutants, consumption of more environmentally sustainable goods, reduction of waste or reduced consumption of natural resources. Thus, market-based policy instruments are promoted as *effective* regulatory tools. But economic policy instruments are also considered the most *cost-effective* form of regulation, as the price signals ensure that pollution abatement will be undertaken by those businesses or business sectors that can cut pollution at the lowest price per unit of reduction (OECD, 2001: 22). Finally, neo-classical environmental theory holds that market-based instruments are also a *welfare-efficient* means for achieving environmental policy objectives, as the level of pollution and consumption will reflect the social preferences of a society; the price mechanism creates an equilibrium between the preferences for consumption and pollution, on the one hand, and for a cleaner environment and preservation of natural resources, on the other (Kolstad, 2000; Sprenger, 2000).

Evolving directly from neo-classical economic models, the prescription to apply economic instruments to environmental regulation thus rests on assumptions that actors are *motivated* by economic incentives, are *aware* of prices, and are able to transform accurately the new prices into optimal decisions. It assumes also that businesses are cost minimisers (Tietenberg, 1990: 21).

Assumptions: are they accurate?

Despite its dominant status, the rational actor model has been widely criticised for resting on an unrealistic model of political or economic actors. Areas of contention involve the nature of motivation and the nature of decision-making processes (see, for instance, Green and Shapiro, 1994; Simon, 1997; Shafir and LeBoeuf, 2002).

As for motivation or goals, critics take issue with the common assumption that actors' preferences reflect unadulterated self-interest. In a widely cited article, Nobel Prize laureate Amartya Sen forcefully argued that actors in single-minded pursuit of self-interest were indeed 'rational fools'. To make it in the long run, Sen pointed out, actors must be able to take into account the social context in which their actions play out (Sen, 1977). Socio-biologists, likewise, have shown that a capacity for cooperation and consideration of others would confer evolutionary advantages on the human species. This means, they argue, that a strict assumption of self-interest is unjustified (see, for instance, Trivers, 1971; Cosmides and Tooby, 1994). While these scholars primarily question the scientific foundations of the rational choice assumption of self-interest, other researchers have demonstrated in empirical settings other-regarding or non-selfish behaviour (see, for instance, Monroe *et al.*, 1991). Hence, critics argue that the self-interest assumption ignores the social context in which decision-making takes place *and* that it simplifies human motivation without due cause.

Criticism of the rational model of *choice* comes particularly from the cognitive sciences. Researchers within the cognitive tradition argue that humans cannot process information as assumed in the rational model (Simon, 1955, 1990, 1997; Jones, 1999, 2001; Kahneman, 2002). Research has uncovered several features of human cognition that do not comport with the rational model of 'economic man'. Firstly, humans cannot easily process large amounts of information, which impedes the kind of comprehensive calculation of optimal choice implicit in the rational actor model. Secondly, humans cannot make the smooth trade-offs among different goals also embedded in the rational consumer model and, thirdly, humans consistently misapply probability principles which means that neo-classical models of decision-making under uncertainty lack empirical foundation. Because neo-classical theory rests on a methodological assumption that all collective outcomes must be explained with reference to the choices of individuals, these criticisms gain importance for economic models of collective decision-makers as well, including business organisations.

Other theoretical schools question even the notion that actors would necessarily be guided in their endeavours by an instrumentalist logic. Hence, cultural theory tends to see rationality as a cultural construct rather than as a universal standard of behaviour (Wildawsky, 1994). Sociological institutionalists argue that humans are guided by their sense of identity and norms of appropriate behaviour, implying that behaviour is based on rules rather than on strategic calculations of utility (March and Olsen, 1995; Madsen and Ölander, 2001).

Assumptions: do they matter?

Proponents of the rational actor model tend not to refute the behavioural criticism of rational choice assumptions as much as ignore it. They argue that the criticism is irrelevant.

Firstly, rational choice theorists, spearheaded by Milton Friedman, contend that the accuracy of the model's assumptions matters less than the theory's ability to generate testable predictions about behaviour (Friedman, 1953). Friedman argues that any theory must abstract features from reality in order to be useful for empirical prediction. The point is not so much whether people actually are selfish or go through the entire reasoning process, but rather whether they choose *as if* they are selfish optimisers (Friedman, 1953). As long as the predictions that follow from these assumptions hold, or at least hold often enough, the theory is validated. In Friedman's perspective, the rational model should be judged on its parsimony and fruitfulness, which denotes the ability of a simple theory to generate widely applicable and empirically testable predictions.

Secondly, economists often argue that deviations from rational behaviour at the level of the individual matter little for aggregate models of behaviour. More or less random deviations will cancel each other out at the aggregate level; individuals learn over time, or non-optimising actors will be driven out of business by optimising ones (see Conlisk, 1996; McFadden, 1999; and Fehr and Tyran, 2005 for (critical) reviews).

These arguments meet with disagreement, particularly from researchers within behavioural traditions who maintain that theories explain little without an empirically based model of human behaviour (Simon, 1997). They suggest incorporating the knowledge generated in cognitive laboratories and other spheres of the behavioural sciences (McFadden, 1999; Jones, 2001).

> Chicago man [homo oeconomicus espoused by the Chicago School] is an endangered species. Behavioural decision theory has accumulated experimental evidence that severely restricts his maximum range, and he is not safe even in markets for concrete goods where he was once thought secure ... The challenge is to evolve Chicago man in the direction of K-T man [Kahneman and Tversky], adopting those features needed to correct Chicago man's most glaring deficiencies as a behavioural model, and modifying economic analysis so that it applies to this hybrid. (McFadden, 1999: 99)

Likewise, Ostrom (1998) argues that inclusion of knowledge from the socio-biological sciences would vastly improve rational choice theory on collective action, so central to political science. Others suggest more generally that models of economic and political behaviour as a matter of principle should build on insights from other more basic sciences about the constitution of human beings, such as biology or evolutionary science (see, for instance, Jones, 1999, 2001; Ostrom, 1998).

This discussion regarding the veracity of the assumptions embedded in the rational model is essentially epistemological, turning on the proper way to develop explanatory theory. Yet, from a public policy point of view, it is of independent interest whether the predictions of the theory hold, i.e. whether market- and incentive-based reforms deliver on their promises.

Do predictions hold? Empirical evidence on market-based reforms

Evaluations of market-based reforms of public management and environmental policy often suffer from a lack of comprehensive and accurate data, particularly data that allow for before-and-after comparison of relevant indicators (OECD, 2001; Boyne *et al.*, 2003: 38–45). Furthermore, it is difficult to identify the impact of reforms separately from the impact of other variables.

Due to such problems of inadequate data, Boyne (2003) draws only tentative conclusions in his reviews of the effectiveness of New Public Management reforms in the healthcare, education, and public housing sectors of the UK. But the overall finding is that reforms have had limited impact; although this is due partly to the fact that policies only partially reflect public choice principles (Boyne *et al.*, 2003: 157). Increased competition has led to small or moderate efficiency gains in the education and healthcare sectors, but not in the housing sector; while the evidence indicates that public institutions have become somewhat more responsive to their users. Christensen (2003b), based on a comprehensive review of the literature, concludes that hierarchical government models and competitive market models perform equally well on the criteria of responsiveness and economic efficiency. While the choice of service provider ensures some responsiveness in the market-based model, this has proven to work primarily for the well-educated (Christensen, 2003b: 190). On the other hand, politicians ensure responsiveness to the public as a whole in the hierarchical model (Christensen, 2003b: 186). Likewise, evidence from healthcare reforms indicates that political control over resource allocation is pivotal to ensuring economic efficiency (Christensen, 2003b: 188). Such political control may also be built into market-based systems. Either way, these reviews neither support nor refute the assertion that markets lead to greater efficiency or responsiveness.

As for the use of incentive-based public management, evidence is also unclear. The OECD (2005) concludes that performance-related pay does not solve the problem of information asymmetry. If the contract between the political leadership and the administrative agency cannot adequately specify standards and performance indicators, it becomes difficult to craft relevant incentive structures or to monitor performance. Furthermore, surveys in both the UK and the United States show that economic incentives generally do not affect the motivation of public employees, who appear to pay little attention to the economic incentives when they go about their jobs (OECD, 2005). However, the OECD concludes that the reforms have had positive corollary effects, as the organisational changes required to institute performance pay schemes have offered a 'window of opportunity' to increase the focus on the goals of the organisation and on management in general. In a previous report, the OECD concluded that performance pay did appear to increase efficiency, but the organisation warned also that economic incentives aimed at managers may undermine a culture of public service and the attention to organisational goals (OECD, 2003). Even so, Christensen (2003c) finds that 'there is no clear evidence' linking executive pay to the economic performance of the organisations or policy sectors they lead.

As for environmental regulation, there are quite a few examples of effective outcomes of market-based instruments, although effects vary considerably and depend critically on policy design (EEA, 2005; Speck *et al.*, 2006). Evaluations indicate that environmental taxes have helped reduce emissions of polluting substances and waste, particularly from industries. But the evidence also shows that tax rates need to be at a significant level to make companies undertake pollution abatement (EEA, 2005: 8; Speck *et al.*, 2006: 225–226). Furthermore, the effect of taxes is often augmented by simultaneous use of other instruments, such as subsidies or voluntary agreements, suggesting again that price incentives in and of themselves have not been sufficient (Enevoldsen, 2005; EEA, 2005). As for tradable emission quotas, evaluation shows that the US system for SO_2 has been both effective and cost-effective. The 400 electricity utilities that were included in the first round of the programme halved their emissions between 1990 and 1999 (Miljøstyrelsen, 1999: 126; see also EEA, 2005). The European system has not yet been evaluated.

In general, however, evaluations of economic policy instruments have suffered from data problems and the difficulty of disentangling the effects caused by economic instruments from other influences. Comprehensive ex-post evaluations are only now beginning to appear (Miljøstyrelsen, 2003; Speck *et al.*, 2006).

This quick overview indicates that the empirical evidence on the behavioural effect of market-based policy reforms is mixed, just as the evidence for improved economic efficiency or cost-effectiveness leaves something to be desired. Studies are often hampered by methodological difficulties, and the empirical applications of the theoretical model are imperfect, as one would expect. This said, it would be reasonable to conclude that the empirical evidence has not convincingly defended the rational actor model against the theoretical challenge to its behavioural assumptions. Yet no clear theoretical alternative has been established. Thus, the theoretical discussion as to whether behavioural assumptions are sufficiently accurate remains unresolved; and also the empirical question as to the effectiveness of market-based policy reforms has not been answered conclusively. This suggests a need for deeper examination and discussion of the rational actor theory as the model for public policy.

Implications for public policy of behavioural assumptions

It matters for public policy whether the behavioural assumptions of the rational model hold.

Firstly, if the rational choice model erroneously ascribes only selfish and economic motives to those whose behaviour is the target of regulation, policies based on the model may set up an ineffective incentive structure. For economic incentives to work in the environmental or any other arena, actors must be motivated by material gain; if they are not, the policies will fail or introduce unwarranted distortions into the economy (van den Bergh *et al.*, 2000). Likewise, in the public sector, if employees are not motivated by higher wages, the incentive may be futile. And, it is possible that economic incentives may even prove counterproductive. Economic incentives could crowd out other motivations, for instance environmental stewardship or a professional ethic (see, for instance, Frey and Oberholzer-Gee (1997) on crowding out of social motivations in environmental policy). In the long run this might require economic incentives to become increasingly stronger in order to have an effect. The claim is not that humans do not respond to economic incentives, but that other values such as environmental stewardship, social bonds or values of professionalism, depending on the target group, may interfere with the workings of the economic incentive. The implication for policy is that it is paramount to understand what motivates actors when designing incentives to regulate human behaviour, perhaps allowing for a multitude of goals. Such knowledge would contribute to more effective design of market-based instruments.

Secondly, even if economic motivation prevails, the decision-making properties of individuals as well as collective decision-making bodies may hinder a smooth adaptation to new incentive structures. Price-based incentives work, if decision makers a) pay attention to prices, and b) are able cognitively or by means of organisational structure to convert the price signal into optimal choices. However, cognitive theory suggests that humans may not respond to incentives completely as policy designers envision; actors may misunderstand the incentive structure created, or they may not even pay attention to a price change (Jones, 2001). And, even if actors are aware of the price change, they may not be able translate this awareness into a behaviour adjusting completely to the new prices. Decision-making is often shaped by habits, and habits are difficult to break. Likewise, organisations often do not operate according to a single goal structure and typically have coordination problems, causing potential distortions in the adaptation to price signals (Cyert and March, 1992). It is claimed that business organisations work inside rather than on the boundary of profit and that organisations in general operate with slack; that is, with inefficient use of resources (Leibenstein, 1966; Cyert and March, 1992; Porter and van der Linde, 1995). This would indicate that actors are less sensitive to price signals and economic incentives than claimed.

The consequence is that policy-makers may not be able to direct the behaviour of public employees, consumers or businesses exactly as expected. While economic incentives are still expected to affect behaviour somewhat, and probably also in a predictable direction, they may not necessarily work to achieve a pre-specified target. Hence, policy-makers would need to ask whether market-based instruments are the best choice if they seek to achieve a specific objective, for instance in the realm of energy conservation (van den Bergh *et al.*, 2000: 55; EEA, 2005).

Finally, unless agents have a stable preference structure and respond consistently to price incentives, economic instruments may not be efficient in the welfare economic sense; as such, Pareto efficiency rests explicitly on the existence of a stable preference ordering (van den Bergh *et al.*, 2000).

This discussion does not invalidate the use of market-based instruments for policy reforms, but it suggests greater uncertainty about the effectiveness of the causal mechanisms implied by the model of economic man than that which is usually assumed in economic theory. It suggests that environmental or any other policy aiming to modify behaviour would benefit from a better understanding of human decision-making and motivation. A better behavioural model might indicate when incentive-based policies are most likely to succeed, and how such policies might be modified or supplemented by other instruments to achieve a higher degree of effectiveness.

Development of an accurate behavioural model

The bounded rationality perspective credited to Herbert Simon suggests that such a behavioural model should allow for differential motivation of actors and that it should also include theory about decision environments and decision processes. These elements derive from studies of individual decision-making carried out in the laboratories of cognitive psychologists as well as from studies of organisational decision-making.

According to Simon, the behavioural model should focus specifically on the interaction between decision environments and decision processes that affect the behaviour of individual or organisational actors (Simon, 1997; Jones, 1999, 2001). As outlined above, decision-makers have difficulty handling large amounts of information, making trade-offs, and integrating uncertainty into their choices. As a result, decision-makers tend to employ a wide range of simple decision rules, referred to as heuristics, or rely on routine solutions (see, for instance, McFadden, 1999; Kahneman, 2002 for overviews of specific heuristics). Simple decision mechanisms allow for quick decision-making and draw efficiently on the experience of decision-makers, but they do not use all of the information available to the decision-maker and therefore may not result in optimal choices. In fact, to compensate for the difficulties associated with boundless information and the need to make trade-offs among multiple goals, decision-makers may satisfice, that is they may settle for a solution which is 'good enough' rather than the optimal solution assumed in neo-classical economics (Simon, 1976, 1997).

Bounded rationality theory further holds that simple decision mechanisms gain importance when the decision environment is complex. Complexity refers both to the complexity of the problem or calculation at hand as well to the circumstances in which the problem must be solved. For instance, time pressure, uncertainty about the outcome of various behavioural paths, and frequently changing information have been identified as important features of a decision environment which may affect decision-making.

The bounded rationality framework thus suggests specific points on which the model of man used in economic and political theory may be improved and, therefore, provides a direction for research. Using this framework instead of the rational actor framework involves a trade-off. The simplicity and precise predictions following from the rational actor model are sacrificed and replaced with a model which allows for multiple types of motivation and complex decision processes but is incapable of precise predictions of particular choices or outcomes. The potential gain would be to end up with a more accurate or true model of individual and collective actors, leading in the end to better predictions about behavioural patterns, better explanations of behaviour, and to more effective public policies and management.

A behavioural study of environmental policy response

Against this background, this book presents a study of responses to environmental regulation. The purpose is twofold. One purpose is to contribute to the discussion of the appropriate behavioural assumptions on which to build policy reforms. The other purpose is to contribute to an explanation of the effect or lack thereof of market-based policy reforms. Thus, drawing on the bounded rationality framework, the study attempts to answer whether the response to environmental regulation is conditioned by the decision context and the decision processes this fosters.

The study thus seeks to ascertain whether a behavioural model based on bounded rationality assumptions of behaviour might represent an improvement over the more simple assumptions of self-interested utility-maximisation in the rational model. Furthermore, by evaluating in depth the behavioural response to a specific example of environmental regulation, the study may contribute to explanations of the outcomes of other reforms based on economic incentives. Specifically, this would serve also to provide input to discussions of neo-classical environmental economics and its policy prescriptions for environmental regulation.

Furthermore, the study has methodological relevance. The bounded rationality framework, although originating with Herbert Simon's study of public organisations (Simon, 1976 originally 1945), has been developed in large measure in cognitive laboratories, where experiments have uncovered many specific simplifying decision mechanisms and demonstrated how they bias choice in relation to a fully rational response. But it has been argued that to improve the relevance of the framework, it is time to take studies of decision processes outside of the laboratories.

> It is important to look for the presence of simple heuristics in settings outside of the laboratory. Discovering how people process information to make judgments and decisions in their everyday lives – as well as how to structure information so that better decisions can be made – can have important real-world implications in domains ranging from deciding guilt in the courtroom to choosing whether or not to have a medical test. (Todd and Gigerenzer, 2003: 154; see also Jones, 2001)

This reasoning extends as well to implications for design of regulatory policies in many domains.

The present study therefore pursues such an empirical path of studying bounded rationality outside the laboratory. It examines decision processes in a field setting in order to ascertain whether simple decision mechanisms can be observed outside the laboratory, and to explore when and how they are applied.

Empirical case

Fertiliser regulation among Danish farmers constitutes the specific empirical case. For years, farmers in Denmark have applied fertiliser in excess of crop needs, leading to nutrient leaching to the surrounding environment (see, for instance, Grant *et al.*, 2000: 44). In this context, excess fertilising represents a waste of resources, and as such the fertiliser practices of Danish farmers constitute a challenge to the rational model of business organisations as cost minimisers bond profit optimisers. The bounded rationality perspective would suggest that farmers either are not motivated by profit objectives alone or that properties of fertiliser management as a task and the decision context affect the decision processes of farmers and cause deviations from fully optimal fertiliser practices.

In the mid-1990s, regulation was introduced which placed a cap on the amount of fertiliser each farm could use, based on a set of fertiliser norms specific to crops and soil type. Fertiliser norms were set at economically optimal levels. This regulation thus does not represent an economic policy instrument, but the fertiliser norms mimic the logic of a market-based instrument in that it seeks to take advantage of the economic logic generally ascribed to businesses.

The case thus plays into the theoretical question of the book with regard to the discussion of behavioural models. But it also offers methodological advantages, because the fertiliser norms specify a precise standard of rational behaviour at the level of the individual. This presents a unique opportunity to apply the bounded rationality framework to studies of decision processes outside of the cognitive laboratories.

Outline of book

The first part of the book lays out the theoretical foundation for the empirical analysis. Chapter 2 discusses in greater detail the main rational approaches, primarily the model of economic man and, as the challenging approach in this context, the bounded rationality model. The chapter lays out the main behavioural assumptions of each, discusses their merits, and relays the most important critical discussions regarding each of the approaches. Using the bounded rationality framework, an analytical model is developed in Chapter 3. The first half of the chapter discusses the key theoretical concepts of 'decision environment', 'motivation', and 'decision processes', and outlines their interaction in an analytical model. The second half of the chapter outlines in greater detail features of simple decision processes in order to generate specific criteria and expectations that may structure the empirical analysis of such processes. Moving towards the empirical analysis, Chapter 4 presents the research design of the study of responses to environmental policies. The chapter describes the data sources used, i.e. a database detailing fertiliser practices of approximately 150 farms and a set of in-depth interviews with farmers about their decision processes. Finally, the chapter discusses shortcomings of the research design and the data.

Chapter 5 marks the beginning of the second part of the book, setting the stage for the empirical analysis through a brief introduction to the empirical context: key features of the Danish agricultural sector, the impact of agriculture on environment and environmental regulation of agriculture. Chapters 6–8 report on the empirical analysis concerning farmers and their responses to environmental regulation, as well as on their decision-making processes. Chapter 6 analyses the effect of decision environment on decisions, specifically the degree to which complex decision environments may explain deviation from optimal behaviour. The chapter moves from a set of descriptive analyses of fertiliser practices to explanatory bivariate and multivariate analyses of the variables included in the analytical framework. Chapter 7 moves into analyses of the decision processes of farmers, building on in-depth interviews. The focus in this chapter is on decisions regarding fertiliser management, aiming to study how decision processes may account for fertiliser practices. Chapter 8 focuses on farmers' decision processes more broadly. The chapter compares decisions in the domain of fertiliser management with decision processes in other domains on the farm, from pesticide application to large investments in machinery and land, and seeks to establish more general properties of these decision processes and how they reflect on the bounded rationality framework. In order to assess the applicability of the findings for other sectors, the chapter briefly analyses responses to energy and waste taxes in light of bounded rationality. Finally, Chapter 9 concludes the book by summarising and discussing the findings of the analysis and their implications for rational models of behaviour as well as for incentive-based public policies.

2
Theoretical approaches to rational behaviour

Economic and rational choice models have provided the theoretical inspiration and justification for many policies adopted in recent years. But the models exist in many versions and may not always be applied stringently in real-world settings. Likewise, the alternative approach of bounded rationality may be associated with a lack of rationality or second-best rationality, which does not entirely comply with the actual theory. In order to lay the groundwork for a study of rational behaviour this chapter therefore reviews the main concepts of each of the two approaches.

Some dispute exists over whether the two even represent different approaches, with bounded rationality simply being seen as a special case of fully rational theory under the *rational choice* heading (see, for instance, Monroe, 1991a). However, the argument of this book is that they differ significantly in their behavioural assumptions, and that these differences hold widely different implications for the formulation of public policy. This said, the two approaches do share the notion that behaviour is generally intentional or goal-driven. In this regard, they are positioned towards one end of a continuum, the other end of which holds the perspective that behaviour is driven largely by a human need to constitute identity within a social and cultural context.

The chapter also focuses predominantly on the micro-theoretic aspects of the rational approaches, that is, the model of individual agents. This reflects the character of the research question of the book and serves to highlight the foundation and the basic building blocks of each approach, but it does not imply a normative positioning in the debate about structure vs. agency. Both rational approaches have earlier been criticised for reductionism, in the sense that behaviour of individual as well as collective organisms was explained exclusively by reference to individualist characteristics, ignoring the conditioning effect of structural factors (Nørgaard, 1996; Peters, 1999: 13–14). This criticism provided impetus for the development of neo-institutional theory, which claims that behaviour cannot be explained without reference to institutions and institutional contexts (March and Olsen, 1984; North, 1989, 1990, 1993; Levi *et al.*, 1990; Ostrom, 1991). In this sense, institutional theories would constitute an alternative approach to the basic rational approaches, and, in fact, they are often treated as such in discussions of rational approaches. But since their emergence, neo-institutional theories have to some degree prompted both neo-classical rational theory and bounded rationality theory to account also for the relationship between institutions and agents. Hence, in this chapter the discussion of institutions will be subsumed under the review of the two rational approaches in terms of how institutions are treated, i.e. the *role* they play.

Neo-classical rational approach: from economic man to rational choice

Rational actor theory originates with classical microeconomics, and its model of individual behaviour is embodied in the proverbial *economic man*. In its most simple form, the model stipulates that actors pursue goals which reflect their self-interest and, furthermore, that actors are able to assess which among several alternatives best serves their self-interest, given the constraints they face in the decision situation. The founder of classical economics, Adam Smith, saw individual pursuit of self-interest as a powerful economic driver that would actually lead to the greatest collective welfare (Monroe, 1991a; Whitehead, 1991; Smith, 1998, 2002: 503[1]). Yet this force needed to be regulated so as not to disintegrate into the chaos otherwise envisioned by philosophers such as Thomas Hobbes. Smith identified the market as the regulatory mechanism that could transform individual self-interest into a collectively rational outcome, defined as the greatest production output possible. Rationality, thus, was constituted at the level of the collective (Whitehead, 1991).

This focus on the *collectively* rational outcome changed with the development of neo-classical economics, which aimed to explain the behaviour of *individual consumers* at a given time; consumer behaviour and the nature of demand became the cornerstones of economic theory (Arrow, 1986: S386; Whitehead, 1991: 63). Building on the ideas of utilitarianism, which identified pleasure and pain as the guiding norms of behaviour, neo-classical economists substituted the self-interest assumption with the notion of *utility*. Hence the neo-classical model held that consumers 'would allocate their income among commodities in a way which would maximise the satisfaction, or utility, from them' (Whitehead, 1991: 63). Utility expresses the value to consumers of the goods they consume and it follows from preferences for different commodities in the consumer model. In later, non-consumer versions of the model this has been reformulated to 'preferences over outcomes'. Although the theory implicitly maintained the assumption of material self-interest as the motivating drive for economic actors, the terms preference and utility were more neutral with regard to the substance of that which was pursued.

With neo-classical theory the rational model evolved from a theory of rational actors to a theory of *rational choice*. Rational behaviour came to be defined as choosing that alternative, be it that bundle of commodities, which yields maximum utility, given preferences and budget constraints. It is implicitly, albeit not very expressly, a theory of decisions and decision-making. It amounts to 'reasoned pursuit of self-interest' (Sen, 1987: 69).

Behavioural assumptions of the rational actor model

The description of rational economic behaviour as 'reasoned pursuit of self-interest' indicates the two main elements of the rational model. They concern assumptions regarding a) the motivation from which utility functions spring, and b) the reasoning by which the actor is able to maximise his utility, i.e. the process of choosing. Each of these assumptions will be reviewed in the following.

Preferences: the content and structure of utility functions
Rational choice theory is generally associated with the assumption that the actions of humans are motivated out of self-interest.

But what does self-interest mean? In modern rational choice theory, the concept is less straightforward than one might expect. In the case of economic pursuits, particularly in the realm of consumer theory, self-interest tends to be prefaced by *material* self-interest. In theories of business behaviour self-interest is generally equated with profits or shareholder value. In domains of non-market decisions, including politics and bureaucracy, self-interest has been operationalised as office-seeking, rent-seeking, budget-maximising, and other bureaucratic perquisites (for an overview, see Mueller, 1997 and 2003). Importantly, self-interest as expressed in these goals connotes *selfish* interest.

While this would probably conform to common assumptions, the literature shows great diversity of definitions on the issue of utility or preferences (see, for instance, Sen, 1977, 1986; Monroe, 1991a; Wildawsky, 1994; Yee, 1997; Opp, 1999). At the risk of misrepresenting some categorisations, it seems that assumptions about motivation can be divided on two dimensions. The first concerns the nature of preferences: do we assume selfish motivation alone or can actions be grounded in other types of motivation, including measures of social preferences? The second dimension concerns whether the content of preferences is specified or left open.

Some rational choice scholars have argued in favour of a wider notion of self-interest, one that may even encompass other-regarding behaviour (see Sen, 1977; Green and Shapiro, 1994; Wildawsky, 1994). If an actor values the welfare of other actors, he may derive utility from considering their interest or welfare in his choice (Sen, 1977; Wildawsky, 1994). In this sense self-sacrificial behaviour could be considered rational. Likewise, some scholars have abandoned the material component of self-interest and included also ideational aspects, such as psychic benefits of doing one's civic duty by voting, when strategic calculations would lead one to refrain from voting (Green and Shapiro, 1994: 59, citing Riker and Ordeshook, 1968, 1973; Yee, 1997).

A related, but different, answer to the question about preferences has been to leave unspecified the goals and preferences of actors. In fact, this is evident in the neo-classical concept of utility, which does not specify the preferences of consumers (Monroe, 1991a; Whitehead, 1991; Green and Shapiro, 1994). The distinctive positions along this dimension have been termed *thick* and *thin* rationality, respectively (Elster, 1983: 1, quoted in Yee, 1997, and Ferejohn, 1991: 282). *Thick models of rationality*, thus, make specific assumptions about the goals and beliefs of actors and in doing so assume that actors generally value the same things, such as wealth, income or power. By contrast, *thin rational models* do not specify goals but assume simply that actors are instrumentally rational in the sense that 'they efficiently employ the means available to pursue their ends' (Ferejohn, 1991: 282). Even so, thin rationalists often 'thicken' their concept of rationality when applying it to empirical analysis, as in rational choice studies of bureaucracy, which tend to assume that bureaucrats pursue leisure or income or power through large budgets (Green and Shapiro, 1994; Wildawsky, 1994). Although the rational choice literature accommodates these different perspectives on preferences, it is fair to say that mainstream rational choice studies tend to rely on the assumption that actors pursue self-interested goals. By and large, the model of economic man rules in rational actor and rational choice studies (Monroe, 1991a; Downs in Wildawsky, 1994: 137).

Assumptions regarding preferences not only concern their content but also their structure. Hence neo-classical economics assumes that every actor possesses an underlying utility function which induces a consistent ordering among all the choices an actor faces (Simon, 1985; Elster, 1986; Green and Shapiro, 1994). It is in this sense that preferences are said to be exogenous in the rational model; they derive from an underlying, stable preference ordering, independent of factors specific to the moment of choice. This preference ordering is complete in the sense that the actor can perform pair-wise comparisons among alternatives and (consistently) rank one over the other or rank them equally, no matter how they are presented. This implies also that the actor knows whether he prefers one alternative over the other or is indifferent. The preference ordering is also transitive, which means that if alternative A is preferred to alternative B, and B to C, then alternative A should also be preferred to alternative C (Sen, 1986; Douma and Schreuder, 1998: 20; van den Bergh *et al.*, 2000). The two requirements of consistency sum to what Arrow termed a weak order of preferences (Sen, 1986; Green and Shapiro, 1994: 15).

The assumption of consistent preference orderings is critical to the neo-classical framework. If individuals do not have such well-ordered preferences, it is questionable whether the market equilibrium that is the crux of neo-classical theory will be obtained (Elster, 1986; Whitehead, 1991: 64; Green and Shapiro, 1994). More generally for rational theory, the existence of well-ordered preferences is essential for the ability to predict specific outcomes (van den Bergh *et al.*, 2000).

Choice: reasoned pursuit of self-interest
The other assumption of the neo-classical model concerns the *rational pursuit* of self-interest. In economic versions, the actual reasoning process is not explicitly described. Instead, the theory implies a standard of rational behaviour, namely that of utility-maximising.

Maximising in neo-classical economics refers to picking that alternative which yields the greatest amount of utility among the available alternatives, given the actor's preferences over the alternatives and constrained by budget only. Rational decision-making, implicitly or explicitly, amounts to a calculation in which the actor evaluates all alternatives synoptically, that is ranking and valuing alternatives on several dimensions, and summing up the comparison in a single measure of optimal utility (Payne *et al.*, 1993; Jones, 2001). To illustrate, a choice among public policy alternatives could be broken down into dimensions of effectiveness, cost, equity and enforceability. In order for the calculation to result in an optimal choice the rational actor must make smooth *trade-offs* among the alternatives, based on the value he assigns to each (Begg *et al.*, 1984; Bettman, Luce and Payne, 1998; Douma and Schreuder, 1998). For instance, a policy-maker should be able to make precise trade-offs among relevant attributes, such as effectiveness and costs of several policy proposals, to arrive at the policy offering the greatest benefit to society.

The model assumes that rational decision-making involves choice among *well-defined alternatives*, be they goods or alternative courses of action. Furthermore, it assumes that actors have *full information* about each alternative and the consequences of choosing each one. Given the obvious impossibility of this assumption, decision theorists interpret the requirement of full information to mean that actors perceive the information available to them in an objectively correct manner (Opp, 1999: 175;

Jones, 2001). However, much decision-making occurs under conditions of uncertainty where actors cannot know the consequences of their choices; in such situations they are expected to estimate the probability that each outcome will materialise and to calculate the expected utility (Simon, 1985; Elster, 1986; Sen, 1987; Monroe, 1991a). Finally, the model assumes constant updating as new information becomes available (Jones, 2001: 94–96).

The role of institutions

Rational actor theory, economic as well as political, has focused on the individual decision-maker and his preference structure as the determinant of behaviour, ignoring any effect of institutions on individual actors (Nørgaard, 1996; Peters, 1999). This owes in part to an epistemological claim that all action, also action by collective bodies, originates with actions of individuals and therefore individuals are the valid point of inquiry (Peters, 1999: 13). But through neo-institutional theory rational actor approaches eventually came to theorise also the relationship between individuals and the institutional context within which they acted. Retaining the notion that the locus of action is with individual actors and driven by their preferences, the rational theory conception of institutions is that 'they establish parameters for individual behaviour' (Peters, 1999: 15). Institutions embody the rules that govern interaction among individuals, and institutions provide incentives that may affect the choices of individuals in given situations (North, 1990; Nannestad; 1991; Hall and Taylor, 1996; Nørgaard, 1996; Peters, 1999). Institutions do matter, but because they shape the playing field, so to speak; that is, they constrain choices by introducing new decision parameters. But they do not fundamentally alter the preferences of actors.

Critical discussions

Given the status of the rational choice theory as largely axiomatic, much of the critical discussion about the model has revolved around the empirical validity of its behavioural assumptions. This concerns the self-interest assumption, as well as the implicit model of choice. Directly related to the discussion of the validity of assumptions is a second long-standing dispute concerning the epistemology ascribed to by the core of rational choice practitioners: does the veracity of assumptions matter for theory building?

Are actors necessarily self-interested?
The assumptions regarding motivation and preferences in the rational choice model represent a contentious issue. Are people by nature selfish, and are their choices necessarily motivated by self-interest?

Nobel laureate Amartya Sen in his treatise *Rational Fools* argues that economic man, who has but one single preference structure, determined entirely by his own self-interest, is 'close to being a social moron' (1977: 336). Real-world actors do not operate in social vacuums, but are integrated into social contexts. At the very least, this means that behaviour is to some extent guided by norms and rules of conduct and in some cases perhaps by sheer consideration of the welfare of others, be it kin, friends, colleagues or society at large, Sen argued.[2] Thus, reducing human motivation to self-interest amounts to a 'wholly arbitrary limitation on the notion of rationality' (1977: 342).This resonates also with cultural theorists, who hold that individual selves are social constructs rather than naturally given. It is implied therefore that the definition of self-interest can only be established with reference to a concrete cultural context and may indeed be quite different from the economic idea of self-interest (Wildawsky, 1994: 139–143).

Empirical evidence for the self-interest assumption is mixed. Experimental game studies have shown that people often choose the unselfish or cooperative course of action, contrary to rational theory predictions (Sen, 1977; Camerer and Thaler, 1995; Mullainathan and Thaler, 200). Take the game of 'divide the dollar', in which a sum of money is given to an appointed leader, who is then asked to divide the money as he sees fit among himself and one or several other players. The other players can reject or accept the offer. If the other players reject the offer, no players receive any money.[3] Rational choice theory would predict that the self-interested, rational leader would calculate the minimum amount necessary to gain the other players' acceptance and, essentially, that any other player would gain by accepting any amount above zero. Yet, the game repeatedly shows that leaders give away more than the bare minimum and opt instead for a fairer division of the money. Camerer and Thaler (1995) review several versions of this game and conclude that the most likely conclusion is that the leaders are driven by social norms of fairness, and that rational choice predictions of strategic maximisation of self-interest tend to fail. Similar results have been shown in studies of real-world politics (for a review, see Jones, 1999: 317; see also Browne, 1991).

Results such as these have led some rational actor theorists to reinterpret the self-interest assumption to incorporate the welfare of others in the utility function (see Sen, 1977: 322–324 for a discussion). Hence, people who share more than what is strictly rational exhibit a preference for sharing, or they derive utility from the welfare of others. So if an agent sacrifices his own welfare for the welfare of someone else, he has simply revealed a preference for altruistic behaviour in this interpretation of the theory. In fact, any behaviour can be consistent with rational behaviour, when the self-interest assumption is reinterpreted in this manner, even suicide (Becker, 1976).

Critics argue that the above renders rational theory empty; it evades the issue (Sen, 1977, 1986; Simon, 1997: 370). In the words of Sen: 'If you are consistent, then no matter whether you are a single-minded egoist or a raving altruist or a class conscious militant, you will appear to be maximising your own utility in this enchanted world of definitions' (Sen, 1977: 323). Furthermore, without prior specification of goals, rational theory loses the ability to predict choices.

Utility functions: are preferences fixed?

Relaxing the assumption of self-interest, the neo-classical model of rational actors maintains the assumption that actors have a fixed ordering of preferences over all alternatives or outcomes, which ensures consistency of choices. This means that choice will be impervious to the presentation of alternatives or other contextual factors. Again, these are laid out as axioms of the theory rather than as empirically derived assumptions about preferences.

However, much research in the cognitive and behavioural sciences suggests that violations of these consistency requirements might be the norm rather than the deviation. In fact, a whole branch of research within cognitive psychology appears devoted to uncovering biases in judgement. Setting the standard were Daniel Kahneman and the late Amos Tversky, who jointly and in countless collaborations with other researchers have produced a virtual laundry list of violations of the consistency requirements (see, for instance, Tversky and Kahneman, 1974,[4] McFadden, 1999; Kahneman, 2002; Shafir and LeBoeuf, 2002). Laboratory experiments have demonstrated that actors are prone to errors, such as being sensitive to the *framing* of the task, for instance loss or gain or adjusting choices to quantitative anchoring cues.[5] In a valuation study of environmental goods Payne *et al.* (2000) found that the sequence in which the goods were presented to the respondents significantly affected their willingness to pay for each alternative.

Although some write off these results as mere artefacts of the research design (discussed in Shafir and LeBoeuf, 2002), the regularity with which the results have been obtained in different settings has led many cognitive theorists to conclude that preferences are not exogenous to the choice situation: preferences are constructed in the moment of choice (Payne *et al.*, 1993, 1997; Bettman, Luce and Payne, 1998; Shafir and LeBoeuf, 2002).

Such findings have significant implications for rational actor theory – they affect methodology and the instrumentalist argument for measuring theory by its ability to produce predictions (van den Bergh *et al.*, 2000). The inconsistencies of choice uncovered by cognitive researchers and the notion of constructed preferences undermine the methodology of many studies which deduce preferences from choice. Without an underlying, consistent utility function, choice cannot serve as the only source of information on preferences. And if a given choice is not evidence of an underlying, stable preference function, then past behaviour becomes an unreliable predictor of future behaviour. Without the assumption of consistent utility functions, neo-classical and rational choice theories lose some of their much-touted parsimony and precision. Scientists are then forced to explore the preferences of actors in concrete settings (see, for instance, Simon, 1997: 278).

Finally, the findings reflect on economic theory and other formalised rational theory. Formal modelling relies on the consistency requirements for the deduction of equilibrium points. If people's preferences change in apparently idiosyncratic ways or if they cannot say which of several alternatives they prefer, there will be no stable point at which demand equals supply or stable political majorities for a certain policy; at least such equilibria will not be analytically tractable (Sen, 1986; van den Bergh *et al.*, 2000).

Fit of the model of choice

The decision process implicit in the model of rational choice also provokes discussion. Critics, many of whom are based in cognitive sciences, point out that the neo-classical model unduly simplifies the decision processes and misrepresents human information processing.

The rational choice model of choice derives its distinct features from the consumer model in which decision-making involves choice among well-defined alternatives, easily recognisable to the actor. Yet, as Simon and others have pointed out, many decisions, be they business, public policy or household decisions, fail to present themselves so neatly to decision-makers. Often, choice is more accurately conceived of as problem solving. In other words, decision-making is considerably more complicated than anticipated by the rational choice model (Simon, see for instance, 1955, 1985, 1997; Conlisk, 1996; Jones, 1999, 2001, 2002). While this may not in and of itself invalidate the rational model, for cognitive theorists this point is important because complexity is precisely what invalidates the rest of the decision-making model.

Researchers within the cognitive tradition argue that humans cannot process information as assumed in the rational model (Simon, 1955, 1990, 1997; Jones, 1999, 2001; Kahneman, 2002). Firstly, humans cannot easily process large amounts of information simultaneously because of the limited capacity of working memory. Secondly, humans cannot make the smooth trade-offs among different goals implied in the rational consumer model. And thirdly, decision-makers are prone to cognitive biases when they process information (for overviews, see Thaler, 1992; Goldstein and Hogarth, 1997; Shefrin 2002; Kahneman, 2002; see also Tversky and Kahneman, 1974; Arnott, 2006). Hence, even when decision-makers aim to optimise, they often fail to identify the optimal solution (Simon, 1997; Jones, 2001).

Epistemological controversies: do assumptions matter?
Proponents of the rational model have deflected these criticisms
by adopting the instrumentalist argument that the accuracy of the
model's assumptions matters less than the theory's ability to
generate predictions. Milton Friedman put forward perhaps the
most forceful, and certainly the most influential, argument for the
scientific merit of this scientific approach in his *Essays in Positive
Economics* (1953). Here, he argued that any theory must abstract
features from reality in order to be useful for empirical prediction;
in fact, the simpler the theory, the more useful it would be: 'Its
performance is to be judged by the precision, scope, and conform-
ity with experience of the predictions it yields' (1953: 4). A
hypothesis is important if it explains much by little. To support
his claim, Friedman used the analogy of Galileo developing the
law of falling bodies by studying the fall of a body in a vacuum.
He pointed out that developing the law under the circumstances
of a vacuum does not amount to assuming a vacuum (1953:
16–18). It merely allows for a test of the hypothesis under the
specified conditions (1953: 23).

Terry Moe (1979) suggested that this represented misuse of the
notion of abstraction. In the Galileo example, the vacuum specifies a *context* within which the law of falling body applies. But in
the rational model there is a direct logical connection between the
'ideal conditions and the behaviour to be explained', Moe argued.
The assumptions of self-interest and maximising represent the
'engine that produces behaviour', not merely a context for behaviour. Therefore, the assumptions cannot be separated from the
theory. Hence, if Friedman and other instrumentalists do not
stand by their assumptions, they have very little theory, according
to Moe.

Simon argued that the veracity of assumptions matters, particularly when predictions are employed for the prescriptive
purposes of designing policy. Countering Friedman's reference to
the law of falling bodies, Simon argued that: 'We can assume
vacuum when studying the fall of bodies in a near-vacuum, but
not when designing parachutes' (1997: 330). Therefore, predictions arising from rational economic theory and the policy
recommendations derived from them must be treated with
caution (1978: 367).

Critics are equally unconvinced by Friedman's argument that

the point is not so much whether actors actually are selfish or go through the entire reasoning process, but rather whether they choose *as if* they are selfish optimisers (Friedman, 1953). Conlisk (1996) contends that this argument turns the issue into an empirical question. Whether or not people act *as if* they are self-interested optimisers can only by tested empirically, and on that point the jury is out; the empirical record of rational actor theories is not overwhelming (Conlisk, 1996: 683). The kind of evidence offered by Friedman himself is conjecture. Curiously, he seems to slip from the 'as if' argument into an evolutionary argument to prove his point: if firms had not profit-maximised, they would not have survived (Friedman, 1953: 23). The market mechanism selects for those who profit-maximise. However, this assumes a perfectly competitive market (van den Bergh *et al.*, 2000: 51). In fact, it would seem to be entirely possible for a company to survive without profit-maximising, as long as its competitors do no better. Furthermore, there is no parallel evolutionary argument for why consumers should maximise utility (van den Bergh *et al.*, 2000).

The bounded rationality approach

According to scientific lore, the germ for the approach came from Herbert A. Simon's first-hand observations of the budget processes of the city of Milwaukee. What Simon observed in the city government of Milwaukee bore little resemblance to the economist's model of comparing marginal returns of competing activities to determine the optimal allocation of resources. Instead of rational comparisons of costs and benefits, public officers allocated funds based on the previous year's budgets, and they would argue for allocations based on their own organisational position rather than the overall goals of the organisation (Simon, 1978; Jones, 2001).

The story is interesting for two reasons: firstly, Simon's observations provided the notion of bounded rationality and secondly, it highlights the credo on which the bounded rationality approach rests – that a model of economic and political behaviour ultimately must capture real-world behaviour. The impetus for the development of bounded rationality theory was empirical observations of the shortcomings of the rational choice model as described above.

Overview: from cognitive limitations to organisational decision-making

Bounded rationality (BR) scholars fundamentally agree that actors are rational, but not in the comprehensive manner suggested by rational actor models. Rather, the approach holds that actors seek to achieve goals and *intend* to make rational choices, but may not always be able to do so (Jones, 2001).

This conceptualisation owes to the theory's roots in the cognitive sciences, which have proven both the lack of realism of the neo-classical model and provided the positive template for a behavioural model of decision-making. Furthermore, the cognitive model has also been extended to studies of organisations which exhibit similar decision-making properties to individuals.

A considerable part of research in bounded rationality has been conducted within the 'heuristics and biases' programme. As mentioned above, Tversky and Kahneman spearheaded this research which has demonstrated the many ways in which decision-makers more or less systematically misinterpret information and misapply heuristics, suggesting serious flaws in the concept of economic man (Tversky and Kahneman, 1974; Kahneman and Tversky, 1979; Kahneman, 2002).

The other main direction within bounded rationality, the Simon tradition as it were, uses cognitive research to build a positive model of decision-making (Simon, 1955, 1990, 1997; Jones, 1999, 2001; Kahneman, 2002).

Cognitive studies have demonstrated that physiological constants determine the speed at which humans can process and compute information; this is relatively slow compared with the amount of stimuli we receive at any given moment (Simon, 1990). One such constant, and a key one, is the limited capacity of short-term or working memory which can hold no more than six or seven pieces of information simultaneously and actually attend to only one or two of them at a time (Simon, 1985, 2001).[6] This means that humans cannot easily process large amounts of information simultaneously and that *the computational capacity* of humans is limited (Simon, 1990; Conlisk, 1996).

Several consequences follow from such cognitive features. Firstly, humans may not process information from the environment as accurately as assumed in the fully rational theory. The boundedly rational actor will pay attention to some external stimuli and ignore others, making his own reproduction of the environment, in effect (Jones, 2001: 9). Selective attention, which follows directly from the limited capacity of short-term memory, plays a pivotal role in the bounded rationality framework (Jones, 1999, 2001), because only those aspects to which the actor pays attention will be integrated into the decision process. In the words of James March (1994: 24): 'If attention is rationed, decisions can no longer be predicted simply by knowing the features of alternatives and desires. Decisions will be affected by the way decision makers attend (or fail to attend) to particular preferences, alternatives and consequences.'

Secondly, human information processing tends to be of a serial nature. While the rational actor supposedly can juggle many different parameters simultaneously, boundedly rational decision-makers will attend to different aspects of decisions sequentially.

Thirdly, humans have tremendous difficulty trading off among multiple goals, particularly when goals are incommensurate or conflicting (Simon, 1997: 297).

However, decision strategies which serve to simplify information processing compensate for the cognitive limitations. Common to these strategies is that they are *learned strategies*, which embody the experience of the decision-maker personally or are passed on through the social contexts in which the decision-maker is embedded. Experience creates knowledge, which is linked by association, in effect expanding the capacity of working memory. And stored strategies enable quick decision-making.

Satisficing

In reviews of bounded rationality, the term 'satisficing' is sometimes used to characterise boundedly rational decision-making. The term grew out of Simon's seminal work *Administrative Behaviour* (1976, first published in 1945) and was conceived perhaps to distinguish bounded rationality from the neo-classical concept of optimising. Simon argued that actors, be they individuals or organisations, do not always optimise, i.e. seek that option which confers the greatest utility. Rather, they may search for solutions until they find one that is satisfactory by some predefined target level, referred to as aspiration level. As such, scholars within the BR tradition, who scoff at reducing BR to satisficing, point out that satisficing should be viewed simply as a heuristic. Yet, clearly, satisficing also embeds a decision criterion and, thereby, a rationality standard: namely the solution that implies a satisfactory (as opposed to an optimal) outcome.

Cognition: limitation or enabler?

The term 'bounded rationality' and its highlighting of cognitive constraints has bestowed on bounded rationality an aura of second-best or flawed rationality. But scholars within the tradition make a point of arguing that cognitive architecture must not be viewed solely or primarily as a limitation on decision-making. The very decision mechanisms that simplify complex and uncertain decisions may also be viewed as cognitive features which actually *enable* decision-making in the face of complex environments (Jones, 2001).

Thus simplifying decision strategies take on a dual character in the bounded rationality approach, i.e. both as enablers and inhibitors of rational decision-making. The key question is the degree of match between the decision strategy and environmental or task features. If there is a high degree of matching, the decision may well approximate a fully rational decision. But the rationality of the decision is contingent on the degree to which the simplifying mechanism is appropriate to the situation. It is *possible* that simplifying decision mechanisms will lead to the same outcome as a fully rational decision process would. But it is *likely* that such mechanisms will deviate from the rational standard sometimes, because heuristics introduce the possibility of distortions in all stages of the decision process.

Organisations

Although the bounded rationality approach has been presented above as a model of individual decision-making, it is as much a theory of organisations. After all, the inspiration for the model came from Simon's observation of organisational decisions. Organisations provide an answer to the cognitive limitations of the individual decision-makers. Through coordination and specialisation of activities, organisations overcome the limitations of the individuals and allow them to become more productive than if operating in isolation as their shared storage of knowledge is increased (Simon, 2001: 12785; Jones, 2001: 131).

But organisations also reflect and reproduce the behaviour of individuals and are thus beset by the same problems of having to make decisions under complex and uncertain circumstances, unable to integrate all information and goals into one simple utility structure. What Simon described in *Administrative Behaviour* was that in response to complex situations, organisations would simplify decisions by focusing on sub-goals or by developing routines which institutionalised experience (Simon, 1976; Jones, 2001). Thus, Simon draws a straight line from the cognitive foundation of BR to a theory of organisational decision-making.

Building on Simon's behavioural model of the individual entrepreneur, Cyert and March developed a theoretical model for the business firm. They emphasised the need for a model focusing on the internal operations of the firm, recognising that businesses are large, complex entities (1992, first published in 1963). Cyert and March theorised some of the aspects raised by the cognitive framework. Specifically, the behavioural theory of the firm developed the framework with regard to the setting of goals, searching for information, formation of expectations and the execution of choice.

In contrast to the neo-classical model, which assumes that all business organisations are profit-maximisers, the behavioural theory of the firm claims that decision-making in business enterprises is not truly geared toward achieving this one simple goal. Firstly, business enterprises, as well as other organisations, constitute a coalition of participants, each with their own goals, likely leading to a conflict of goals, which is resolved through bargaining (Cyert and March, 1992; Douma and Schreuder, 1998). Hence, Simon (1997: 223) questioned whether employees would operate according to a profit motive. Secondly, even if the organisation does have one overriding goal such as profit, it must be divided into operational sub-goals, often matched to sub-divisions of the organisation. If each sub-division seeks to fulfil its goals, again conflicts of goals may very well follow. Hence, the bounded rationality framework assumes that organisations will pursue several goals at once, and importantly that they may do so in a sequential fashion, attending to one (sub-)goal at a time.

Behavioural assumptions of bounded rationality

What motivates
In line with its general empirical approach, bounded rationality holds that the goals pursued by actors can only be determined empirically in each and every case. This implies that an *a priori* assumption of self-interest as the motivating force in decisions is ruled out. In fact, Simon admonished that 'an empirically grounded theory would assign comparable weight to other motives' (1997b: 264). Simon arrived at this principle through an affirmative argument. He drew on evolutionary theory to show that humans do not only operate out of self-interest, but may be predisposed to other-regarding behaviour (1997: 257ff.). Such behaviour may evolve as groups improve their evolutionary fitness through social learning, because learning from others helped overcome the inevitable limitations in the information cognitively available to them.[7] 'As long as social influence on balance increases individual fitness, altruism can thrive' (Simon, 2001: 12785). The claim is not that humans are predominantly other-regarding but that the possibility of such motivation requires empirical determination of goals.

Furthermore, the BR approach theorises preferences as endogenous, moulded in a social context, and subject to change over time and in response to evolving events. Experimental evidence suggests that preferences are constructed during the decision process and that they are responsive to the framing of the problem at the moment of problem-solving (Payne *et al.*, 1993: 8; Bettman, Luce and Payne, 1998). Hence, the BR tradition rejects the neo-classical assumption of exogenous preferences reflecting an underlying value structure. In the words of Simon, 'theory must make room for tulip crazes, responses to oil shocks, or the unexpected rise of ethnicity' (1997: 264).

Do decision-makers even pursue goals?
Bounded rationality generally assumes that actors pursue goals and evaluate decisions based on their consequences in terms of the goals. Hence, the intentionality of action has been offered as the reason for defining bounded rationality as rational (Jones, 2001). But March and Olsen in their work on organisations came to question this view. They argued that individuals and organisations follow rules and

procedures seen as appropriate to the situation they are in, in order to fulfil identities (March, 1994: 57). Hence, rules and identities rather than preferences and consequences guide decision-making in this perspective (March, 1994: 57–59). Instead of asking, 'How will this alternative fulfil my objectives?', decision-makers seek to match the situation to their perceived identity or the identity of the social context, and to rules for behaviour. This 'logic of appropriateness' was developed as a critical response to what was seen as excessive focus on the individual within rational actor theory and behavioural theory, and a corresponding neglect of the social context within which much decision-making occurs (Hall and Taylor, 1996; Nørgaard, 1996; Peters, 1999).

Such a focus on rule-following rather than on goal-seeking would seem to be incompatible with the bounded rationality perspective. Yet it has been argued that the bounded rationality approach can accommodate both logics (Jones, 2001).[8] The logic of appropriateness adds 'a moral constraint to choice' in addition to the cognitive constraints; hence it affects the alternatives that actors would include for consideration (Jones, 2001: 205).

Choice as problem-solving: the character of decision processes
Whereas decisions in rational choice models are essentially about choice, the bounded rationality approach uses the notion of problem-solving or decision processes. This implies that decision-making involves far more than a (simple) choice among preconceived alternatives. In many cases, decision-makers must become aware that they have a problem to solve or a decision to make; then they must form an understanding of the problem or the decision parameters, and seek out information about different options; only then begins evaluation and calculation of the preferred option (Simon, 1976, 1985; Bendor, 2001; Jones, 1999, 2001). Theoretically, this clarification of the model is important, because it amplifies the complexity of decision-making.

Comprehensive or simple decision processes?
Even so behavioural theories do not rule out the idea of synoptic decision-making. In this perspective, decision-makers will, under the right circumstances, be able to calculate the optimal solution to a problem. In so doing, they undertake a comprehensive decision strategy paying full attention to all relevant aspects and

alternatives. Yet much of the time decision-makers take shortcuts, drawing on stored knowledge and learned strategies to handle a multitude of decision tasks (Simon, 1990). Prepared strategies enable actors to make decisions where the complexity of a situation, the abundance of information, and time constraints might otherwise induce a cognitive meltdown. Prepared strategies simplify decisions and problem-solving by providing ready-made solutions to previously encountered problems without conducting a complete search and decision process. They are in other words cognition-efficient strategies. For the sake of illustration and to clarify their function, two types of prepared strategies will be discussed here: habits and heuristics.

Habits form from repetitive behaviour. Faced with new tasks, actors must devote significant cognitive resources to accomplishing these tasks. However, once the same task has been performed several times, some or all aspects of the behaviour can be carried out with significantly less conscious effort or attention. Habit takes over from attention (Simon, 1976). 'Habit performs an extremely important task in purposive behaviour for it permits similar stimuli or situations to be met with similar responses or actions' (Simon, 1976: 88). Habits draw on *pattern recognition* (Bendor, 2001, 2003). Actors well experienced in a specific problem domain have a store of knowledge pertaining to tasks in that domain, i.e. a system of problem categories and associated solutions. Facing a decision problem, these actors in a manner of speaking scan their stored knowledge for a similar situation and, thereby, quickly generate a problem definition and an associated solution. That is, they recognise a pattern in the available information from previous exposure to such problems (Simon, 1990; Bendor, 2001, 2003). Pattern recognition applies to mundane everyday behaviour, such as driving, as well as to what is more often associated with true expertise, master level chess – one of Simon's favourite subjects of analysis. Cognitive scientists argue that the reason master chess players can outperform less experienced players in multiple parallel games is that they have committed countless combinations and plays to memory simply by spending many hours at the board. This enables such experienced chess players to recognise quickly particular plays and retrieve the appropriate solution, i.e. a good move, from memory without lengthy analysis (Bendor, 2003).

In lieu of habits, boundedly rational decision-makers may apply simplifying decision rules, also known as heuristics. Heuristics offer rules for how to search for information, when to stop and by what criteria to choose, and they allow decision-makers to economise on the calculation process (Gigerenzer, 2001: 43; Jones, 2001: 50). For instance, 'party affiliation' represents the classic heuristic for voters trying to decide among candidates. This cue presumably offers the voter much information at low cognitive cost. Likewise, rather than evaluating all alternatives in parallel for optimal utility, the boundedly rational decision-maker may assess alternatives sequentially based on a subset of parameters; this is referred to as a lexicographic decision strategy.

Satisficing – a standard of rationality and a heuristic
As mentioned above, satisficing has come to epitomise bounded rationality, especially among researchers outside the BR tradition. In this sense, satisficing is perceived as a contrast to optimising; the actor chooses not the alternative which confers optimal utility but one which offers a satisfactory, i.e. a good enough, solution.

But in the BR approach, satisficing refers to a particular type of decision process. Actors who satisfice set an aspiration level or a target for the solution overall or for each of their sub-goals and then evaluate each alternative based on this. Once an alternative is found which matches the aspiration level for each goal, the alternative is chosen and the decision process is stopped regardless of whether all alternatives have been examined. Hence, the BR approach largely views satisficing as a heuristic (Bendor, 2003). In this regard, satisficing is a decision rule. March theorised the role of satisficing in search for information and alternatives. In this view, satisficing 'specifies the conditions under which search is triggered and stopped' (March, 1994: 27).

As satisficing implies that decision-makers may content themselves with less-than-optimal solutions, the concept also speaks to the overall intent of decision-makers. Contrary to the neo-classic version of business firms and the market, businesses in the bounded rationality tradition may not be entirely efficient. Hence the bounded rationality approach claims that businesses may operate under slack, that is, with sub-optimal use of resources. Importantly, this occurs primarily when performance exceeds expectations, which lowers the motivation of decision-makers to improve their information and decisions. Chapter 3 will deal with this concept in greater detail.

The role of institutions

Although the bounded rationality perspective is entwined with organisational theory, its theoretical origins enjoy a stronger association with the behavioural school and its analytic focus, the micro-foundation of behaviour. Hence the concept of institutions did not feature with much clarity, if at all, in original models, and Simon has been criticised for neglecting the role of institutions in shaping behaviour (Dequech, 2001: 921). In fact, a bounded rationality view on institutions was developed most forcefully with the new economic institutionalists, such as North and Williamson, who arguably drew on bounded rationality insights in order to explain the emergence and role of institutions (Douma and Schreuder, 1998). These new economic institutionalists recognise that human interaction and behaviour is constrained by uncertainty and complexity. Institutions help reduce these problems by structuring information as well as behavioural options. In the bounded rationality perspective, institutions may simplify the task environment (Jones, 2001: 21).

In the economic version, institutions largely feature as incentives and rules that shape the decisions of utility-maximising or goal-pursuing actors; although North in particular places equal emphasis on informal and formal constraints on behaviour (North, 1990; Denzau and North, 2000). Yet an alternative version of institutions exists within, or rather overlapping with, the bounded rationality approach. In this version, institutions are seen as 'collections of norms, rules, understandings, and perhaps most importantly routines' (Peters, 1999: 28). This approach, which was first conceptualised by March and Olsen, perceives behaviour differently from the rational approach of strategic calculation. Sociological in its origin, this approach claims that much behaviour consists of rule following, because human beings are embedded in social structures and depend on these for meaning and identity. In this regard, institutions serve to identify appropriate behaviours in different settings or roles. Because institutions assign meaning and interpretation to situations, they provide not only normative prescriptions, but also cognitive templates for how to act in a given situation (Hall and Taylor, 1996: 948; Denzau and North, 2000). The notion fits well with the bounded rationality framework because social and cultural norms, let alone routines, serve to simplify behavioural choices. They could be construed as heuristics. As such, the concept does merge the original bounded rationality framework with its focus of simplifying decision strategies with a cultural or sociological view of what motivates human decision-makers.

While institutions in the BR perspective thus serve to simplify complex and uncertain circumstances, they may also develop into a constraint on rational action. Institutions can be 'sticky', not changing smoothly with changes in the circumstances that shaped them (Jones, 2001: 170–171). Hence, the institution that initially serves to overcome bounded rationality may, over time, inhibit rather than promote rational decisions. Institutional changes also require that actors pay attention and reorient themselves and, in this sense, institutions may at least temporarily reduce the value of learned strategies. Hence also the treatment of institutions revolves around the match between environmental features and features of the decision-making system.

Critical discussions

The theory of bounded rationality typically encounters two kinds of criticism; the first holds that the theory really does not differ substantially from the rational actor model, while the second questions its status as a theory at all.

Bounded rationality: maximisation under constraints?

Some scholars within the neo-classical rational tradition responded to advances by the bounded rationality approach by adding a cost-of-information function to the general utility calculus (Becker, 1976/1986: 121; Conlisk, 1996). A rational human being would take into account the cost of acquiring information and of deliberating and comparing it to the pay-off of search and deliberation. This has been referred to as 'optimisation under constraints' and it has been argued that the theory of bounded rationality and its notion of satisficing can be reduced to, or rather replaced by, such an information cost function (see Conlisk, 1996; Gigerenzer and Selten, 2001).

Bounded rationalists are quick to point out that information constraints simply exacerbate the computational demands, which cause the decision-maker to resort to heuristics in the first place. In the words of Simon (1997: 296):

> In a formal sense, a process of satisficing could always be converted into a process of optimising by taking into account the cost of search and only searching up to the point where the expected gain derivable from another minute of search is just equal to the opportunity cost of that minute. However, that conversion imposes a new, possibly heavy informational and computational burden upon the chooser: the burden of estimating the expected marginal return of the search and opportunity cost. Solving these estimation problems may be as difficult as making the original choice, or even more difficult.

Logically, the maximising-subject-to-constraints argument leads to a situation of infinite regress: calculating the optimal decision point, that is the utility of extra information versus the cost of further deliberation, induces further search and deliberation, hence continuously changing the optimal solution (Conlisk, 1996: 686–688).

Furthermore, the types of reasoning and judgement errors uncovered under the Kahneman and Tversky tradition suggest that there is more to bounded rationality than economising on cognitive effort. Phenomena such as the loss/gain value asymmetry, the winner's curse, and lack of information updating have been replicated under many different circumstances, including various payoff structures (Thaler, 1992; Camerer and Thaler, 1995; Mullainathan and Thaler, 2000; Jones, 2001). If errors owed to cognitive economising alone and were unrelated to the decision-makers' cognitive processing, the errors should be arbitrary or reflect information available only, but one would not expect systematic error patterns to show up. Likewise, the information constraints argument cannot account for the trade-off difficulties humans exhibit (Jones, 1999).

Bounded rationality: a theory?
Perhaps the main criticism levied against the bounded rationality framework is that it is underspecified as a theory. Lupia,

McCubbins and Popkin (2000: 10) argue that Simon was most specific about the definition of bounded rationality in his treatment of irrationality, but offers no precise theory for defining the boundaries of rationality. Because of its open-ended nature, the bounded rationality approach cannot produce precise and falsifiable predictions of behaviour (Lupia, McCubbins and Popkin, 2000: 10). Without more systematic conceptualisation, bounded rationality theory will not lead to better predictions or better explanation, they argue (see for instance, Lupia, McCubbins and Popkin, 2000).

This questioning of the status of bounded rationality as a *bona fide* theory does not ring entirely foreign to scholars within the tradition. Simon himself referred on several occasions to a research programme or 'a sequence of theories with overlapping sets of assumptions' (Simon, 1955; Bendor, 2001). The bounded rationality approach is entrenched in a behavioural framework, suggesting that theory must be built from empirical observation. The criterion for a good theory is how well it matches real-world conditions. Clearly, the ambition to build a fully fledged theory has not yet been accomplished. The framework points to specific components and dynamics that begin to form the contours of a theory, but reflecting the complexity of the undertaking and of the empirical phenomena under study, it appears illusory to build a simple model that can make precise testable predictions about a large range of phenomena. At this point it appears feasible to develop a theory that specifies some general causal relations and points to central mechanisms which condition outcomes. The most well-developed aspects of the theory concern the conditions under which BR can be expected *vis-à-vis* full rationality and also describes systematic properties of human decision processes.

Rational actor and bounded rationality approaches compared

This comparison focuses on the main similarities and differences of the two approaches as they conceive of motivation, decision processes and scientific aspirations. Clearly, this review has highlighted the differences between the two. If compared against other theories, for instance non-instrumentalist theories of behaviour, the standard of comparison would shift, and the two rational approaches would lie at the same end of a continuum, near the instrumentalist pole. But the differences are significant enough to have implications for research as well as for policy-making.

As outlined above, rational actor models vary in terms of how they conceive of the preferences that motivate decision-makers to act and choose. Typically, rational actors are infused with self-interest, which shapes their preferences and hence their choices. The self-interest assumption followed naturally from theorising about actors in an economic market. In thin-rational and neo-classical models the self-interest assumption has been relaxed and replaced by the concept of a utility function, specified only by a set of consistency requirements, but mute on the content of motivation. However, when it comes to empirical analysis even thin-rational approaches are inclined to formulate auxiliary assumptions, which typically ascribe self-interested goals to the objects under study (Green and Shapiro, 1994; Simon, 1997).

The bounded rationality approach distinguishes itself from the rational actor approach in three ways. Firstly, it does not make *a priori* assumptions about the motivation of decision-makers. These are to be ascertained by empirical investigation. Secondly, however, it rejects the notion that actors are motivated only by self-interest.[9] Thirdly, the approach does not assume a fixed set of preferences from which choice springs. Preferences change over time and may be moulded in a social context; and they are susceptible to features related to the decision process such as the framing of alternatives or the sequence in which they are presented.

This said, the main difference between the two approaches relates to the role of decision processes. In rational actor models decision processes are essentially confined to *choice*, and that choice embodies optimal utility. The processes by which decision-makers transform preferences into an optimal choice are not spelled out. Theories of consumers and companies suggest that decision-making resembles the solving of an algorithm involving several alternatives which are ranked across a range of dimensions, and that trade-offs are involved.

Decision-making in the bounded rationality model differs significantly from the one implicit in the rational actor model. Firstly, choice is redefined as problem-solving, which is a more complex undertaking than choosing among given alternatives. Secondly, the BR approach claims that decision-makers may not use all the information available, and that they may combine information in a manner which does not optimise their utility. This occurs when and because decision-makers tend to use simplifying decision strategies. Thirdly, the adaptiveness of the decision to the environment, i.e. the rationality of the decision, depends on the match between the environmental features and the decision strategy. Boundedly rational outputs occur more frequently under complex and uncertain circumstances and a high time pressure. Fourthly, decision-makers may not pursue optimal outcomes; they may choose alternatives that live up to a predefined aspiration level and in this sense are satisfactory – they satisfice at times.

Implications for research

The neo-classical or rational actor approach arrives at its insights via analytical deduction and hypothesis testing. It offers a simple set of axioms, which would lead to a set of precise, testable predictions. Just how simple these predictions are would depend on the empirical context, however. Some familiar domains lend themselves to predefined auxiliary assumptions such as profit-maximisation (votes in the political realm), while others would be less clear. Applying the rational actor approach to empirical study of responses to environmental regulations, one would identify analytically the goals of the decision-makers, deduce rational responses to the environmental incentives and examine empirically whether the prediction held.

Under the bounded rationality approach, goals and decisions cannot be assumed but must be established empirically. And while the focus of rational actor studies is choice itself, the bounded rationality approach is concerned with the processes that lead to decisions as much as with the actual choice (Simon, 1997: 293). This does not imply that bounded rationality studies are confined to inductive or descriptive studies. It is possible to formulate testable hypotheses, which would predict boundedly rational behaviour following from a) certain circumstances, and b) certain types of decision process. Predictions about bounded rationality would take the form of comparative statics or marginal predictions, i.e. predictions about the direction of deviation from fully rational responses in response to changes in environmental circumstances (Green and Shapiro, 1994).

However, such theory testing is confined to decisions for which it is possible to identify an optimal response against which to compare actual behaviour.

It also follows from the empirical orientation of the BR approach that research will lean toward descriptive, hypothesis-generating studies. Such research must be based on observation of behaviour. But it needs not result in 'a blind accumulation of facts' (Simon, 1997: 362). Building on insights from cognitive sciences about information processing, it is possible to focus research on key points of development for an empirically based theory about economic and political decisions (Simon, 1997; 362). Among the areas Simon points to as ripe for theorising is knowledge about what directs attention to particular aspects of a decision.

Implications for policy

Different policy implications flow from each of the two approaches. The rational actor model is concerned chiefly with incentive structures; and it ascribes largely utility-maximising motives to actors. Hence from this approach one would assume that environmental or other regulation would be effective if building on economic incentives that would play into the preference structures of decision-makers.

Following the bounded rationality approach, policy-makers might also use economic incentives, but they would take into account the cognitive features affecting decision-making and policy design in accordance with these. Hence, policies should take into account the role of selective attention to information which might imply disproportionate or delayed adaptation to the economic incentive imposed by, say, an environmental tax. Generally, policies should be designed with simplicity in mind.

BR-based policies would also take into account that decision-makers generally have difficulties making trade-offs. Environmental behaviour may offer many situations in which humans encounter social dilemmas – having to trade off their personal preferences for consumption with socially benign behaviour, such as resource conservation, for instance. Behaviour in social dilemmas is often guided by norms rather than by self-interested calculation (Thøgersen and Gärling, 2001: 214). In this situation, policies might do better if they aim to influence social norms rather than cater to economic self-interest.

Notes

1 Vernon Smith points out that Adam Smith did not view human actors solely as motivated by self-interest; he was merely concerned with the function of self-interest in *market* exchanges (Smith, 1998: 1).
2 Sen proposes that a distinction be made between two forms of other-regarding behaviour: behaviour which implies that an actor derives welfare from the welfare of others, which he denotes 'sympathy', and behaviour which occurs out of a sense of commitment to a person or a principle regardless of its effect on the actor.
3 This version of the game is also known as the 'ultimatum game', cf. Camerer and Thaler (1995).
4 The paper, entitled 'Judgment under uncertainty: heuristics and biases' and first appearing in *Science*, laid the foundation for this branch of research.
5 See McFadden, 1999, or Kahnemann, 2002 for lists of such errors.
6 Pieces of information are referred to as 'chunks'. The size of a chunk is not constant and may increase with learning (Simon, 1990).
7 The argument mirrors that of evolutionary theorists such as Trivers (1971) and Cosmides and Tooby (1994), but Simon linked them directly to bounded rationality.
8 In fact, there have been calls for a merger or partial merger of the two approaches; see for instance Nørgaard, 1996 and Ostrom, 1991.
9 In this regard, the approach does not differ from many neo-classical economists.

3

A positive model of bounded rationality: from theoretical approaches to analytical model

> To describe, predict and explain behaviour of a system of bounded rationality, we must both construct a theory of the system's processes and describe the environment to which it is adapting. (Simon, 1990: 6–7)

Bounded rationality is a model of interaction; its focus is the interface between the cognitive architecture of a decision-maker and the environment in which he operates. Todd and Gigerenzer liken bounded rationality to a pair of scissors, with the mind as one blade, and the structure of the environment as another: 'To understand behaviour, one has to look at both and how they fit together' (2003: 146). This implies that the cognitively based constraints on rational decision-making gain importance in some circumstances more than in others.

The underlying idea is that rational decisions and problem-solving are essentially about adapting behaviour to environmental incentives. Fully rational behaviour, therefore, is behaviour that is optimal in the sense that it is in complete correspondence with environmental incentives and constraints, as well as the preferences of the decision-maker. Boundedly rational behaviour, by implication, is not fully adapted to the information present in the decision environment. This is because the cognitive make-up of humans is such that we cannot perform equally well in all environments; information-rich environments and complex tasks are notoriously difficult to tackle for the human cognitive apparatus. Humans can process only limited amounts of information at a time; in fact, the boundedly rational actor is a disproportionate information processor, paying attention to some external stimuli and ignoring others. Hence, 'objective information is transformed in the process of thought. It involves the tendency of people to react differently to identical information depending on the circumstances' (Jones, 2001: 9). Decision-making becomes a process of selective attention and serial information processing and is often shaped by simplifying decision mechanisms. All in all, this leads sometimes to fully rational decisions and sometimes to boundedly rational decisions.

This chapter draws on key insights and theoretic elements from the bounded rationality approach to develop an analytical model applicable to empirical study. Thus, the framework must have a dual focus on decision environments and the processes by which decisions are reached. Firstly, the framework must specify features of the decision environment that are conducive to rational or boundedly rational behaviours, respectively. Secondly, the framework must specify key features of decision-making processes, of individuals as well as organisations, and how these interact with different decision environments. Thirdly, the framework must consider criteria for how to define boundedly rational behaviour.

Decision environment

The decision environment may be understood as 'the opportunities and constraints that affect an individual's efforts toward goal accomplishments' (Jones, 2001: 7). Douglass North has suggested that fully rational behaviour, i.e. goal accomplishment, could be expected in situations characterised by simple problems, complete information, repetitive situations and high motivation (North, 1993). The first three conditions relate to the decision environment, whereas motivation is an attribute associated with the specific subject of decision as well as the decision-maker. These conditions mirror roughly the conditions specified by bounded rationality theory as determinants of boundedly rational behaviour. In other words, when the problem is complex, determined in part by the fluidity and uncertainty of the information environment, when time is scarce, and when multiple objectives conflict, decision-makers will be more likely to exhibit bounded rationality rather than full rationality (Simon, 1985; Jones, 2001).

Decision environments vary in *complexity*. Problems that involve many alternatives and must be compared across many dimensions are cognitively demanding and may exceed the computation skills of actors (Simon, 1990; Payne *et al.*, 1993; Jones, 2001; Bendor, 2003). Selecting the proper or most relevant features in an information space becomes more difficult the more complex the task, and computing the optimal response given one's preference structure even more so. Whereas the neo-classic model of rationality may allow for *lack of information* as a constraint on full rationality, the bounded rationality approach rather points to *information overload* as a condition which causes complexity.

Complexity is amplified when decision environments change frequently. According to Denzau and North (2000: 27), complexity is inversely related to the familiar. Hence, the *degree of stability* of the decision environment affects performance. Stable environments offer actors the opportunity to learn and adapt, reducing complexity over time, while fluid and suddenly changing decision environments impede rational adaptation, because actors cannot rely on stored knowledge in such environments. Novel concepts may seem complex, because the decision-maker has no stored mental models of them, while rather complex ideas may appear simple if the decision-maker has previously been exposed to them and thus recognises them (Denzau and North, 2000; for background, see also Simon, 1976: 88 on the role of habits and Bendor, 2003, on the role of expertise).

Uncertainty about the outcomes of various actions further affects the complexity of the task. Often actors cannot know with certainty whether an outcome will materialise or not. In those situations actors must assess different alternatives, not only in terms of their preferences but also with regard to the probability that these outcomes will actually materialise. As demonstrated time and again by researchers within the Tversky and Kahneman tradition, such judgements under uncertainty cause decision-makers great difficulty, often leading to systematic reasoning errors (Tversky and Kahneman, 1974, wrote the seminal article; see also Hastie, 2001 for a recent overview).

Pressure for time greatly compounds the cognitive challenges outlined above. Newell distinguished between information processing in the cognitive band vs. processing in the intendedly rational band (Jones, 2001). In the cognitive band, 'knowledge can be brought to bear on a problem, but problem search is constrained – the response is pre-programmed at the level of the deliberate act or involves rapid pattern recognition at the level of operations and units task' (Jones, 2001: 56–58). In the rational band, actors more consciously assess the task at hand and look for appropriate solutions. The implication is that behaviour is more likely to be adaptive, i.e. fully rational, when processed in the rational band. Time is one determinant of which of the two bands is activated. This implies that time available for a given task or decision will affect how adaptive it is.

The final condition under which boundedly rational behaviour may be expected is when *multiple* and particularly *conflicting goals* are at play. Contrary to the assumption of neo-classical economic theory, decision-makers cannot easily substitute seamlessly among objectives to define an optimal combination of parameters. Trading off is particularly difficult when objectives conflict, for instance, when a choice involves a gain on one dimension of an alternative and a loss on another dimension, or when the choice involves a good outcome under one contingency and a bad one under a different contingency (Simon, 1997: 297). Behavioural research has shown that decision-makers faced with conflicting objectives often either fail to make decisions or choose by the most salient objective exclusively, rather than trading off among several objectives (Jones, 2001).

Yet while these circumstances are more likely to bring about boundedly rational decisions, they do not necessarily determine such an output. The rationality of the decision is contingent also upon the decision process which constitutes the other independent variable in the framework.

Decision process

Not only do decision environments vary, but decision processes do as well. Decision mode denotes the manner in which information processing and choice transpire, and in their pure forms can be either impression-based and intuitive or memory-based and deliberative (Payne *et al.*, 1993).

Intuitive decision-making implies that decision-makers draw on stored knowledge, learned strategies and heuristics (Simon, 1990). Such strategies simplify decisions and problem-solving by providing ready-made solutions to previously encountered problems without conducting a complete search and decision process. Thus, they will be referred to here as a simple decision mode. A simple decision mode implies also that the decision process will incorporate only some dimensions of the problem, and that the use of information will be selective. Prepared, or learned, strategies enable actors to make decisions where the complexity of a situation, the abundance of information and time constraints might otherwise induce a cognitive meltdown. They enable decisions to occur without exhausting the attention capacity.

Simple decision modes may, and often will, take the form of satisficing, cf. Chapter 2. This implies that the decision-maker predefines an aspiration level, a target, for a good enough outcome and stops the search for information and alternatives once this aspiration level has been met. In other words, the decision-maker stops short of achieving an optimal outcome. The features of the simple decision mode will be further elaborated on later in this chapter in order to facilitate empirical analysis.

Alternatively, decision-makers may employ a synoptic decision mode, drawing consciously on the knowledge stored in memory. This has been referred to as deliberative decision-making (Payne *et al.*, 1993; Jones, 2001). In this context it will be referred to as *comprehensive* decision-making. This is the decision-making model embedded in, although not explicitly described by, the rational actor model. It is characterised by a conscious consideration of all relevant parameters, weighting their relative importance to arrive at an optimal outcome completely adapted to environmental incentives and circumstances.

The bounded rationality approach claims that most decision-making is to some extent intuitive in the sense that it draws on learned strategies and known solutions (Jones, 1999, 2001). The many simultaneous claims on the attention of decision-makers make this necessary. However, decision-makers also can and do employ the comprehensive decision mode.

Determinants of the decision process: motivation and time
High motivation has been identified as important for rational decision-making, as it increases attention to the decision (North, 1993; Denzau and North, 2000). In other words, motivation may prompt a switch from a simple and routine-oriented decision mode to a comprehensive decision-making mode. This is in line with Tversky and Kahneman's conclusion that economic or other incentives work in decision-making experiments because they prompt decision-makers to increase attention and consideration given to the decision (1986, cited in Payne *et al.*, 1993: 111).[1]

Denzau and North, taking a psycho-sociological approach, point to two sources of motivation (2000: 27). One source of motivation is that the decision is central to the identity or self-assessment of the decision-maker. The other source of motivation is the confidence of the decision-maker that his choice will affect the outcome of a situation. Denzau and North refer here to decision situations involving multiple actors (auctioning experiments) or collective decision-making bodies. But this argument would seem to apply also for parametric decisions characterised by uncertainty. In situations of great uncertainty about outcomes even individual decision-makers may feel less confident that their choice will bring about a desired outcome, which could reduce motivation.

Other researchers have linked decision mode to emotional states. Specific emotional states are directly related to decision modes. Studies have found that positive emotions prompted a more easygoing decision process, using shortcuts and heuristic search, while negative emotions, particularly anxiety, prompted actors to switch into a more comprehensive decision process (Marcus and MacKuen, 1993; Schwarz and Bless, cited in Oatley, 2001). However, anxiety is episodic and rare, which suggests that the influence of a negative effect is sporadic (Marcus and MacKuen, 1993). Much of the time decision-making proceeds without actors paying much attention to it, letting habit and simple decision rules guide. But every now and then, environmental features will evoke emotions that prompt actors to pay closer attention to the decision. In those situations they will switch into a comprehensive decision mode. Shifts in or new external stimuli grab the attention of actors, but only if they evoke emotional responses, particularly anxiety. This implies that the affect associated with certain situations offers a clue as to what type of decision process will ensue (Jones, 2001).

In addition to motivation, the decision process is also determined by the amount of time available for decision-making. Hence, a simple decision process is more likely to occur when decisions are made on the fly or otherwise time constrained as opposed to when there is adequate time for consideration.

Decisions – rational or boundedly rational?

While the analytical framework holds that boundedly rational decisions are more likely under conditions of complexity and uncertainty, and when employing the simple decision mode, it is not possible to specify a simple causal relation between these conditions and the character of the choice. Even complex circumstances may be overcome or compensated for through a comprehensive decision mode. Likewise, simple decision mechanisms such as heuristics may result in optimal decisions. In fact, Jones points out that heuristics should not be viewed as 'the key limitation on our decision-making capacity' (2001: 73).

Heuristics, routines, pattern matching and other stored decision mechanisms compensate for the cognitive limitations of boundedly rational decision-makers in complex decision environments (see for instance Bendor, 2003: 459–460). Such prepared strategies embed lessons learned from previous, similar experience and, therefore, offer solutions without requiring cognitively demanding decision processes. They may yield rational outcomes when the strategy fits the situation. When, on the other hand, these decision rules are not appropriate to the tasks, the outcomes will more likely be boundedly rational. It is *possible*, then, that decision by prepared strategies will lead to the same outcome as a fully rational decision process would. But this is far from ensured, because simplifying decision mechanisms introduce the possibility of distortions in the decision process. However, the theory does offer pointers as to when the boundedly rational decision mode is likely to produce a fully rational decision, even in a complex decision environment.

When do simple decision rules yield rational outcomes?

Simple problems, ample time, reasonably predictable outcomes and single goals accommodate a happy marriage of circumstances with intuitive decision modes, one that is more conducive to a fully rational decision despite simple decision modes.

But features related to the individual decision-maker also affect the relationship between circumstances, decision mode and decision output. *Experience* on the part of the decision-maker increases the chances that a decision, even arrived at on the fly, will approximate a rational decision. This is because the very notion of prepared strategies indicates that actors can learn effective responses to given problems, as they gain experience in a particular problem domain. Learning, therefore, expands an actor's cognitive capacities and improves his information processing in this domain. Experienced actors, experts as it were, are more likely to have appropriate strategies on hand and to apply them more accurately. The implication for empirical study is of course that one should expect actors' experience in a given problem domain to influence their performance, so that more experienced actors should be closer to a fully rational standard of behaviour than less experienced actors. When measuring performance *over time*, the expectation should be that each actor would improve his performance relative to the rational standard.

However, there is one caveat, and an important one, to this proposition. Learned strategies may become outdated. Because actors do not update information continuously or in complete synchronisation with changes in the environment, prepared strategies that work well under one set of circumstances may cease to work as circumstances change (Jones, 2001). When the prepared strategies no longer fit the circumstances they will not yield optimal responses. This means that learned strategies will probably be less adaptive in decision contexts characterised by a high degree of change and fluidity. This leads back to the effect of the decision environment in that the stability of the context conditions the rationality of the outcome.

Standards of rationality
The analytical frame begs the question of how to ascertain the rationality of a decision, particularly in an empirical setting. Fully

rational decisions are those which maximise the utility of the deci-sion-maker, reflecting their preferences as well the constraints they are faced with, such as budget size. Hence, in order to assess the rationality of a decision, the analyst must assume, deduce or gain concrete knowledge of the particular preferences of the actor.

Boundedly rational decisions also reflect in some measure the objectives or preferences of the decision-maker. But boundedly rational decisions do not follow linearly from the preferences of the decision-maker and, therefore, bounded rationality cannot be identified in terms of a unique decision output or a point predic-tion. A boundedly rational choice deviates from the optimal response, but by how much or in what direction is not necessar-ily predictable.

This means that in an empirical context boundedly rational decision output can be established primarily as deviation from optimal decisions. This does not distinguish bounded rationality from a lack of rationality or irrationality. Unfortunately, there is no way to draw a line here other than with reference to the deci-sion process. Bounded rationality is therefore also established by the presence of simple decision mechanisms in the decision process. Another criterion which may serve to distinguish bounded rationality behaviour from non-rational behaviour is whether or not the actor pursues goals.

Satisficing conceivably represents a specific standard for boundedly rational decisions. Although March (1994) points out that satisficing should be viewed more as a decision strategy, the concept does incorporate a standard of rationality: a choice is boundedly rational if it fulfils a predefined aspiration level but falls short of representing an optimal choice. In fact, Simon in some contexts referred to *satisfactory* decisions as an alternative to optimal ones (see, for instance, 1997: 295). Using this standard for empirical analysis requires that decision-makers consciously define such aspiration levels, and that such information is avail-able for the assessment of rationality.

But in most empirical studies two options are available for determining deviation from fully rational behaviour: all non-optimal behaviour is defined as boundedly rational, which is not a satisfactory solution, or the evaluation must take into account also the character of the decision process.

The role of institutions

As this study aims to understand responses to environmental regulation, the role of institutions must necessarily be included in the analytical framework. Institutions enter the analytical framework in several ways. Firstly, formal institutions, such as regulatory measures, constitute decision parameters. As such they alter the problem definition and incentive structure facing the decision-maker. For instance, a CO_2 tax on energy would affect decision-makers' evaluations of different sources of energy. In this capacity, institutions affect the complexity of the decision environment. Secondly, institutions constitute decision rules. Laws, organisational standards or professional or social norms embody templates for how to go about certain problems; they structure information, reduce uncertainty and may direct attention to certain features of the decision environment. As such they may reduce decision and other transaction costs by simplifying decisions (Jones, 2001: 18–21; see also North, 1989, 1993). However, institutions may also increase complexity, either substantively or because institutions change, destabilising the decision environment in the process.

Institutions thus affect the complexity of the decision environment; they may define the types of decision rules available, and the degree of stability in the institutional context affects the chances that a simple decision rule actually matches the environment and results in a rational decision.

Model of analysis

Figure 3.1. outlines the main variables and causal chains of the analytical framework that will be applied to the empirical analysis later in the book.

The framework generally assumes that decision-makers, particularly in economic and political realms, are guided by goals and that they *intend* to make optimal decisions. However, actual decisions are conditioned by the decision environment framing the decision and by the decision processes employed, and specifically by the degree to which the two match. Decision environment and decision process thus comprise the primary independent variables of this framework, while decision output represents its dependent variable.

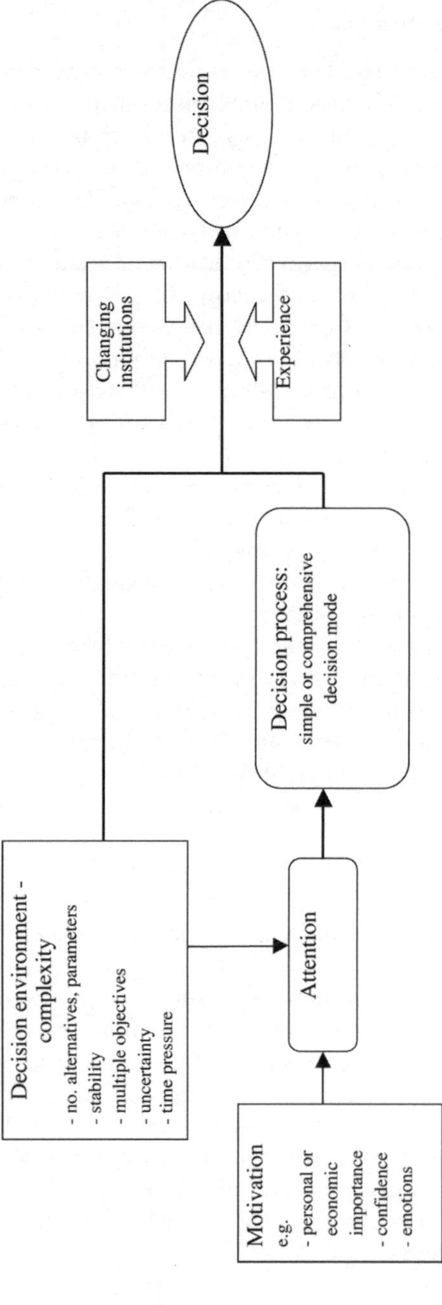

Figure 3.1   *Model of analysis*

Table 3.1 presents an ideal-type matrix of the overall relationships between circumstances and decision processes. The matrix is stylised in the sense that it provides an overview of the reasoning implied in the framework, but in empirical analysis it would be practically impossible to categorise decision environments and decision processes in a dichotomous manner. Both variables are more likely to be continuous. However, the matrix provides a skeleton for analysis of relationships between decision circumstances, decision processes and decision outputs. Firstly, one would expect a comprehensive decision process in a simple decision environment to result most often in fully optimal responses. Secondly, combining comprehensive decision modes and complex decision environments would lead to some deviation from optimal responses. The same goes for simple decision processes in simple decision environments. Finally, the most deviations from optimal behaviour should be expected when decision-makers apply simple decision strategies to complex decision environments.

Returning to Figure 3.1, the framework also indicates some preceding as well as conditioning variables. Firstly, the framework specifies that decision mode is determined by attention. Hence when decision-makers pay attention to a problem, they are more likely to switch into a comprehensive decision mode. Attention, in turn, is affected by the degree to which the decision-maker is motivated or alerted to pay attention to a specific situation. But attention, and by implication decision mode, is also partially a function of the decision environment. A decision-

Table 3.1   *Matrix of likely decision outputs for combinations of decision environments and decision processes*

Decision environment	Decision mode	
	Comprehensive	*Simple*
Simple	Fully rational decisions or few deviations	Moderate degree of deviation from the fully rational
Complex	Moderate degree of deviation from the fully rational	High degree of deviation from the fully rational

maker facing a multitude of tasks of great complexity will necessarily have less time for each of these tasks, and time pressure and
frequently changing conditions will lead to more decisions being
processed in the simple decision mode. In other words, the two
independent variables are also in part causally related, although
complexity in this broad sense does not definitively determine the
decision mode. Decision mode constitutes an independent as well
as a dependent variable in the framework.

Finally, Figure 3.1 indicates that the relationship between decision mode and decision output is determined also by the
experience of the decision-maker as well as by the degree of
change in the decision environment. Experienced decision-makers
may be able to make fully rational decisions more often than
inexperienced ones, even if they apply heuristics or other simple
strategies. This is because they have learned the most appropriate
strategies for different situations. Experience thus constitutes a
conditioning variable.

But learned strategies are useful only as long as the decision
environment remains stable or largely stable; hence, the degree of
change in the decision environment and the institutional context
is also likely to affect the match between a simple decision strategy and a decision output. Institutions affect the degree of
complexity; hence they form part of the independent variable
decision environment. But because *changes in institutions* affect
the usefulness of learned strategies they also constitute a conditioning variable in the framework, positioned between the two
independent variables, decision environment and decision
process, and the dependent variable, decision.

The framework gives rise to a set of analytical hypotheses
which will guide the empirical analysis.

- Boundedly rational behaviour will occur more often when the
  decision environment is complex in a broad sense, i.e. characterised by many decision parameters, information abundance,
  uncertainty and time pressure.
- Boundedly rational behaviour will occur more often when
  decision-makers employ a simplifying decision mode than
  when they employ a comprehensive decision mode.
  - A simplifying decision mode is more likely to occur when the
    decision-maker has low motivation.

- ○ A simplifying decision mode is more likely to occur when the decision-maker faces a multitude of tasks or must make decisions under time pressure.
  - ○ A simplifying decision mode will occur more often when the decision-maker operates with a multitude of objectives (or conflicting objectives).
- Boundedly rational behaviour will decrease over time as decision-makers learn, provided that the decision environment remains stable. However, frequent changes in the decision environment will lead to fluctuations.

The expectations will be specified in the context of the empirical case, once this has been introduced and discussed in the following chapters.

Features of boundedly rational decision processes

Empirical study of decision processes requires a more detailed description of the defining elements of simple decision processes. This will allow for proper identification of such behaviour in an empirical context and thus provide a better foundation for empirical test of the analytical framework. A framework for analysis of decision processes must account for the role of objectives in decision-making, specifically how decision-makers negotiate multiple and conflicting objectives. Further, the framework should outline the use of information and, finally, the model must specify the mechanisms by which the decision-maker ultimately settles on a choice of course of action. The general framework as outlined here applies to singular decisions as well as to the overall operations of a business organisation.

Objectives

The framework assumes that decision-makers pursue goals and that they pursue multiple, and sometimes conflicting, goals. This is no different from the rational actor approach. The difference lies in its conceptualisation of how decision-makers cope with multiple objectives. In the bounded rationality framework objectives are both incomplete and inconsistent, i.e. they do not reflect a complete preference structure and, therefore, cannot guide decision-makers toward optimal utility. When decision-makers cannot make trade-offs among multiple objectives they use a number of shortcuts. They may consider just the most salient objective or consider several objectives sequentially. In the first case, referred to as a lexicographic choice, alternatives will be evaluated based on how well they fulfil this particular objective; in the second case, referred to as elimination by aspects, objectives will be considered one at a time until one yields a clear choice (Jones, 2001: 70). Neither approach ensures an accurate weighting of objectives that reflects the overall preferences of the decision-maker in the neo-classical sense. Such sequential attention to objectives may occur in a business organisation when each department makes decisions guided exclusively by the objectives of that department, whether or not they coincide with the overall objectives of the organisation (Cyert and March, 1992; March, 1994).

Conflicting objectives are particularly difficult to handle. Choices may involve conflicting objectives when they involve gains in one dimension of a problem but losses in another dimension, or where the objectives of one section of an organisation can be met by a certain choice which works against the objectives of a different section of the organisation. In such situations, decision-makers may choose alternatives which are satisfactory with regard to all objectives but are not optimal, akin to a lowest common denominator approach. In some cases, decision-makers will postpone or altogether avoid making the decision or launch a search for other solutions (Simon, 1997: 297; Jones, 2001).

In order to mediate among multiple objectives, decision-making organisms may set aspiration levels which refer to a predefined target of utility. Instead of searching for an alternative that fulfils optimal utility given several objectives, decision-makers define a minimum level of goal attainment that will be satisfactory. If an alternative meets this level it may be chosen (March, 1994; Simon, 1997: 296; Jones, 2001).

In the context of empirical analysis, then, sequential attention to stated objectives or disjointed integration of objectives in the decision may be taken as evidence of a boundedly rational decision process. Specifically, the framework holds that decision-makers will express their objectives in terms of aspiration levels, that is, in terms of acceptable outcomes rather than in terms of optimality.

Information processing

The mismatch between the amount of available information and the information processing capacity of decision-making organisms directs attention to the way in which decision-makers select and combine information.

First of all, search for and use of information is limited in part by the problem at hand, or more specifically by the decision-maker's definition of the problem. A decision is framed; that is, it is given a specific interpretation which includes some aspects and excludes others (March, 1994: 14). Frames and similar devices such as stereotypes and categorisations are heuristics, which simplify information search. They structure the selection of information by pointing attention to and imparting meaning on certain features of a situation or task.

The objectives pursued by the actors provide an immediate framing of the task which is mirrored in information processing. But objectives may follow from the decision-maker's perception of the problem, which can have many sources.

In experimental studies, Newell and Simon found that decision-makers form problem definitions based on the instructions given, and on information available in the environment, as well as on experience from previous and similar tasks and experience with other tasks which has been transformed into general-purpose problem-solving skills (Newell and Simon, 1972, cited in Jones, 2001: 65). Thus the current task is matched with previous decision problems, which yields not only a problem definition, but also entails a set of potential decision strategies and perhaps even solutions. Decision-makers reason by analogy (Jones, 2001: 72).

Frames may also follow from the context in which the decision takes place. In the words of March, frames tend to be narrow or local (1994: 14). Thus, when a business organisation faces increased competition, the sales department may frame the challenge in terms of how to increase or maintain sales while the production manager may see the challenge as cost-cutting. This is because each sub-unit is defined partly by the means and methods they bring to bear on the tasks concerned, but also because each sub-unit pursues different sub-goals. Actions following from each of these frames may be compatible and work in the same direction, but are not necessarily so. Local frames are more likely to prevail where tasks are subdivided to cope with complexity, as in setting up specialist units within organisations. They are also more likely to result in sequential attention to and inadequate integration of sub-goals.

Finally, problem definitions may be framed by the social context in which the decision-maker operates. Humans learn socially from groups with which they identify; hence they may derive their perceptions of particular situations from these groups, be it family, profession or local community (Simon, 1997: 248–250; Jones, 2001: 116). This resembles March's and Olsen's notion that humans follow rules in order to derive meaning and identity (March and Olsen, 1989, 1995; March, 1994). But in the framework applied here it does not go so far as to exclude intended rationality; decision-makers may still apply a conse-quentialist logic, but the means by which they judge consequences may be socially derived, as may in fact the substance of the goals.

Experience, professional frames, heuristics or similar means simplify information processing, but these features also entail that not all relevant information is sought or all alternatives consid-ered (March 1994; Simon, 1997).

Satisficing
According to March (1994), satisficing may be interpreted as a heuristic used in information search. As such it 'specifies the conditions under which search is triggered and stopped' (1994: 29). In this perspective, search for new solutions and information is triggered primarily by failure in a particular area. Decision-makers set performance targets and monitor performance in relation to these targets. Only if performance falls below expec-tations will they look for improvements. Furthermore, the search for alternative solutions continues only until an alternative is found which meets predefined aspiration levels. If the search does not produce alternatives that meet the aspirations, these will be lowered, but if a satisfactory alternative is found quickly, aspira-tion levels may be increased (Simon, 1997: 295–297). As such, search aims to produce alternatives which are better than those used in the past.

Choice

In a comprehensive decision-making mode, the actor seeks to integrate all of their objectives and all available information in a synoptic, calculating fashion. The simple decision mode, in contrast, considers objectives sequentially and selectively and uses largely simple decision mechanisms.

Heuristics feature prominently in the assessment of different courses of action. Heuristics allow decision-makers to make conjectures based on available information, which in turn facilitate decisions that might otherwise be difficult to make (Tversky and Kahneman, 1974; see also Shefrin, 2002, for an overview of heuristics in the finance industry). For instance, decision-makers typically look for an anchoring value when they assess the outcome of a given choice (Tversky and Kahneman, 1974). An anchor serves as a baseline value, and when such anchors are available, decision-makers tend to adjust their own valuations, such as a price they are willing to pay, either up or down from this anchor. The resulting prices are likely to be quite different from the prices they would have arrived at in open-ended decisions, as has been shown in many a valuation study (Hansen, 1997; Payne *et al.*, 2000).

Loss aversion and differential assessment of risk also play a significant role in evaluation of alternatives. Firstly, decision-makers typically evaluate alternatives differently if they are presented as gains rather than losses (Jones 2001: 71; see also Thaler *et al.*, 1992; Payne *et al.*, 1993). This implies that decision-makers tend to value the status quo too highly and that they value what they have more than what they might gain. For instance, experiments have shown that people who are given an object typically value this object at a much higher price than people who are not given the object (see Thaler *et al.*, 1992). Loss aversion is also related to differential assessment of risk. Faced with a loss, decision-makers are prone to take a larger risk than when faced with the possibility of a gain (Kahneman and Tversky, 1979).

Some decision mechanisms reflect an aversion for making trade-offs among objectives. Thus, as described at the beginning of the chapter, a decision-maker may choose simply by the most salient objective, known as a lexicographic approach, or may evaluate choices based on one objective at a time, until one yields a clear choice in a process of elimination (Jones, 2001: 70). Or the decision-maker may simply try out an alternative and stick with it if it works. Thus trial-and-error also represents a simple decision rule.

Satisficing represents the iconic example of simple decision strategies. It also describes a simple criterion for choosing among alternatives: the first alternative which meets aspiration levels on one or all decision parameters is chosen, and the criterion of choice is that an alternative must be satisfactory rather than optimal (Simon, 1997: 295).

In addition to these *cognitive* shortcuts to choice, decision-makers use *social* cues to evaluate alternatives; they look to those around them to learn what works or what is valued in a given community. This is sometimes referred to as a bandwagon effect (Jones, 2001).

Typical errors in decision-making

It has been repeated throughout these last two chapters that simple decision strategies may well be adaptive in the sense that they lead to optimal or reasonably optimal decisions. But behavioural research has also demonstrated systematic reasoning errors that typically affect decision-making and decision-making organisms.

Heuristics and biases

Heuristics are cognitive devices that facilitate decision-making. For instance, the value of social cues is expressed in the saying 'there is no reason to reinvent the wheel'. But heuristics may also systematically bias decisions when they do not fit the circumstances. In a literature review, Arnott identified 37 specific biases (2006: 59–60). Among the more commonly recognised biases are:

- Confidence – decision-makers tend to overestimate the precision of their information. Consequently, they may not estimate realistically worst and best possible scenarios. For instance, studies have shown that private investors are overconfident in their abilities to outperform the market and therefore trade much too often, but similar biases are common among professional traders and analysts (Klayman *et al.*, 1999; Shefrin, 2002: 18, 132–133).

- Confirmation – decision-makers tend to pay more attention to information which confirms the alternatives to which they may be predisposed and do not look for disconfirming information (a risk which is very real also in the domain of research).
- Loss aversion – while loss aversion may result in carefully considered decisions, it also frequently induces decision-makers to hang on to losing propositions for too long or, as has been found in behavioural finance studies, to sell winners too early (Shefrin, 2002: 107–117).

While these biases are presented with reference to individual decision-makers they may apply also to organisations and other collective decisions. Hence, large corporations may be just as loath to loss aversion as the individual investor. Shefrin (2002: 24–25) recounts how Apple Computer Inc continued to invest many years and large sums in the development of a palm computer, Newton, despite evidence that it would never live up to early promises. Apparently, it took a change of CEO, who was less attached to the project, to cancel the project (Shefrin 2002: 24–25).

Slack

Because organisations satisfice, they are most likely to look for new solutions when they are performing below their aspiration levels or when stimulated by indication of some failure. Hence, during good times organisations tend to incur slack, defined broadly as sub-optimal use of resources. As March observed: 'Performance adapts to aspirations by increasing search and decreasing slack in the face of failure and increasing slack when faced with success' (March, 1994: 29).

The bounded rationality perspective emphasises that slack occurs because organisations should be viewed as coalitions of participants, each staying with the organisation as long as the payoff meets their aspiration levels. When some participants, through bargaining, achieve higher payoffs than necessary to induce them to stay in the organisation, the organisation incurs slack (Douma and Schreuder, 1998: 91). This is possible because there is information asymmetry about the true objectives or aspiration level of the coalition partners, and management in successful organisations is under less pressure to figure out the true aspiration levels necessary to keep employees in the organisation. Another source of slack stems from sub-units of an organisation growing beyond what is justified from a strict calculation of additional costs and benefits (cf. Cyert and March, 1992). In either case it requires some indicator of failure, i.e. decreasing performance or performance below expectations, for organisations to reduce slack. In the same vein, Leibenstein (1966) has analysed the use of resources in business organisations and concludes that there are often considerable possibilities for efficiency gains: what he terms 'x-efficiency'. He argues that firms do not cost-minimise on their own, but require competitive pressure or other sources of motivation to reduce cost. Hence, companies must receive some environmental stimuli such as increased pressure from competition or 'adversity', i.e. a downturn in economic fortunes, in order to pay attention to cost functions; they do not operate at the margins of profit. Again, the importance of motivation for performance is emphasised.

Decision processes: criteria for empirical analysis

The features of decision processes outlined here may serve as indicators of simple decision modes; hence boundedly rational decision-making. To recap:

- Decision-makers juggle multiple objectives but attend to objectives in a sequential manner. Objectives are typically stated in terms of aspiration levels, and choice mechanisms may reflect aversion to trade-offs. In contrast, fully rational behaviour would manifest itself in that economic objectives override and integrate other objectives.
- Information processing is selective. The search for information is framed by objectives, and it is guided by cognitively as well as socially derived rules of thumb and other learned strategies. In contrast, fully rational behaviour would show as continuous updating of information and use of all available information.
- Choice is simplified by heuristics for evaluating alternatives and by simple decision rules, which may serve to avert explicit trade-offs. Satisficing is the iconic example of simple strategies. In contrast, fully rational behaviour implies synoptic processing and precise calculation.

This framework for analysis of decision processes suggests that decision processes in organisations as well as by individual decision-makers is largely characterised by rule following. But these rules may be of a cognitive as well as a social character (Jones, 2001: 200). In other words, the framework makes room for a consequentialist logic as well as a logic of appropriateness. In both frameworks, rules supply decision strategies and, as such, they represent means – either to goal achievement or to identity building.

Note

1 However, Kahneman and Tversky's general point is that many reasoning errors are hard-wired, i.e. they result from perceptual illusions, and therefore economic or other incentives will not always lead to better decisions.

4
Research design

Research in bounded rationality is driven in part by an ambition to build a theory which accurately reflects the complexity of real-world behaviour. This leads in the direction of descriptive and explorative studies. On the other hand, researchers within the tradition strive to build a model capable of generating specific predictions which can be subjected to empirical test. This leads to studies of decision domains where behaviour can be predicted more precisely. This sometimes leads to a dilemma between developing the theory, while at the same time proving its value as a theory. The question is whether the contradictory tendencies can be lessened. This chapter sketches a research strategy for a study of bounded rationality that may reasonably accomplish both.

Empirical study of bounded rationality

Research on bounded rationality has proceeded largely along two parallel tracks: experiments on individual decision-making carried out in cognitive laboratories, and case studies of organisational decision-making. The former approach was pioneered by psychologists Kahneman and Tversky and has been labelled the 'heuristics and biases' approach, because researchers in this approach have systematically demonstrated how human decision-making deviates from the neo-classical assumptions – specifically, how the use of heuristics may lead to sub-optimal outcomes (see, for instance, Kahneman *et al.*, 1982). As for organisational decision-making, the best known examples are synthesised in Simon's *Administrative Behaviour* (1976; see also March and Simon,

1958) and Cyert and March's *A Behavioural Theory of the Firm* (1992, originally 1963). Both rely on in-depth studies, using direct observation as the main source of data.

Each approach has its advantages and disadvantages, but neither has adequately bridged the gap between theory building and theory testing. Laboratory studies enable a close-up study of decision-making processes, which may yield quite precise knowledge of the interaction of human cognition with the decision environment. This is important for theory development and determination. Furthermore, experiments allow the researcher to frame the decision in such a manner that the fully rational response is clearly defined and thus may serve as a standard of choice against which the choice of the decision-maker may be measured. Precise prediction is a requirement for a proper test of a theory (Green and Shapiro, 1994: 38). However, critics have argued that these experiments have been more suitable for a test of rational choice theory than for bounded rationality theory, as they have shown how decision-makers do *not* fit the model of full rationality. At the same time, experimental studies have been criticised for a lack of empirical relevance in the sense that few problems in real life mirror the tasks of the laboratory (Shafir and LeBoeuf, 2002; Gigerenzer, 1996).[1]

The criticism does not invalidate the insights generated in the laboratory, but indicates that experimental studies should perhaps be formulated with greater empirical relevance, including realistic time frames and motivation structures (Simon, 1997: 289; Jones, 2001: 27).

However, a weightier objection to the use of laboratory experiments in this context is that bounded rationality concerns the very interaction of human cognition with a decision environment, which unlike laboratory experiments is anything but controlled. Therefore, Jones advocates the use of field study.

> While great strides have been made in recent years by psychologists and behavioural economists studying choices in the controlled arrangements of the laboratory, only serious field study can indicate how real choices are made in the 'structured, yet dynamic' environments of real choice situations. (Jones, 2002: 271)

Studies of decision-making in organisations, in contrast, generally do rest on in-depth case observations 'in the real world'.

These studies offer insights into the causal mechanisms of human and organisational decision-making and as mentioned above have produced the core concepts of the BR model. But in the words of Simon, who knew this first-hand, field studies are also 'extremely costly and time-consuming' (Simon, 1978: 354), which has limited their number. These relatively few studies lean toward the explorative and toward theory generation, whereas actual theory test has been scant. But the lack of theory testing in a field setting is not due simply to the resource demands of such studies. It lies also with the level of specificity of the BR model, which makes it difficult to make precise, hence falsifiable, predictions about a boundedly rational decision in a specific empirical setting.

Jones (1999, 2001) proposes an alternative approach which draws on the methodology of experimental studies, but applied to the field setting. He calls for 'studies explicitly organized around the limits of rational adaptation' (2001: xii). This involves comparison of observed behaviour with the behaviour predicted by rational theory and thus requires study of decisions where the decision environment is sufficiently structured to allow for a determination of the optimal response (Jones, 1999: 312). This is essentially what experimental economists do when they set up a specific incentive structure, such as a game, and study the reasoning processes and responses of the participants. In the field, structured institutional settings may mirror the experimental set-up, as institutions generate incentive structures which can be understood and modelled for quantitative testing (Jones, 1999: 312, 319). Where decision-makers do not respond as expected in the fully rational model, Jones speaks of 'bounded rationality showing through' and suggests that researchers should study more closely 'adaptive behaviour and its failure in particular situations' (Jones, 2001: xi; see also Jones, 1999: 319 and 2001: 63). As such, this approach links the study of decision outcomes to studies of decision processes, and it offers a direction for theory building.

But the approach also offers a strategy for testing bounded rationality theory. The bounded rationality framework maintains that deviations from rationality are linked to the human cognitive architecture and specifies circumstances when bounded rationality is more likely to come into play. This permits drawing up predictions as to when bounded rationality will show through.

These predictions can be tested precisely on those decisions that allow for a reasonable specification of the fully rational choice. However, Jones and scholars working in this tradition do not generally advocate testing against predictions of specific choices (point predictions), but prefer instead studies of frequency distributions of large decision outputs. Bounded rationality is better suited for marginal predictions, i.e. predictions about movements in response to changes in the decision context. Hence, propositions such as 'actors are more likely to deviate from optimal behaviour in unstable environments than in stable environments' are testable marginal predictions that would follow from the BR framework. Using this research approach, Jones and others have carried out large quantitative analyses of agenda setting (Baumgartner and Jones, 1993, cited in Jones, 2001) and budgeting (Padget, 1980; Jones *et al.*, 1996, cited in Jones, 2001), among others.

The research strategy suggested by Jones thus offers the promise of bridge-building between the rather narrow experimental approach, with its focus on specific decision mechanisms or processing flaws, and the more exploratory studies of organisational decision processes. This approach of 'studying the limits of rationality' seems quite appropriate for the current level of specificity of the bounded rationality framework, because it builds specifically on the insights generated both in laboratories and single case organisations but aims to develop these into a more coherent theoretical perspective on decision-making (Jones, 2001: 25–26).

The present study draws on this strategy, but returns from the study of institutional decision output to the micro-foundation of rational studies, i.e. the level of the individual decision-maker. But in contrast to previous research on individual decision-makers, this study uses field data in order to enhance its relevance for incentive-based regulatory theory. In order to do so, the study must identify an arena of decision-making that is sufficiently structured to determine a criterion for fully rational decisions against which the actual decisions may be compared. Furthermore, as the theoretical framework posits that the decision environment partially conditions decision outcomes, the case selected should encompass variation in such environmental circumstances. Finally, as Jones suggests that the deviations from rational behaviour indicate opportunities for theoretical development, the case should be amenable to the study of decision processes.

Making the case for a case: fertiliser practice

Fertiliser practice among Danish farmers makes for an appropriate, if slightly untraditional, case for a study of boundedly rational decision-making, because it fulfils all of the criteria set out: rational decisions must be identifiable, decision environments and decision processes must vary, and decision processes can be studied in depth.

As for the rational standard, a set of norms for economically optimal nitrogen levels exists. These incorporate research findings gathered over 20 years showing variations in crop yields under different climatic and soil conditions as well as agricultural practices and technologies. Thus, the norms represent the best available knowledge as to the most appropriate level of fertiliser for each crop, adjusted according to soil type and climatic zone. Importantly, the norms reflect the *economically optimal* level, as they take into account also crop prices and fertiliser costs (Hansen, 1990). In other words, the norms are calculated along marginalist economic principles where optimal input level is determined by balancing the cost of an extra unit of input factor with the value gained by extra units of physical output. The fertiliser norms were introduced as an environmental regulation in 1994, placing a cap on the use of nitrogen. This means that each farm has a nitrogen quota which aggregates the economically optimal nitrogen level for each field. In years with unusual weather conditions the norms are adjusted up or down to ensure that crops are allotted the appropriate amount of nitrogen. Furthermore, farmers who have a track record of above-average yields for their area are allowed to adjust norms upwards to reflect these yields. Prior to 1994, agricultural advisory services produced a set of recommended norms, largely calculated according to the same principles.

Fertiliser norms – a valid indicator of rational behaviour?

Nitrogen norms appear to represent the very standard of rationality, so rarely found in field research, against which actual behaviour may be compared. Even so a few issues require consideration as they do not represent a flawless standard of rational behaviour.

First of all, the norm is crude. It cannot take into account different soil types within a single field, or topographical differences, which the individual farmer knows to make a difference. But for the present study of decision-making the point is not to determine whether or not farmers fertilise optimally (i.e. point predictions), but rather to study whether they deviate *more* or *less* from norms as predicted by variation in circumstances and decision processes, i.e. the approach undertaken here will be to analyse in terms of comparative statics (Green and Shapiro, 1994; see also Bendor, 2003). For this purpose the norm may be considered a valid yardstick for optimal behaviour.

Secondly, although the regulatory norm appears rather sophisticated in its marginal approach, there are costs which it does not incorporate, specifically relating to transport of fertiliser. Presumably, transportation costs in fertiliser planning would affect the optima, particularly of livestock farms as well as manure-importing crop farms, as transport of manure is costly. However, as regulations force farmers to use the organic fertiliser produced on the farm and as the nitrogen quota assumes a minimum use of nitrogen from livestock for these farms, they do have an incentive to use this form of fertiliser. Thus, transportation cost could affect the relative allocation of artificial and livestock fertilisers across fields, but should not affect the level of fertilisers.

Fertiliser norms do not constitute a perfect standard of rational behaviour, but a suitably designed study may get at the effect of crude norms and transportation costs, and thus the norms may be considered appropriate indicators of optimal behaviour.

Variation in decision environment and decision processes

The theory holds that deviation from fully rational behaviour is more likely in complex decision environments. To test this prediction, fertiliser management must be complex and contextual circumstances must create variations in the level of complexity. Furthermore, the theory holds that variations in decision processes affect deviation from fully optimal behaviour.

How to determine the right amount of fertiliser: complexity of the task

In the institution-free world (i.e. a world without fertiliser norms), determining the right amount of fertiliser involves two questions: 1) what is the physically optimal level of fertiliser, i.e. what is the amount of fertiliser that produces the highest physical output, and 2) what is the economically optimal level of fertiliser, i.e. where does the marginal cost of an extra unit of fertiliser equal the marginal value of physical yield produced by that unit of fertiliser?

As for physical output, the right amount of fertiliser depends first of all on the crop to be grown and the soil and climate conditions under which it is grown. But it also depends on what was grown on the field previously, as different crops affect soil nutrient storage differently. Even when measuring optimal fertiliser strictly in physical terms (not including economic or environmental criteria), it is possible to apply too much fertiliser. Fast-growing crops may 'lodge' (bend or fall), and too much fertiliser may reduce the quality of the crop. For crops such as barley and wheat, quality is measured in terms of protein level, which requires just enough but not too much fertiliser. As for the economically optimal level of fertiliser, the farmer must calculate according to marginalist principles the value of the yield of the crop against the cost of fertilisers. Hence, fertiliser management is by all accounts a complex affair.

However, fertiliser regulation has reduced the complexity of the task considerably, indicating both an optimal level for each field and putting a cap on the overall amount of fertiliser. One way to ensure variation in complexity is, therefore, to analyse fertiliser behaviour over time, i.e. before and after introduction of the norms.

Furthermore, complexity of the decision environment may be as important for outcomes as the complexity of the task itself. And complexity varies across farmers with regard to decision context. Some farmers have more activities competing for their time and attention than others. The regulations require high util-isation rates of manure, which increases the complexity in fertiliser planning for farmers with manure but not for farmers without. Likewise, the institutional context changes repeatedly, which also increases complexity and allows for analysis over time.

Variation in decision processes

Farmers may also vary in decision processes. Some may undertake comprehensive calculations of proper fertiliser levels and follow them precisely; others may go by rough estimates of what is needed. Some may change the plan from year to year; others may follow the same plan from year to year, making only minor adjustments. Some may evaluate carefully the practice and incorporate this year's lessons into next year's practice. Generally, the case represents many potential sources of variation also in decision processes.

Most-likely or least-likely test

One criterion for evaluating the strength of a theory is the difficulty of the test to which it was put (King, Keohane and Verba, 1994: 209). At issue is whether the case represents a least-likely or a most-likely observation of the theory.

The fertiliser case cannot be defined uniformly as a most-likely or a least-likely test of the bounded rationality framework. It is a most-likely case of the theory in that fertiliser decisions are quite complex. There is also uncertainty about the outcome of fertiliser decisions, which would tend to increase deviation from optimal behaviour. Finally, the institutional context is changed frequently enough to increase complexity. All of these factors improve the probability that a boundedly rational outcome will materialise and therefore point to a weak test of the theory.

On the other hand, the norm in and of itself tends to simplify the decision, working against the predictions. Likewise, farmers are professionals who have typically received formal training, and thus know how to calculate optimal fertiliser levels. Presumably farmers are also motivated to optimise economically (although in the framework this is truly an empirical question). All of these factors put the theory to a strong test, and in this sense fertiliser management is a least-likely case.

Description and discussion of quantitative analysis

Translating the analytical framework into the empirical context of the case, the question for this study is whether deviation from optimal fertiliser levels can be explained by complex circumstances and simple decision strategies. Ideally, the study would have data on all of these variables for all units of analysis. However, this poses practical challenges. The relationship between the independent variable 'decision environment' and the dependent variable 'decisions' are best assessed in a large-N study, using statistical analysis to infer an underlying causal relationship. In principle, statistical evidence could also be obtained about decision processes, but categorisation of decision processes requires in-depth analysis and, within the resource constraints of the current study, it is not practically feasible to undertake such analysis of a large number of units.

Hence, the study will use two different research strategies: a quantitative, multivariate analysis for examination of the relationship of circumstances on decisions, and a qualitative, interview-based analysis for examination of decision processes. The qualitative study of decision processes will produce knowledge about the effect of circumstances on decision processes and decisions. But the numbers will be too small for statistical test. As such the analysis will not be able to *test* the entire analytical framework. Rather, the ambition is to *make plausible* the explanatory power of the analytical framework and to explain the role of each variable through methodological and analytical triangulation. Such triangulation may improve studies of complex phenomena (Andersen, L., 2005). In this case, the synthesis of the two approaches is flawed, because methods and sub-questions split along the same lines. Yet the final word on the study's suitability for analytic generalisation can only be spoken in the context of the actual analysis.

Data for analysing the effect of decision environment

As part of a national monitoring programme implemented from 1988–89, Denmark's National Environmental Research Institute (NERI) has gathered detailed data about farmers' fertiliser practices in order to assess the effect of environmental regulation on the use of fertiliser and ultimately on the link between farm practices and nutrient leaching from fields (for a description of the study, see for instance Grant *et al.*, 1995). Data have been collected from approximately the same farms every year since 1990, although *farmers* may have been substituted due to changes in ownership. The dataset will be used for a multivariate, quantitative analysis of fertiliser patterns.

The Agricultural Monitoring Catchment Programme – or to use the simple Danish acronym, 'LOOP' – comprises seven waterway catchment areas, all dominated by agriculture (Grant *et al.*, 2001). Farmers with land within these catchment areas have been interviewed annually to uncover agricultural practices. Each interview maps out all information necessary for a complete picture of the fertiliser patterns of the farm. The result is a database containing, for each farm, precise information about acreage, livestock herds, field sizes, crops grown, fertiliser levels, the exact mix of artificial and natural fertilisers, and yields (DMU, 2000/2001). Field level data are key as they enable comparison of actual fertiliser levels with the economically optimal fertiliser norms. The data therefore allow for quantitative analysis of decision outputs.

The database does not include economic data, nor does it include personal information about each farmer such as age, education level or how many years the farmer has owned the farm. The interviews also do not include questions about the actual decision processes.

The study consists of anywhere from 165 farms in 1990 to 128 farms at the lowest in 1997. Each farm was included in the study *qua* its physical location in the catchment areas that were chosen for the study. Catchment areas were selected to achieve the best possible representation of the national farm population on parameters such as soil types, climate, size, livestock intensity and crop composition (Grant *et al.*, 1995: 9). The study population is largely representative of the population of Danish farms with regard to their distribution across farm categories and size, but the livestock intensity is higher for the study population than for the at-large population of farms (Grant *et al.*, 1995, 1997). In 1998, one catchment area with just a few farms was replaced with another area with more farms. This reduced the livestock intensity in the study population to levels matching those of the farming population as a whole.

The primary guideline is that all farms with more than two hectares of land participate in the study. Some farms straddle the border of a catchment area and may participate with all of their fields or just those located in the catchment. Livestock farms are typically included with all of their fields. This poses a potential problem for comparison involving different farm types, as it is impossible to know whether aberrant fertiliser patterns for crop farmers reflect actual differences or measurement errors related to partial data from this type of farm. Yet there is no reason to believe that this introduces a systematic bias in terms of large or small deviations from optimal behaviour. A field is included in the study if it is located inside the catchment area, a circumstance presumably unrelated to the fertiliser decisions of the farmer.

Data collection

The interviews were conducted on site by agricultural advisers in most cases, but also by county officials or by a private contractor in forest and landscape management. Since the mid-1990s interviewers have been typing answers directly into a special version of a computer program, which is used by many farmers for planning and management. Interviewers cross-check data with the annual fertiliser accounts that farmers must submit to national authorities as well as with interview data from the previous year (DMU, 2000/2001). Data are also checked against updated field and property maps. Any discrepancies are double-checked with the farmers and corrected if necessary. Such standardisation of data collection and the frequent cross-control against other data sources serve to limit measuring errors and increase reliability (Hellevik, 1977: 156).

One question that needs consideration, however, is whether participation in the study creates a Hawthorne-like effect, i.e. the phenomenon that participation in the study affects the behaviour of study objects (see, for instance, Babbie, 1989: 214–216). In this case such an effect is conceivable and actually in line with the theoretical framework, that being interviewed about fertiliser practices increases the attention paid to these practices among the study objects and thereby reduces deviation from optimal behaviour. In this sense, the case constitutes a conservative test of the theoretical framework; there may be a bias against measuring the effects predicted. If such interference does occur, it is more likely an issue for the first years of the study. However, an analysis indicates that data from LOOP catchments are comparable to national averages (Andersen, J.M. *et al.*, 2005: 18).

To be able to generalise the findings of the study to the theory, i.e. analytical generalisation, the empirical variables must accurately reflect the theoretical concepts. Operationalisation of the independent variables is accounted for in conjunction with the analysis in Chapters 6 and 7, and issues pertaining to validity will be discussed in those chapters.

On a general note, however, LOOP data are considered valid for a cross-section analysis of variation in decision context and their effect on fertiliser decisions. Although the LOOP database includes data for more than 15 years, it is *not* valid for individual-level analysis across time. This is due to promises of anonymity and the organisation of data, which prevents identification of individuals throughout the data-series and therefore precludes control for autocorrelation. Likewise, personal variables such as age and education were not gathered for the study, and it has not been possible to collect such data after the fact. These data would have made useful control variables.

Data for measuring decision processes

The analysis of decision processes relies on in-depth interviews with farmers about their decision processes, both decisions relating to fertiliser management as well as other management issues and more strategic decisions. The unit of analysis in the qualitative study is decision processes rather than farmers.

Ideally, perhaps, one would observe farmers in the process of decision-making, producing a verbal protocol – a process tracing method in the field, so to speak (no pun intended). This would prevent obvious problems of post-rationalisation, memory distortion and other ills following from self-reporting about occurrences in the past. Yet it is inherent in the concept of decision used here, that a decision may not necessarily be isolated to a moment neatly confined in time; it is a process. Observation is also a very time-consuming data collection method. Thus observation presents some practical problems. Moreover, direct observation embodies its own problems, as the object of study may respond to the observation and change behaviour (Babbie, 1989). Qualitative interviews, properly planned, conducted and analysed, can give both reliable and valid data about decision processes.

The qualitative study encompasses twenty farms distributed throughout Denmark. Twenty interviews are considered enough to ensure a range of respondents for relevant variables, whereas it was considered impossible within the practical confines of this study to analyse adequately a larger number of interviews. The respondents cover all agricultural branches and differ with regard to the size and category of the farm, but also the age of the farmer. The purpose is not to produce statistical representation but to provide range in the material, as the theoretical framework suggests that farmers vary in their decisions according to such factors. The selection is strategic and aims to cover all relevant themes. In order to ensure this type of spread, farmers were contacted through agricultural advisers, who would be able to point to farmers with different characteristics. The drawback of this approach is that at least some advisers appear to have suggested people who had been particularly active in agricultural organisations, or who otherwise had significant contact with the advisory system. This potentially biases the study population toward a high degree of awareness about professional issues. To compensate for this, a few participants were also recruited through private contacts. Furthermore, participants were recruited through livestock advisers, crop advisers and economic advisers. Asking only crop advisers might have produced a sample of participants biased in their interests toward crop production. The interviews lasted anywhere from $1^{1}/_{2}$ to $2^{1}/_{2}$ hours and were carried out on the farms.

Interview strategy

At a fundamental level, the purpose of this research project is to improve the understanding of a phenomenon in the world, namely decision-making and how it affects responses to economic incentives. In this sense the scientific position is essentially realist (Wengraf, 2001: 4), assuming that there is an objective reality to be understood, but this position is implemented with an appreciation that the social world is also constructed; it is what its participants see, or perhaps *how* they see it. The two positions merge in the sense that the farmers' perception of decisions and the way they make sense of them constitutes the objective reality for the researcher to understand. Thus the interviews seek descriptions of decision processes in order to understand how farmers perceive and carry out decisions in a particular realm. They are both accounts of reality and of the meaning ascribed to them by the individuals carrying out the interviews.

Interviews were carried out in a semi-structured fashion, deducing themes and questions from hypotheses, but retaining flexibility so as to capture data not falling within the purview of the research model. Thus semi-structured interviews were considered most appropriate for the task at hand (see, for instance, Wengraf, 2001). Semi-structured interviewing thus requires an interview guide, which reflects the themes of the interview but also the type of data sought. Generally, qualitative interviews are considered appropriate for questions of what, how and why; questions aimed at understanding the meaning of a phenomenon. Researchers of a hermeneutical bent suggest that meaning is uncovered through descriptions of specific situations and processes (Olsen, 2002). The interview strategy followed here leans on this approach in so far as the interview is generally designed to get detailed descriptions of decision processes rather than synthetic assessments. Descriptive accounts allow the researcher to interpret the data within a pre-defined theoretical framework, while synthetic assessments to a larger extent reflect the *frame* of the interviewee. But where necessary or appropriate, the interview also asked both evaluative and factual questions. The guiding principle is that questions should be designed to elicit the kinds of data necessary to answer the research questions.

The main research question to be examined by the qualitative analysis is whether farmers use simplifying decision strategies and if so, how these affect fertiliser management. The analysis also examines the role of motivation for the choice of simple or comprehensive decision strategies. Finally, the study analyses decision strategies more broadly to uncover the presence and the function of simple decision strategies. Thus, the main theoretical variables for this part of the study are decision mechanisms and motivation. The interview guide represents an operationalisation of the theoretical concepts; it elicits accounts of how farmers make decisions on fertiliser management as well as other decision domains.

Analysis of data

Following the interview, each interview was transcribed verbatim. A short summary, recapping how the farmer carries out fertilising, how he decides on other issues, motivating factors and value statements, as well as facts about the farm, was later sent to each farmer, allowing him to comment and perhaps catch mistakes. No comments were received.

Interviews were coded to enable systematic analysis. A set of codes was identified, based on the interview guide and therefore reflecting the theoretical concepts as well as the research question. For the purpose of theory testing, data analysis was carried out deductively. Analysis of the data moved back and forth between a vertical and horizontal reading of the interviews. First, each interview was read in its entirety to achieve a comprehensive understanding of the farmer's decision style. Subsequently, the interviews were analysed thematically across interviewer, i.e. horizontally by relevant coded text segments for each question. This reading continued the coding process, but moving from a thematic coding to a theoretical coding by variables and attributes. For instance, interviews were analysed to identify theoretically defined decision mechanisms, such as calculation or trial-and-error, in order to determine decision modes. Likewise, the variable motivation was coded by categories of motivation. This type of categorisation served largely to analyse the range and nature of decision processes in the material. However, to understand how these decision mechanisms worked and when, they needed to be analysed also in context. Likewise, an interviewee might mention several objectives pursued in fertiliser management. But to tease out conditions for when one or the other objective prevailed, or how the farmer made trade-offs between them, the analysis had to include the overall picture. Therefore each interview was again read vertically, that is, in its entirety, to put the overall decision strategy back together again, but with the structures now clearer. Complex phenomena such as decision process or motivation are not easily reduced to an analytical category or concept. In order to capture such complexity, analytical conclusions build on a comparison of direct statements with descriptions of actions. Typically, descriptions of actions weigh more heavily in the conclusion.

Reliability and validity

Data collection must abide by standards that ensure reliability, but this is interpreted differently by different scientific approaches. One approach sees reliability as replicability (Olsen, 2002). By this standard, the findings of a given study should stay the same, if the study were replicated with the same methods. This requires that the researcher explicitly accounts for and therefore makes transparent all methodological choices. The other approach hails consistency, implying that interpretations of data should remain consistent over 'different observers or over different occasions by the same observer' (Olsen, 2002: 146). This requires that the researcher makes explicit *analytical procedures and choices.*

The preceding sections, describing how data were collected and analysed, lay open the procedures by which this study aims to produce reliable data. M*ethodological transparency* is attempted by making available the interview and coding guides as well as by describing interview strategies and selection of interviewee. *Consistency* has been sought throughout all phases of the analysis: in the interviews, interpretations were checked iteratively with the interviewee; in the data handling phase, interviews were transcribed, transcriptions were checked against the tapes, and data were structured according to a set of standardised codes. Finally, consistency of interpretation represents perhaps the biggest challenge in qualitative interviewing. In order to achieve this, operationalisation of theoretical concepts provided a set of criteria to be applied, and the continuous switching from horizontal to vertical readings of the data also aimed to provide consistency. Furthermore, throughout the analysis, criteria for different interpretations will be laid out, and evidence for each interpretation will be supported by extensive quotation from the interviews. Documentation is thereby discursive, allowing the reader to assess the interpretation.

Discussions of validity within the context of qualitative analysis tend to be broader than within the quantitative research traditions of the positivist bent. Definitions and categorisations abound (Kvale, 1989; Olsen, 2002: 144). But they generally revolve around the relationship between the scientific claims and the empirical conditions they concern.

One standard concerns the *correspondence between* the scientific claims and the real world, expressed as 'the extent to which an account accurately represents the social phenomena to which it refers' (Hammersley, in Olsen, 2002: 145). This is essentially the criterion of external validity, i.e. 'measuring what we think we are measuring' (King *et al.*, 1994: 25). Thus it revolves around the process of translating theoretical concepts into empirical indicators and inferring back to the theoretical concepts. One way to assess validity here, then, is to ask whether proper criteria have been applied to the interpretation and categorisation of statements and actions. For instance, in this study one may ask whether the operational definition of simple decision mechanism accurately reflects the theoretical meaning of the concept.

But validity also hinges on whether interpretations are correct, that is whether the criteria were applied to data in a proper way. 'Proper' means consistent, credible and without bias. In this sense, validity may also be assessed by whether the scientific claim is *coherent* (Kvale, 1989; Olsen, 2002).

Validation of each interpretation cannot be carried out generally; it is specific to the analytical context. Hence, validity must be established throughout the analysis as specific concepts are operationalised and applied to interview data. However, one aspect of validation can be discussed in general terms here. Validation depends on the reading or perspective applied to a given statement (Kvale, 1989/1992: 212). In this study, interviews are generally given a veridical reading; statements are interpreted as accounts of how things are, i.e. what farmers do when they make decisions. Veridical interpretations are generally validated by triangulation; that is, other sources of information about the same phenomenon, whether other informants or other methods. In this study, the validation consists of analysing *different types of information within each interview.* For instance, if a farmer states that economic considerations determine the decision arrived at, this statement is compared with the descriptive accounts the farmer gives of actual decisions. If the two correspond, the statement is considered validated. If they contradict each other, the analysis looks for further sources of evidence in the data, but generally descriptive accounts of decisions weigh more heavily in the interpretations, as actions rather than attitudes are the main point of interest.

This raises the question of the validity of self-reported evidence. Self-reporting may be false (Kvale, 1989/1992: 212), either because the interviewer cannot report the reality or does not wish to report the reality. So the first question is whether farmers are able to report on their decision processes. As most questions are asked in terms of descriptions of practices, this yields a fairly straightforward yes. The closer the questions are to what and how, i.e. to descriptions rather than assessments, the more concrete and less deliberated the answers seem.

The second question is whether farmers want to report the truth. There may be personal sources of bias, such as wanting to seem rational or competent, or there may be political sources of bias, such as framing one's answers to put fertiliser regulation in a bad light, for instance. Personal sources of bias have been checked to some extent through the comparisons of different accounts and statements, but short of direct observation, bias cannot be ascertained completely. As for politically loaded answers, the farmers do make direct political statements about fertiliser regulation (positive *and* negative statements), but there seems to be no connection between such statements and accounts of actual fertiliser practices.

Conclusion: research strategy

In conclusion, the case of fertiliser management offers a rare opportunity to test a model of bounded rationality in a field setting, due to the rational standard embodied in fertiliser norms. At the same time this permits a focused study of decision processes. Applying both quantitative and qualitative research methodologies, the study will make for a thorough examination of key concepts in the bounded rationality approach. Two main sources of data provide the empirical foundation for the analysis: a database with detailed data about fertiliser levels in relation to norms, following fertiliser patterns over time. The other dataset consists of twenty in-depth interviews with farmers. Combining this test of the framework with a theory-guided examination of the decision processes, the study allows for empirical foundation and development of the framework. Finally, the case allows for a theory-guided evaluation of fertiliser regulation as it has been formed in the Danish context.

Yet the case also has clear limitations. Data do not allow for a single test of the entire framework, including all variables. It is necessary to assess decision environment and decision processes in separate analyses and with different participants. Furthermore, the lack of individual-level data prevents control for obvious variables such as education, age or income. Hence, the data may at best make plausible the value of the framework.

Note

1 See also Kahneman and Tversky's discussion of these criticisms (1996).

5

The empirical setting – agriculture and environmental regulation

In the mid-1980s dramatic TV images of dead lobsters, suffocated due to eutrophication, landed the agricultural sector at the very top of the Danish environmental policy agenda (Andersen and Hansen, 1991). This followed decades of structural change and intensification in this sector bringing with it increased use of fertilisers and pesticides, with a detrimental effect on the environment but with relatively little regulation. The dead lobsters provided the momentum for policy-makers to begin regulating agricultural pollution.

To set the background for the study of fertiliser, this chapter outlines the developments in the agricultural sector and the impact on the environment as well as development of fertiliser regulation.

From family farm to big family farm

Danish agriculture has undergone significant change over the last 50 years. The structural development in Danish agriculture, as in so many other western countries, is a tale of fewer and larger, of specialisation and of significant increases in productivity. These developments would affect the decision environment facing the farmer. While concentration in larger farms might increase the complexity of running a farm, all other things being equal specialisation would simplify farm operation, as this allows the farmer to focus on fewer activities and develop expertise.

In 2006, the number of farms was less than 25 per cent of the number of farms that existed in 1960, but the remaining farms grew in size almost correspondingly. Mean acreage increased from 16 ha to 60 ha over the same period. The mean masks some differentiation. Half of the farms are small, owning less than 30 ha of land, while more than half of *farmland* is owned by farms with more than 100 ha.

In a European context Danish farms are relatively large. In 2004, among the EU-25, the mean per farm acreage of Danish farms was topped only by the Czech Republic and the United Kingdom (Landbrugsraadet, 2006: 8). Even so, family ownership remains dominant, accounting for 90 per cent of farms, while another 8 per cent are owned by partnerships or limited partnerships, often consisting of just a few farmers (Landbrugsraadet, 2004).

Livestock holdings are also growing in size. The average pig farm more than tripled its livestock herd between 1990 and 2006 alone, while cattle-rearing farms nearly doubled their herds. In fact, livestock density is rather high in Denmark compared with other European countries. In 2003, only the Netherlands and Belgium had higher livestock densities than Denmark (EURO-STAT). According to EUROSTAT, Denmark had a livestock density of 1.7 livestock units (lu)/ha in 2003, up from 1.4 lu/ha in 1990. This pales in comparison with the Dutch figure of more than 3 lu/ha and the Belgian livestock density rate of 2.8 lu/ha, but it is still well above the mean of the EU-15 of 0.89 lu/ha.

Concentration has been matched by specialisation. The traditional mixed family farm has almost disappeared since the 1970s. Half of the farms are pure crop farms, while the share of farms that have both cattle and pigs decreased from 75 per cent in the 1970s to 4 per cent in 2006 (Statistics Denmark). Nonetheless, livestock farms are bigger and dominate also economically. More land has been concentrated under livestock farms.

Generally considered a story of success, the structural development has however not been without cost. Environmental degradation has become a thorny issue for agriculture.

Agriculture and the environment

As has been the case generally, modernisation of Danish agriculture has been accompanied by an increase in the use of chemical inputs, particularly artificial fertilisers and pesticides. Between

1950 and 1984 total consumption of nitrogen in fertilisers increased nearly six-fold from about 70,000 tonnes of nitrogen per year to about 410,000 tonnes of nitrogen (Landbrugsministeriet, 1991: 129). The amount of nitrogen applied from manure also increased, but only from 137,000 tonnes of nitrogen in 1960 to 168,000 tonnes of nitrogen in the early 1980s (Danmarks Statistik, 1989). Per hectare, total nitrogen application increased from 40 kg per ha in 1960 to 198 kg per ha in 1984, a level at which it stabilised for the remainder of the 1980s. Consumption of phosphorous in artificial fertilisers remained fairly stable over the period, while the amount of phosphorous applied through manure increased from 46,000 tonnes in 1960 to 68,000 tonnes in 1984 (Danmarks Statistik, 1989).

Pesticides were introduced after the Second World War, but were not accounted for in statistics until the early 1970s. In 1974 the sale of pesticides amounted to 6,200 tonnes and peaked 10 years later at 7,000 tonnes of active ingredients, but then gradually declined again (Landbrugsministeriet, 1991: 156).

Nitrogen in the environment

While both nutrients and pesticides are absorbed by plants, some of each is lost to the surrounding environment and often migrates to surface waters, such as lakes, streams or coastal waters, but increasingly also to groundwater. Surplus nitrogen, that is nitrogen not absorbed by crops, increased from about 200,000 tonnes in 1960 to more than 500,000 tonnes in the late 1970s, a level at which it stabilised throughout most of the 1980s (Knudsen, 2000). A significant share of the surplus ends up in the aquatic environment. According to an estimate, in 1984 more than 60 per cent of the nitrogen surplus, or 311,000 tonnes, was leached to the environment (Grant and Waagepetersen, 2003: 15).

Excessive amounts of nitrates, which form from nitrogen, are dangerous to human health (Miljøstyrelsen, 1984). But large nutrient inputs also harm natural ecosystems. Nutrients in surface waters such as streams may lead to large-scale production of algae, which depletes the oxygen content of the water and ultimately deteriorates conditions for aquatic life. This process, known as eutrophication, may kill life in a water body, temporarily or permanently.

By the early 1980s concerns were mounting about the increasing pollution of waters caused by nutrients. According to a 1983 survey, the median value for nitrate concentration in Danish groundwater increased from 4 mg/l in 1960 to about 13 mg/l in the early 1980s (Miljøstyrelsen, 1984: 17). Groundwater is the dominant source of drinking water in Denmark. The monitoring of waterworks indicated that 8 per cent of the drinking water supply exceeded the EU maximum limit of 50 mg nitrate/l, while 19 per cent exceeded the guiding limit of 25 mg/l. For watercourses, monitoring showed that discharges of slurry and manure, while illegal, were a dominant source of water pollution. The report noted some improvements, but also evidence of deteriorating conditions in the environmental quality of watercourses throughout the 1970s. Furthermore, eutrophication resulting in high fish mortality was considered a threat (Miljøstyrelsen, 1984, cited in National Agency of Environmental Protection, 1984: 4).

Thus, in policy circles there was a growing recognition that agricultural discharges of nutrients had to be curbed to protect the aquatic environment.

Environmental regulation of fertiliser

The mid-1980s saw the first in a long line of action plans and regulatory initiatives, all designed to curb nutrient leaching from agricultural sources. Some were preceded by and some were later matched by EU regulations, such as the Nitrates Directive (Council Directive 91/676/EEC of 12 December 1991).

National regulation

The main focus of the plans has been to improve the use of fertiliser from livestock and as a consequence reduce the use of artificial fertiliser. In order to achieve this, the plans have employed a mix of strategies from emission limits to behaviour modification, cleaner technology and structural measures (Anker, 1996; Grant *et al.*, 2002).

In 1985, the Danish parliament adopted a plan to curb 'pollution due to nutrients and organic matter' (Parliamentary decision of 31 May 1985, cf. Anker, 1996: 104). The most important measures in the plan included requirements for improved storage of livestock manure and restrictions on the timing and conditions for application of liquid fertiliser (Anker, 1996: 106). Furthermore, the plan imposed a cap on how much livestock manure could be spread per hectare.

However, problems with eutrophication in the summer of 1986, culminating in the news story featuring dead lobsters mentioned above, propelled the issue of nutrient pollution back onto the public agenda (Andersen and Hansen, 1991; Anker, 1996). Thus, in the spring of 1987 a new plan, the Action Plan for the Aquatic Environment, was adopted (Rude and Frederiksen, 1994; Anker, 1996). For the first time, this plan laid out a specific goal for reduction of nitrogen discharges, as much as 50 per cent by 1993, while phosphate discharges were to be reduced by a full 80 per cent within the same timeframe (Anker, 1996; Grant *et al.*, 2002). The action plan aimed to improve overall fertiliser management, introducing as a tool mandatory *fertiliser and crop rotation plans*. These plans, which would take effect in 1988, were to include information about crops grown on each field and the total fertiliser demand for the farm based on recommended nitrogen norms for each crop, adapted to circumstances on the farm. The plans were defined as 'an inventory of the demand for nitrogen and phosphate fertilisers at *economically optimal fertiliser levels*' (Bekendtgørelse no. 469, 1988: §5).

While the measures covered a wide spectrum, the dominant approach of the action plan was voluntary, appealing to farmers to reduce nutrient pollution through 'good agricultural practice', a term also found in the EU Nitrates Directive of 1991 (Grant *et al.*, 2002). In fact, there was no requirement to actually *follow* the fertiliser plan once it was drawn up and sanctions for failing to make one were not imposed (Landbrugsministeriet, 1991: 445; Bekendtgørelse no. 469, 1988). The voluntary approach rested on the assumption that it would actually serve the economic interest of farmers to use fertiliser more efficiently and thus reduce the use of artificial fertilisers. A random sampling in 1989 showed that more than 80 per cent of the farmers did draw up the plans (Landbrugsministeriet, 1991: 443).

Thus, farmers did generally abide by the compulsory elements of the plans, but fertiliser management did not improve adequately to achieve the objective of a 50 per cent reduction in nitrogen discharge (Anker, 1996; Grant *et al.*, 2002). An evaluation of the action plan estimated that introduction of mandatory fertiliser plans had reduced excess fertiliser application by about half of the level that had been expected (Landbrugsministeriet, 1991).

This led to further tightening of requirements in yet another action plan, the Action Plan for Sustainable Agriculture in 1991. To reduce the overall use of fertiliser, the action plan focused on the fertiliser plans as a primary tool. It tightened previous requirements, but the main change was a stipulation that the total amount of nitrogen applied on the farm could not exceed the total nitrogen demand calculated *qua* the inventory. Contrary to the practice hitherto, a regulatory agency would set rules for the appropriate levels of nitrogen for specific crops (Bekendtgørelse no. 1095, 1992: §6). The norms reflected years of research on how to improve yield against optimal levels of input factors. In essence, then, the regulation introduced a nitrogen quota, based on a set of mandatory nitrogen norms. Furthermore, the regulation stipulated a share of nitrogen from livestock manure that must be counted toward the nitrogen quota; the share was differentiated by type of animal and was subject to successive increases. In 1993, for instance, a pig farmer had to count 45 per cent of the total nitrogen in manure towards his nitrogen quota. Only farmers who were able to achieve the required degree of mineral utilisation from manure were able to take full advantage of their quota. Rules for how to calculate the amount of manure and determine its nitrogen content were set by the regulatory agency, the Danish Plant Directorate. The Danish Agricultural Advisory Service, owned by the farmers themselves, was to make recommendations on these rules as well as on the specific nitrogen norms. Finally, a key new element in the regulation was that fertiliser plans were to be followed up by fertiliser *accounts*, which were to be subject to formal control, while lack of compliance was to be subject to fines (Bekendtgørelse no. 1095, 1992: §8–9). The regulation did not specify the levels of the fines. From *c.* 1998 the fines were 10 DKK per kg nitrogen above the norms, and for excesses above 30 kg per hectare, the fine increased to 20 DKK per kg nitrogen. This is considerably above the price of artificial fertilisers, but the strict economic incentive in a fine would have to be assessed against the potential income forgone by not fertilising.

The main regulatory changes, i.e. the nitrogen quota, the

fertiliser accounts and the required utilisation rates for nitrogen were to take effect in 1993–94. The story repeated itself again, leading to successive reformulations of the regulatory requirements, the most important of which was a second Action Plan for the Aquatic Environment in 1998 (Miljø- og Energiministeriet, 1998). Notably, the plan lowered nitrogen norms by 10 per cent below the previous, economically optimal, norms (Bekendtgørelse no. 523 of 8 July 1998 and subsequent changes). Subsequent action plans have largely built on these plans, so that the regulatory instruments implemented in the 1990s largely remain in place.

As of 2005, the European Union instituted a principle of cross compliance which implies that a farmer who does not comply with a specified regulation, including the Nitrates Directive (91/676/EEC), will lose his or her right to receive agricultural subsidies.

EU regulation

EU regulation of fertiliser practice has been limited or indirect. The Drinking Water Directive (Council Directive 80/778/EEC) establishes limits for the nitrate content in drinking water (Anker, 1996), but does not directly regulate fertiliser application. The Nitrates Directive (Council Directive 91/676/EEC), as the title indicates, does address fertiliser management, but again not in a particularly direct manner. The directive obliges member states to identify waters that are or could be affected by nitrate pollution and to designate vulnerable zones, i.e. land areas which drain into these waters and contribute to the pollution (91/676/EEC: Article 3). For these vulnerable zones, member states must set up action programmes, involving provisions for storage capacity and transport of livestock manure, limitations on fertiliser applications taking into account soil conditions and climatic conditions, and crop rotation practices (91/676/EEC: Annex III). Additionally, member states are required to establish a code of good agricultural practice to be implemented by all farmers on a voluntary basis (Article 4). The directive offers considerable flexibility to member states as to how to implement these plans; the only specific requirement in the directive is a cap on the application of fertiliser of 170 kg nitrogen per hectare per year, but this was to be phased in gradually (Anker, 1996: 149).

Denmark has designated the entire country as a vulnerable zone and the requirements of the Nitrates Directive by and large match the rules in place in the aquatic action plans (Anker, 1996).

Effect of regulation

While regulations had to be adjusted repeatedly throughout the late 1980s and the 1990s, evaluations indicate that the policies have been fairly successful. The use of mineral, i.e. commercial, fertilisers decreased slightly in the latter half of the 1980s, but mostly due to changes in crop composition. But during the 1990s, mean application of mineral fertilisers dropped from 142 kg per ha in 1990 (DST) to 97 kg per ha in 1999 and to 77 kg per ha in 2002 (Grant and Waagepetersen, 2003). And while nitrogen *consumption* was slow to decrease, nitrogen surplus and nitrogen leaching did begin to drop from the mid-1980s (see Figure 5.1). Surplus, i.e. nitrogen not absorbed by crops, may be affected through agricultural practices, such as the timing of manure application. Leaching is that part of the surplus nitrogen that is released into soil and eventually into water. The amount of nitrogen leaching was reduced from 311,000 tonnes to an estimated 168,000 tonnes in 2002, a 46 per cent reduction (Grant and Waagepetersen, 2003: 15).

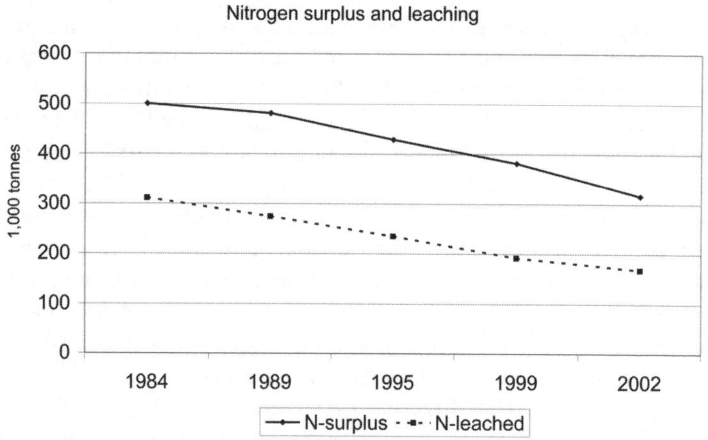

Figure 5.1   *Development in the nitrogen surplus and nitrogen leaching over time. 1,000 tonnes N*

Source: Grant and Waagepetersen, 2003: 15.

The effects of this reduction in leaching appear to be showing in the environment. Samples of nitrogen in the upper layers of groundwater show an increase from 34 mg/l in 1990 to 50 mg/l in 1998, but with a subsequent decrease to 35 mg/l in 2002 (Anderson, J.M. *et al.*, 2003: 27). Yet most of the groundwater monitored in these samples was formed prior to 1990, which means that it is not a completely reliant gauge of the effect of changed fertiliser practices since then (NERI, 2003: 27). Looking only at young groundwater, i.e. groundwater formed within eight years of measuring, the nitrate concentrations have decreased in approximately one-third of the samples (NERI, 2003: 27). Likewise, the share of waterworks with nitrate problems has remained stable throughout the 1990s and by 2000 nitrate problems were even declining (Danmarks Statistik, 2004).

Also the nitrogen concentration in watercourses is falling; NERI estimated a 30 per cent reduction in nitrogen concentration between 1989 and 2002 in watercourses in cultivated catchments, from 8 mg/l total nitrogen to 6 mg/l. By comparison, watercourses in natural areas displayed a concentration of 2 mg/l (Andersen, J. M. *et al.*, 2003: 35). Phosphorous concentrations are determined to a greater extent by wastewater discharges, which have also decreased considerably. Algae concentrations have also fallen. Even so, there is no sign of decreased eutrophication.

Empirical studies of farmers

International as well as Danish literature on farming is extensive, but much of it is within the agricultural sciences or agro-economics and aims largely to provide a better foundation for agricultural practices. As Öhlmér *et al.* noted, 'most research and teaching has been in how farmers *should* make decisions' (1998: 273, emphasis added). Descriptive or explanatory studies on farmers' decision behaviour are harder to come by, but a few do exist.

One group of studies consists of case studies of decision-making processes among farmers. For instance, Öhlmér *et al.* (1998) studied 18 Swedish farms, uncovering the decision phases and decision mechanisms. The farmers were interviewed about different decision problems, including how they adapted their farms to the lower prices following deregulation of the agricultural market. The main conclusion drawn by the authors is that decision processes should be seen more as a matrix of different steps and sub-processes rather than as a linearly progressing process from problem definition to choice. Generally also, the approach was incremental and risk avoidance was achieved through small tests rather than wholesale moves. More specifically, they found that farmers set aspiration levels, typically anchored in current conditions; aspiration levels *were* updated continuously from new information or experiences, but typically in a qualitative manner. Hence, the farmers used a qualitative approach in forming expectations and in estimating consequences. Expectations were typically stated in terms of a *direction* from the current condition (Öhlmér *et al.*, 1998: 286). On the contrary, they were not likely to use budgeting tools or computer models in their decision-making. Generally, the farmers in the study preferred a 'quick and simple approach to a detailed, elaborate one'. Ex-post evaluations of decisions were undertaken only if the outcome of the particular decision could still be influenced. Learning from present or past decisions for the benefit of future decisions seemed less common. Overall, then, the study revealed decision processes with many elements reminiscent of the bounded rationality framework.

A study of decision-making among Danish farmers suggests similar decision mechanisms. Through qualitative interviews with 25 farmers, Jacobsen (1994) examined the decision processes related to purchases and compared these to the ideal rational decision-making process. He distinguished among different types of purchasing decisions based on the temporal scope of the good in question. Hence, short-term decisions were exemplified by fertiliser and feed purchases; medium-range decisions concerned purchases of machinery, and for long-term decisions he examined land acquisition and expansions of the livestock production. Jacobsen concludes that farmers do intend to be rational and do couch their purchases in the language of economic rationality, but the extent to which they achieve the rational decision-making ideal varies with the scope of the decision. Short-term decisions, which are the least complex and less uncertain, come closer to full rationality than do the longer-term decisions. Even so, there is evidence of satisficing rather than optimising. The farmers interviewed tend to stop searching for deals on fertiliser and feed once they have achieved a predefined price, even though the search costs of checking further would be minor (Jacobsen, 1994: 45). In other words, farmers set an aspiration level. Also, loyalty and a sense of security in knowing the dealer are important to the farmer.

Aspiration levels are evident in medium-term purchases of machinery, as farmers set the price they are willing to pay based on hearsay about prices, while they 'do not seem to be based directly on economic calculations' (Jacobsen, 1994: 55). Generally, the farmers in the study have difficulty conducting accurate economic assessments. Several use simple back-of-the-envelope calculations or loose estimates, while others do use more comprehensive calculations. But it appears that the assumptions and considerations employed prevent accurate economic calculations. For instance, farmers in the study tend to value a high buy-back price for their old equipment, despite the fact that this inevitably entails higher prices at the time the equipment is purchased, overall higher machinery costs and not least unclear cost levels (Jacobsen, 1994: 53). Purchasing decisions also seem to be guided unduly by tax considerations (Jacobsen, 1994: 59), while maintenance costs on old equipment are typically over-estimated, justifying perhaps replacements sooner than proper economic considerations would dictate (other parameters such as comfort not withstanding) (Jacobsen, 1994: 71). Hence, Jacobsen calculates that the farmers in his study on average underestimate annual machinery costs, typically by 25 to 30 per cent.

This study therefore also shows evidence of the mechanisms predicted by the bounded rationality model, such as simple calculations, rules of thumb and anchoring. The question is whether decision-making has changed since the early 1990s due to improved education and intensified agricultural consultancy.

While both Öhlmér *et al.* and Jacobsen investigate decision processes assuming that farmers strive to optimise economically, a number of sociological studies have sought to uncover more broadly the values and motivations of farmers (Noe, 1998). These studies indicate that farmers vary in terms of the degree to which economic optimisation seems to guide their decisions. Factors such as lifestyle are quite important to some farmers. But farmers also vary in terms of what or how they optimise. Hence, Noe identified three 'value styles', which he labelled the craftsman style, the manager style and the entrepreneur style, each representing different visions of farming and each entailing different production approaches as well. It follows that one should expect farmers with different value styles to approach decisions differently and potentially to optimise according to different criteria.

Studies of fertiliser management growing out of policy monitoring programmes have shown that nitrogen consumption decreased slightly between 1983 and 1989, but mostly as a consequence of substitution towards crops requiring less nitrogen (Miljøstyrelsen, 1990). The study also found that nitrogen consumption varied considerably across fields and farms. Inappropriate management of farmyard manure was singled out as the cause of excess fertilising. Too many farmers would bring out livestock manure at times when plants could not adequately absorb the nutrients, let alone benefit from them. In essence farmers underestimated the nutrient content and value of manure, applying instead artificial fertiliser up to or even exceeding optimal levels (Miljøstyrelsen, 1990: 28). Over time, there has been a downward trend in over-fertilising, measured as the area that is fertilised with at least 20 per cent more nitrogen than in the norms, but in 1999 when fertiliser norms were lowered, the acreage that was over-fertilised increased according to the new norms, although it remained stable relative to the old, optimal, norms (Grant *et al.*, 2000).

Finally, studies have examined the potential for using economic incentives in fertiliser regulation. One study evaluates empirically the effects of various regulatory instruments on agricultural economics and fertiliser practice (Hasler, 1998). Assuming that farmers do optimise economically, the study concludes that a tax on commercial fertiliser will be effective, as it creates incentives to improve the utilisation rates of manure, substituting away from artificial fertilisers. Yet a tax would induce economically optimising farmers to switch to different crops which would dilute some of the beneficial environmental effect of a tax. Hence, a tax would need to be supplemented with regulatory measures to counteract such crop substitutions (Hasler, 1998: 222).

Furthermore, an analysis of fertiliser use under the auspices of the Danish Environmental Protection Agency compared price elasticities for artificial fertiliser demand for different types of farms (Miljøstyrelsen, 1999). This study found higher price elasticities for pig farms than for other farms, indicating that pig farms would be more likely to substitute farmyard manure for artificial fertilisers in response to a price increase in the latter (Miljøstyrelsen, 1999: 49). Furthermore, the study also examined fertiliser patterns for the years 1990–96 in order to assess the effect of transportation costs on fertiliser allocation. This cursory study suggested that fields closer to the manure storage facility were more likely to be fertilised than were fields farther away, and there was a small tendency for fields closer to the farmhouse to receive excess fertiliser than fields farther away (numbers were not included in the report). An analysis of transportation costs showed that pig farms had lower transportation costs per kg nitrogen than cattle farms due to the properties of nitrogen in pig manure, and that pig farms did transport manure over greater distances. This would suggest that the cost of transporting manure could explain some over-fertilisation (Miljøstyrelsen, 1999: 55). However, the analysis covers 18 farms, and the results must be viewed as preliminary.

Pointers for the empirical study

The structural change as well as the change in the regulatory set-up offers some pointers as to how fertiliser management should have developed.

It follows from the increase in specialisation and intensity in agriculture that farming has become much more complex over the period studied. In and of itself this would affect the propensity for deviation from optimal fertiliser application. The question, of course, is whether other factors, such as increased advisory activities with regard to fertiliser practice or improved education, would counteract this. Quite obviously, the period has seen a surge in computerised decision tools, also in the area of fertiliser management. This chapter also shows that there have been considerable and frequent regulatory changes, which would tend to outdate fertiliser routines. On the one hand, however, the fertiliser norms introduced would make clear the optimal fertiliser levels. On other hand the frequency of the institutional changes would complicate adaptation to new norms as would uncertainty regarding the fertiliser value of manure. Finally, if farmers deliberately choose to deviate from norms in single crops or fields, the fertiliser quota forces trade-offs among fields and crops. Such trade-offs are difficult according to bounded rationality theory, and it may create unstable fertiliser patterns.

Economic studies modelling farmer behaviour show responses to price incentives but these vary across farm categories. But, generally, modelling studies assume optimal adaptation to price incentives. However, these studies do suggest that the economically optimal fertiliser norms might have to be adjusted for manure application costs.

While these studies indicate that farmers respond to price incentives, studies which focus on decision processes suggest that they may not do so in an optimal manner. Several studies indicate that farmers exhibit simple decision strategies and set aspiration levels rather than aim for optima. Finally, the sociological studies indicate that it may be possible to divide farmers into different groupings based on farming style or motivation. In this case, some variation would follow from motivation and personality rather than from structural variables, or similar. But there is also an indication that farmers vary in the degree to which they optimise, not just due to cognitive properties but also substantive or normative differentials.

6

Fertiliser application around optimal norms: effect of decision environment

Fertiliser application is one of the core activities in farmers' efforts to achieve a good crop. Fertilisers boost the yield of the crops and therefore affect the economic outcome of working the fields. But there is not a straight linear relationship between the amount of fertiliser and output; at a certain point the plants no longer absorb the fertiliser, or they absorb a smaller share of it so that the marginal yield from a unit of nitrogen starts to decline. Fertiliser which is not used by the plants may end up in waterways or evaporate to the air as ammonia. This causes environmental problems, but also represents a waste of resources. An economically optimising farmer, therefore, is expected to fertilise at the level where the value of the marginal yield from a unit of fertiliser equals the marginal cost of that unit of fertiliser, all other things being equal. This is obviously a complex decision, and within a bounded rationality framework we would therefore expect farmers to deviate from optimal fertilising, substituting simple rules of thumb or old habits for precise calculation of the economically optimal amount of fertiliser.

However, fertiliser norms indicating appropriate levels of fertiliser under various circumstances would serve to simplify fertiliser management. Hence, from a bounded rationality perspective, farmers would generally follow the norms. In fact, considering that the norms have been calculated to be economically optimal for each field and considering that they reduce information costs (the costs, including time, associated with acquiring information about and calculating proper fertiliser levels), farmers would be expected to follow the norms also from an economic rationality perspective.

On the other hand, the frequent changes in fertiliser regulation throughout the 1990s represent a counteracting force: complexity. Likewise, other factors which compete for the farmers' attention would make for some deviation from rational behaviour. This implies that one would expect fertiliser practice to vary around the optimal norms according to variations in the decision-making context, i.e. the decision environment.

The analytical question as to whether farmers economically optimise their fertiliser application thus translates into the following empirical question: 'Do farmers follow fertiliser norms?' The empirical analyses in this chapter revolve around this question. But more to the point, the analysis examines whether deviations from optimal behaviour vary with changes in the theoretically defined variables *complex decision environments* and *regulatory change*. In preparation for the analysis, the following sections discuss how to measure complexity and deviation from fertiliser norms. The analytic sections are introduced with a brief descriptive overview of fertiliser patterns, and then proceed to present the evidence and discussion on each of the explanatory factors. The first section analyses responses to institutional changes, thus also accounting for fertiliser patterns over time; the following sections analyse the effect of complex circumstances on fertiliser decisions, including bivariate as well as multivariate tests.

Complexity of the decision environment: the independent variable

Complexity inhibits, but does not rule out, an actor's ability to adapt decisions optimally to environmental features. Complexity relates to the decision itself but also to the context in which the decision takes place; together these are referred to as the decision environment. The more complex a decision, the harder it is for a decision-maker to pick the optimal choice out of a range of options, let alone solve a problem without predefined choices, as is more often the true nature of decision-making. Complexity tends to increase with the amount of information available, with the number of decision parameters, and when the decision-maker pursues multiple goals which require trade-offs. Furthermore, uncertainty about the outcomes of different choices augments the cognitive challenges.

In the present context of farming, several indicators may be used to measure complexity. Firstly, complexity is expected to increase with *farm size*, the rationale being that size increases the number of activities competing for attention and the number of decisions to be made. Farm size will be measured in hectarage and in some instances in number of livestock units (lu), a standard measurement.

Furthermore, *fertiliser type* affects complexity. Natural fertilisers[1] are more difficult to work with than artificial fertilisers and the uncertainty is greater as to how much nitrogen plants actually will absorb from manure compared with artificial fertiliser. Application technologies, application methods and timing require consideration. This makes artificial fertilisers simpler to handle both in the decision-making phase as well as in the field.

Finally, *farm category* has been identified as an indicator of complexity, based on three considerations. Firstly, specialisation is expected to correlate positively with simplicity, because it reduces the number of parallel but perhaps unrelated activities. Particularly, arable specialisation reduces the competition from other tasks in relation to field work. Farmers may also specialise in livestock and often do. But most livestock farms also grow crops, partly due to regulatory requirements that they own land, but also because they need forage crops or supplementary income from crop sales. Hence, it is reasonable to assume that livestock farmers divide their attention between animals and fields. A second reason that farm category would vary systematically with complexity is that different categories of livestock may vary with regard to labour intensity. Cattle, dairy cattle at least, tend to require more daily care and attention than pigs, implying a higher degree of competition with regard to attention given to fertiliser management. On the other hand, pig farms may also vary in labour intensity depending on whether they raise feeding pigs or sows (interview data). Thus differences between livestock farms as to intensity may not be great. Poultry and fur farms are not required to have much land compared with the number of animals. This may simplify the task of fertilising, but would also indicate, at least tentatively, that field work is not prioritised. The third consideration that leads to the use of farm category as an indicator of complexity relates to the use of manure which represents more of a challenge than artificial fertiliser. This means that crop farmers *a priori* face a simpler task of fertilising, as only this farm type may choose not to use manure as a source of fertiliser. But some crop farmers choose to import manure, either as a cheap or free source of fertiliser, or because manure has other valued properties.

Farm category turns out to be a source of systematic variation among the other independent variables. Crop farms differ from livestock farms, the average crop farm in the sample having only about half as much land as those in the main livestock categories. Poultry farms are rather small, while mixed farms vary in size from year to year. As for manure, cattle farms tend to have more manure than pig farms. Some crop farms import manure from livestock farms, but do tend to have less manure than the livestock farms. There is a proportional relationship between the size of the livestock herd and *the share of nitrogen* which derives from manure.

Altogether, such systematic relationships among the independent variables suggest a specification of the causal model, where farm type precedes the other independent variables and where number of livestock units also affects share of manure. To the degree that each of these variables do vary systematically with the tendency to deviate, such co-variation would tend to intensify the effect of farm category, as there will be a direct as well as an indirect effect of this variable.

How to measure deviation from norms: the dependent variable

Environmental regulation aims to curb excess fertilising, i.e. fertiliser levels above the optimal norms; consequently over-fertilising has been the focus of most empirical analyses of fertiliser management (see, for instance, Grant *et al.*, 1997, 2000; Hasler, 1998; Hansen and Christensen, 2000). However, in the current theoretical context any deviation from economically optimal behaviour, be it fertilising above or below norms, is relevant. The following discussion therefore concerns the merits of using a combined measure of deviation versus separate measures of above-norm and below-norm fertilising (hereafter referred to by the terms over-fertilisation and under-fertilisation, respectively).

Deviation vs. over-fertilising and under-fertilising: when and why

Rational economic theory predicts that actors optimise their activities. Accepting as a premise that fertiliser norms embody optimal levels of nitrogen, optimisation implies that farmers follow the norms. *Bounded rationality theory* assumes that actors *aim to* optimise their activities, but predicts that they will deviate from optimal behaviour under certain circumstances. This is also the claim of this book. Consequently, from a theoretical point of view any kind of deviation from optimality, be it under-fertilisation or over-fertilisation, is relevant. Deviation thus constitutes the basic dependent variable.

This said, it is possible that the independent variables might lead to different patterns of over- and under-fertilisation, respectively. Uncertainty is one component of complexity which may particularly increase the tendency to over-fertilise. While the fertiliser norms are based on extensive scientific documentation and thus represent the best standard for how much nitrogen crops need, scientists cannot incorporate abnormal climate factors ahead of time. Even though the norms do allow for some adjustments in extreme cases, an element of uncertainty goes with the territory of farming. Farmers may therefore apply a rule of thumb of giving more fertiliser than strictly necessary to ensure against loss of nitrogen. Uncertainty would also be greater for farmers using livestock fertilisers, who might therefore also over-fertilise to a greater extent than farmers not using livestock fertilisers. This reasoning applies more strongly prior to the introduction of the nitrogen quota, which forces attention on over-fertilisation.

Under-fertilisation on the other hand may be related to selective attention in a rather straightforward manner. Under-fertilisation is more likely to occur in circumstances where selective attention plays a significant role, and by the logic of the theoretical framework this would occur when circumstances are more complex. Hence, the independent variables may affect under-fertilisation to a greater extent than over-fertilisation, particularly after the introduction of the nitrogen quota.

Furthermore, using amount of manure as an independent variable also suggests that over- and under-fertilisation should be studied separately. The more manure a farm has per hectare, the less the farm will be able to under-fertilise, as farms must dispose of manure.

In conclusion, therefore, the theoretical considerations determine that deviation from norms will be measured as a composite measure that designates the overall degree of deviation from norms, integrating over-fertilising as well as under-fertilising. But theoretical considerations also indicate the merit of conducting separate analyses using over-fertilisation and under-fertilisation as dependent variables. Hence, the analyses will use all three indicators.

How to measure deviation

The indicator of deviation from norms to be used here is a weighted numerical mean, which may be interpreted as the *mean deviation per hectare for each farm*, where positive and negative deviations both count. Firstly, deviation must be calculated in a relative manner, as norms vary with crop and soil. Therefore deviation is calculated as a percentage of the norm. Secondly, as pointed out in previous chapters, rational behaviour is a feature linked to actors, in this case farmers. To reflect this, a valid indicator of deviation should aggregate deviations on fields at the level of the farm.

To ensure that positive and negative deviations from norms do not falsely add up to a low aggregate number, the measure 'mean deviation' is based on numerical values instead of absolute values. With a fertiliser quota this measure risks seemingly magnifying deviations because over-fertilising inevitably leads to under-fertilising as well, in a sense counting the deviation twice. But it is possible to offset a large amount of excess fertiliser on one field by spreading the deficit across several fields, resulting in smaller deviations on each field. This means that the numerical mean does accurately rank farmers in terms of their tendency to deviate from norms.

Finally, deviation on each field is weighted by its size to prevent a large rate of deviation on a small field distorting the true degree of deviation from norms across the farm. Weighting leads to a more accurate representation of the general tendency to deviate from norms.

The measure of over-fertilisation weights the hectarage of each over-fertilised field against the entire hectarage of the farm. Using the total hectarage of the farm for the calculation yields a measure of over-fertilisation that represents the mean percentage of over-fertilisation per hectare on the farm (and likewise for under-fertilisation). This allows for comparison between groups and for grasping the overall trends in over- and under-fertilisation. But using total hectarage as the denominator also dilutes the number with regard to the actual rate of over- or under-fertilisation on each field, which hampers an intuitive understanding of the levels of over-fertilisation. Hence, in a few select cases the analyses will weight the area of the over-fertilised fields against the over-fertilised area of the farm (and the same for under-fertilised fields); this renders a measure of the degree to which fertiliser is concentrated on the fields, but also risks over-weighting a few extreme values.

Fertiliser levels

Economic theory would expect farmers to fertilise in an economically optimal manner, while scholars within the bounded rationality tradition claim that even economic actors will deviate from economically optimal behaviour, if the decision-making conditions are less than ideal. The first part of the analysis therefore serves to give a quick overview of how observed fertiliser levels compare with economically optimal levels as the latter are embodied in the regulatory norms. The data are pooled over the entire period. Table 6.1 divides deviation into intervals based on the degree of deviation.

Table 6.1   *Deviation from fertiliser norms, calculated by farm. Weighted numerical means*

Per cent deviation per hectare	*Share of farms*	*Frequency (N) farms*
0*	0	0
>0–19.9	40.5	768
20–49.9	43.6	827
≥50	15.9	302
Total	100	1897

Note: *Exactly 0. Pooled sample. N = number of farms.

A first, simple observation is that no farms follow the norms precisely on all of their fields, i.e. no farm has a mean deviation of zero. About 41 per cent of the farms deviate modestly from norms by up to 20 per cent, while as many as 59 per cent of the farms show medium or large mean deviations from optimal norms. In other words, mean deviation per hectare is at least 20 per cent for six out of 10 farms in the pooled sample.

Under-fertilisation is more prevalent than over-fertilisation: see Table 6.2 Almost 90 per cent of the farms under-fertilise on at least one field, while 76 per cent over-fertilise on one or more fields. When over-fertilisation and under-fertilisation are separated modest degrees of deviation dominate. Almost 60 per cent of the farms over-fertilise modestly, i.e. less than 20 per cent, and the same trend applies to under-fertilisation. Even so, 12 per cent of the farms under-fertilise by more than 50 per cent, while only 3 per cent over-fertilise by this much.

Table 6.2   *Degree of fertilising above or below norms. Weighted numerical mean*

Per cent per hectare	Over-fertilising share of farms per cent	Frequency N	Under-fertilising per cent	Frequency (N) farms
0*	24.1	457	11.5	218
>0–19.9	57.5	1090	58.0	1100
20–49.9	15.7	298	18.8	356
≥50	2.7	52	11.8	223
Total	100.0	1897	100.0	1897

Note: *Exactly zero. Pooled sample. N = number of farms. Calculated against total farm hectarage

Explaining deviation by change and stability

In the fully rational model, actors are assumed to update information continually and to adapt behaviour to changes in circumstances so that they always optimise. In the bounded rationality model, actors are assumed to rely on routines. While such routines may be conducive to optimal behaviour under stable conditions, they may not fit when circumstances change. The decisions of boundedly rational actors may be out of sync with optimal decisions, because they update information more intermittently due to selective attention. This means that farmers would change fertiliser behaviour when pertinent conditions change, but they may not do so immediately, and they may also not adapt entirely to the new circumstances. Incomplete adaptation is more likely if the changes increase complexity or uncertainty of fertiliser decisions. In the present study the main source of change would stem from new regulation.

As outlined in Chapter 5, fertiliser regulation changed substantially and frequently between the late 1980s and the beginning of the 2000s. These regulatory changes would affect fertiliser patterns in a somewhat predictable pattern. For the early 1990s farmers were not bound by nitrogen norms, and farmers would be expected to follow routines according to the bounded rationality framework. Deviations could take the form of both over-fertilisation and under-fertilisation. Given the uncertainty about the effect of fertilisers, a likely rule of thumb would be to apply somewhat higher levels than prescribed by norms. But some under-fertilisation would also follow logically from the framework, explained by a lack of attention and/or motivation. The main prediction following from this would be that farmers as a matter of routine deviate from norms, and that they do so at a rather stable level over the first few years. The general political focus on fertiliser reduction and the adoption in 1991 of an action plan for sustainable agriculture, which increased focus on mandatory measures, may have heightened awareness among farmers about fertiliser levels. An alternative hypothesis, one which is also compatible with the theoretical framework, is therefore that deviations from norms begin to decline during this period.

The introduction of a fertiliser quota in 1994 more forcefully focused attention on fertiliser management. To avoid economic sanctions from violating the quota, farmers had to be on top of the situation with regard to fertiliser levels. Theoretically, the norm also simplified fertiliser decisions, suggesting quick adaptation to the fertiliser norms;[2] although any change in circumstances usually embodies a transition period marked by temporary deviations from optimal behaviour. Furthermore, the requirement to update fertiliser plans in spring to conform to the nitrogen prognosis may also slip by some farmers, thus delaying adaptation to the fertiliser norms. Thus, these counteracting forces lead to the expectation that deviation from norms will fluctuate somewhat in the first couple of years after 1994, but gradually decline, as farmers learn to work with the regulatory norms.

Over-fertilisation is expected to decline gradually as the regulation itself, let alone the threat of sanctions, should serve to focus attention on this activity. As for under-fertilisation, predictions are not as simple. For farmers who have not under-fertilised before, the quota may enforce an increase in the rate of under-fertilisation, because any over-fertilisation must be offset by under-fertilisation. But for those who have under-fertilised as a matter of ill-fitting routines, under-fertilisation should decrease, as the quota forces their attention on fertilisation. However, it is possible that farmers would make sure not to over-fertilise to any great extent but would be less careful about under-fertilisation. Thus, the best prediction is that under-fertilisation will fluctuate initially due to the many changes in the regulation, possibly followed by gradual decline, but generally exceeding the level of over-fertilisation.

Finally, the sub-optimal norms implemented in 1998–99 render theoretical predictions difficult. On the one hand, the scarce nitrogen quota focuses attention on fertiliser behaviour, presumably leading to stable and low deviations from norms. Yet, the norms no longer represent a clear-cut rational standard of behaviour. The sub-optimal norms, therefore, present farmers with a dilemma. They can either apply optimal levels of fertiliser on some fields, i.e. privilege some crops or fields at the expense of significantly under-fertilising other fields. This is referred to here as strategic over-fertilisation. Or they can follow the norms closely, spreading the scarcity evenly across all fields. Such dilemmas tend to increase fluctuation and deviation from optimal behaviour. Hence, the bounded rationality framework does not yield unequivocal predictions for over-fertilisation. Under-fertilisation is expected to remain stable or decrease somewhat as nitrogen becomes a scarce resource; although a possible increase in over-fertilisation could force up the rate of under-fertilisation as well. Predictions are summed up in Box 6.1.

<table>
<tr><td colspan="2">Box 6.1   Predictions regarding responses to regulatory changes</td></tr>
<tr><td>Time period</td><td>Fertiliser pattern</td></tr>
<tr><td>Until 1994</td><td>Routines?
Deviation from norms will be stable or, deviation may decline.
Over-fertilisation will exceed under-fertilisation due to uncertainty.</td></tr>
<tr><td>1994–98</td><td>Fluctuations?

Fertiliser patterns will fluctuate due to changes.

Over-fertilisation will decline.

Under-fertilisation will decline due to increased attention, but could also increase due to fear of exceeding the quota.</td></tr>
<tr><td>1999–2002</td><td>Uncertainty?
Initial fluctuation due to regulatory change.
Otherwise unpredictable.</td></tr>
</table>

Fertiliser patterns over time

Fertiliser patterns do generally follow the expected trajectory, but there is also considerable noise in the pattern, (see Figure 6.1). Observed fertiliser levels deviated considerably from norms for the first period; they declined following introduction of the quota in 1994 and generally remained below the pre-quota level until 1998, which marks a rather large jump in deviation. From 1999 onwards, deviation was quite stable but at a slightly higher level than the average trend in the years prior to 1998.[3] Developments within each of these periods as well as the general level of deviation, however, fit expectations less well.

Before 1994: routines?
In the early 1990s, farmers, as expected, typically did not follow fertiliser norms. In other words, if farmers followed routines,

these did not conform to optimal behaviour. But it is not obvious that deviations can be explained by inadequate attention and routine behaviour, since the level of deviation is not stable over the period. Mean deviation decreases by a full 10 percentage points from 40 per cent during the first year only to increase again to 36 per cent in 1993. The decrease in deviation is set against a context of intense political debate about nitrogen leaching, which may have increased farmers' awareness about, and hence attention to, appropriate fertiliser levels. But the 1993 increase does not fit with such an explanation.

1994–1998: fluctuations

The years immediately after introduction of the nitrogen quota are marked by fluctuations in fertiliser patterns. Deviation decreases in 1994, but in the following years continues to oscillate around 30 per cent. Fluctuations are compatible with the prediction that adjustment to norms would be uncertain in the first few years, but it is noteworthy that deviations were closer to the norms in 1994 than any other year in that period and that deviation increased in 1995, 1996 and 1998. Considering the

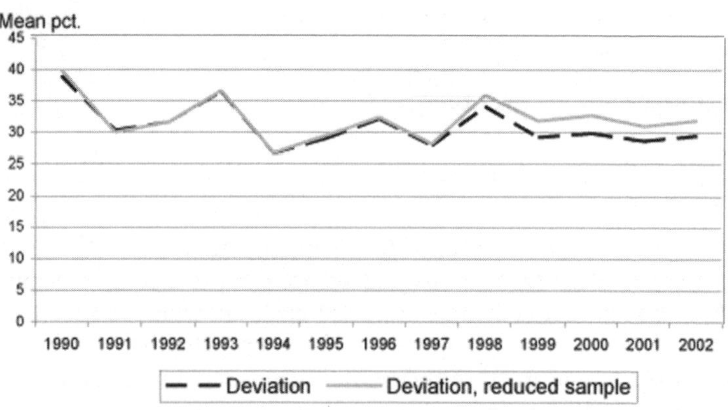

Figure 6.1 *Deviation from norms by farm, weighted numerical means.*

Note: 'Deviation, reduced sample' includes only farms from catchment areas that participate in complete time series. N in reduced sample varies from 109 farms in 2002 to 153 in 1990. N in full sample varies from 128 in 1997 to 165 in 1990.

many regulatory changes that took effect in these years, the pattern remains within the realm of expectations.

Patterns for 1999–2002: increased uncertainty?
Mean deviation drops a few percentage points in 1999 to remain fairly stable over the following years. The fact that deviation generally shifts upward compared with the previous period fits one of the predictions derived from bounded rationality, i.e. that sub-optimal norms would increase complexity and therefore deviation. The overall level of deviation is higher than expected, however. The increase in deviation could also be compatible with the rational expectation that farmers over-fertilise strategically. To examine this issue properly requires decomposition of deviation into over-fertilisation and under-fertilisation.

Over- and under-fertilisation over time

Separate analyses of over-fertilisation and under-fertilisation add important detail (see Figure 6.2). Before 1994, over-fertilisation and under-fertilisation tend to follow each other fairly closely, i.e. displaying an initial decrease followed by increases until 1993. Over-fertilisation is a little higher than under-fertilisation. But from 1994 onwards, over-fertilisation and under-fertilisation follow disparate courses with a tendency for the two to move in opposite directions. This does not match predictions.

Generally, the development in over-fertilisation is characterised by fluctuation rather than by gradual decline. There are striking peaks in 1996 and 1998. But looking at the overall trend between 1993 and 1997 the mean rate of over-fertilisation does decline considerably and approaches norms during this period. As expected, then, the cap on nitrogen forces farmers to pay attention to over-fertilisation, while the fluctuations are somewhat consistent with the notion that adaptation to norms would be uncertain due to the many regulatory changes during this intermediate period. However, the increases in 1996 and 1998 are so large as to suggest that there may be additional factors at play.

The pattern in under-fertilisation fits expectations somewhat better. One hypothesis was that uncertainty about exceeding the nitrogen quota would lead to an overreaction in terms of under-

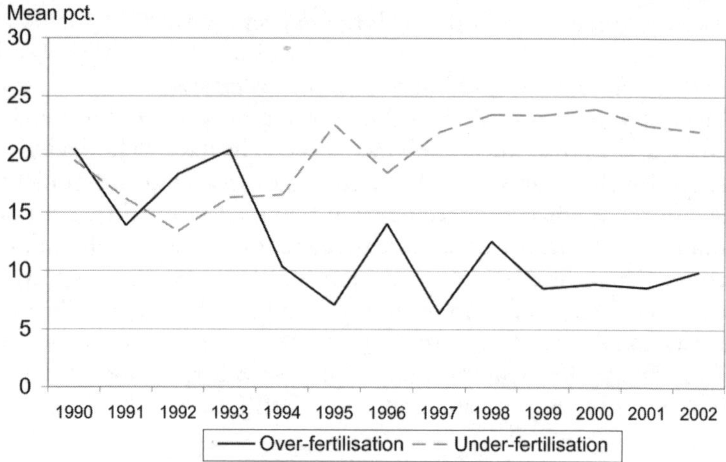

Figure 6.2   Over-fertilisation and under-fertilisation over time

Note: Reduced sample, includes only full-period catchment areas. Calculated against total area of farms. N = 109 to 153.

fertilising. Thus, following an initial decrease, under-fertilisation increases to a mean about 23 per cent in the mid-1990s and remains there for the remaining period. The increase seems quite large, even allowing for this explanation. In fact, the relatively stable level of under-fertilisation following the initial fluctuations does indicate routine behaviour and perhaps a lack of attention to some fields. Lack of attention may also explain the relatively high rate of under-fertilisation even after the lowering of norms in 1999. Yet, it remains somewhat puzzling, as one would expect the sub-optimal nitrogen norms to force farmers to use up their quota. Again, this suggests that alternative or supplementary explanations may be at play. Lack of motivation is an obvious one. This will be further explored in the analysis of decision processes in Chapter 7.

The findings do not indicate strategic over-fertilisation to any noticeable degree. The concentration of over-fertilisation actually drops in 1999 and the overall degree remains stable. An analysis of fertiliser levels for individual fields shows that the share of fields over-fertilised by 10 per cent remains stable throughout the entire study period (data not shown here).

Unexpected patterns of fluctuation

There is a tendency for over- and under-fertilisation to fluctuate in opposite directions for the years 1995 to 1997/1998. Within the confines of the quota system, one would expect the two types of deviation to develop in tandem: if over-fertilisation goes down so would under-fertilisation, partly because attention to fertiliser should manifest itself in both types of deviation, and not least because the quota ensures that any over-fertilisation must be matched by a corresponding degree of under-fertilisation. Of course, as seen here, the quota does not prevent farmers from under-fertilising more than they over-fertilise. The implication of the latter is that farmers do not use their entire nitrogen quota, which appears to be the case on aggregate, particularly for the years 1994 to 1998. In fact, a test shows relatively little correlation between over-fertilisation and under-fertilisation and the correlation is negative. This suggests that different factors drive over- and under-fertilisation, respectively.

Lack of attention to the pre-season updating of nitrogen norms could be another explanation for the opposite movements of over- and under-fertilisation. This adjustment was introduced in 1994. It would work like this: if, for instance, the farmer plans fertiliser application with normal levels of fertiliser, while the update calls for an increase over this level, the farmer would end up with relatively more under-fertilisation and relatively less over-fertilisation. In fact, the years between 1994 and 1997 included several years with significant modifications of the fertiliser quota. Most strikingly, in 1996 norms were lowered by about 10 per cent on average due to an extremely dry winter (Landskontoret for Planteavl, 1996). By the logic of inattention one would expect over-fertilisation to increase and under-fertilisation to decrease. This is exactly what happened in that year. The pattern also fits for 1995, although in the opposite direction. From 1997 there is no longer any correspondence between norm adjustments and over- and under-fertilisation patterns, but arguably farmers would have learned to pay attention to norm adjustments at this point.

Effect of regulatory changes on fertiliser

The overall prediction following from bounded rationality – that behaviour deviates from optimal behaviour – holds. Overall trends also generally follow the prediction that changes in circumstances affect behaviour, and the decline in 1994 as well as the slight increase in deviation in 1999 fit expectations in terms of the direction they take. The norms in 1994 would simplify the task of identifying optimal levels of fertiliser, whereas the sub-optimal norms complicate fertiliser decisions. The fact that adaptation is not instant but rather leads to fluctuations also fits expectations. Yet fluctuations, particularly in the first period, are greater than expected, and the pattern in the intermediate period also suggests that uncertainty and selective attention, important drivers in the bounded rationality framework, do not explain all of the behaviour.

The analysis underlines the value of analysing over-fertilisation and under-fertilisation separately. Assuming that norms are optimal, over-fertilisation that occurs prior to the introduction of the nitrogen quota is consistent with the notion that uncertainty leads to deviation from optimal behaviour; the nitrogen quota then clearly forces some adaptation to optimal norms as the level of over-fertilisation decreases over the period, while sub-optimal norms again increase uncertainty and raise the rate of over-fertilisation to some degree. Nothing in the analysis indicates the rational hypothesis that farmers in general over-fertilise strategically after 1999. Generally, fluctuations are great for the first two periods studied, and particularly the peak in 1998 seems to require explanations other than those following from the bounded rationality framework.

As for under-fertilisation, the level is higher than expected, but stabilises after initial reactions to the regulatory changes. This pattern is consistent with both uncertainty about the fertiliser quota, but also with a lack of attention to fertiliser. But as the regulatory changes were expected to focus attention on optimal behaviour, as seen with over-fertilisation, the rate of under-fertilisation is higher than expected. This suggests that other explanatory factors are also at play. Further analysis may be able to uncover these.

Explaining deviation by complexity

As outlined, deviation from the economically optimal norms is expected to vary to a greater extent when the circumstances surrounding fertilising are more complex. This section explores the bivariate relationships between complex decision environments and fertiliser patterns. The effect of independent variables is expected to be stronger before the introduction of the fertiliser quota in 1994, as the quota seemingly would serve to increase attention to fertiliser practices, thereby moderating the effect of complex circumstances.

Farm category

As argued in the introductory sections, farm category is an indicator of the degree of specialisation and suggestive of the amount of attention the farmer can devote to fertilising.

In line with conventional classifications in agricultural regulation and statistics, livestock farms are defined based on the share of livestock units, using a 2/3 rule. Thus, a cattle farm is so classified if cattle comprise at least two-thirds of the livestock units and so forth for other livestock categories (see, for instance, Plantedirektoratet, 2004: 28). In the present analysis, to distinguish clearly among the farm categories with respect to degrees of complexity, crop farms are defined as farms with less than 0.1 livestock units per hectare, following the definition used by the National Environmental Research Institute (NERI) in their analyses of the LOOP data.

By these criteria crop farms comprise the largest single group of farms included in the dataset, making up 42 per cent of the farms in 1990 and nearly half of the farms by 2002. Cattle farms make for the second largest group of farms. Over the years, their share of the sample ranges from 40 per cent in the early 1990s to just 26 per cent in 2002. The last of the three major farm categories, pig farms, typically average 17 per cent of all farms. As for the poultry and mixed categories, the dataset includes rather few farms, which introduces a problem in comparing statistics for these groups to the other three groups when the sample is split into years. One or two outliers may significantly affect composite numbers for these groups. Therefore, the analyses will focus on the three main farm groups, but poultry farms and mixed farms will be commented on when appropriate.

Table 6.3   *Distribution of farms by category. Selected years. Column per cent*

Farm type	1990	2002
Cattle	36	26
Pig	13	17
Poultry	4	7
Crop	42	49
Mixed	4	2
Total %	99	101
N	165	145

Note: N = number of farms per year.

Overall, the expectation is that the less specialised the farmer is, the more likely he is to deviate from optimal fertiliser levels. Crop farms would be the most specialised and according to the theoretical framework should deviate the least from norms. But there may be systematic variation also among livestock farms. Cattle farms may deviate more from norms than other farms, as cattle, at least dairy cattle, are typically more labour intensive than other types of livestock, according to interviews conducted for this study. This would leave the cattle farmer less time for field work than his pig farm counterpart. However, pig farms also vary with regard to the amount of time required with the animals, with feeding pigs being the least labour intensive. It is possible, therefore, that differences in complexity are not large enough to cause differences in fertiliser patterns.

Initial analysis comparing crop producers to all livestock farms confirms expectations that crop farms deviate less from norms than do farms with livestock. Typically, livestock farms deviate from norms by 10 to 15 percentage points more than crop farms, and differences are statistically significant in each year.[4]

Analysing the main farm categories reveals differences also among livestock farms. Figure 6.3 presents mean deviation for each farm category over time.[5] Cattle farms deviate more from

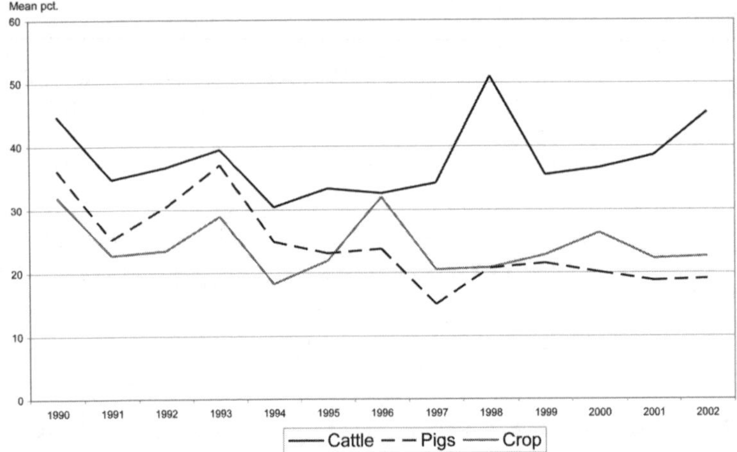

Figure 6.3 *Deviation from fertiliser norms for different categories of farms, over time. Weighted numerical means*

Note: Full sample. N varies from 128 farms in 1997 to 165 in 1990.

norms than do crop farms and pig farms. But, unexpectedly, pig farms are no more likely to deviate from norms than are crop farms. Tests show that the differences between cattle farms and crop farms are statistically significant in many years, whereas the differences between crop and pig farms are not. The findings fit, partially, expectations that crop farms deviate less from norms than other farm categories, while at the other end of the spectrum cattle farms, which experience greater competition for attention to different tasks, deviate the most from norms. The pattern for pig farms defies expectations, however.

Separate analyses of over- and under- fertilisation to some extent repeat these patterns, but also uncover underlying differences: see Figures 6.4 and 6.5.

Thus cattle farms and pig farms generally over-fertilise more than crop farms. A noteworthy exception to this pattern, however, is the marked increase in over-fertilisation for crop farms in 1995–97, when they surpass cattle farms. In fact, both pig farms and crop farms dramatically increase over-fertilisation in 1996. In contrast, cattle farms noticeably decrease over-fertilisation rates in these same years. These behavioural patterns

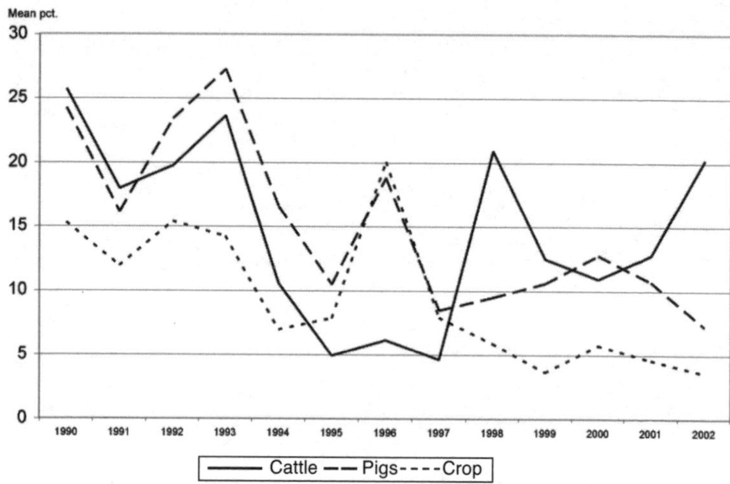

Figure 6.4   *Degree of over-fertilisation for different farm categories, over time. Weighted means*

Note: Full sample. N varies from 128 farms in 1997 to 165 in 1990.

cannot be directly accounted for by different degrees of specialisation, but suggest causes outside the analytical framework. Poultry farms show a rather erratic path, which could indicate inconsistent attention to fertilising, but also may simply reflect the vulnerability to outliers. Statistically significant differences between farm categories occur mostly in the mid-1990s and towards the end of the data series, and typically for crop farms compared to other farms. For 1996, of course, the relationship is the opposite of the one predicted. These findings do not suggest a strong relationship between farm category and over-fertilisation.

As for under-fertilisation, the relative patterns among farm categories remain largely stable throughout the period, (see Figure 6.5).

Cattle farms show a higher propensity for under-fertilisation than other farm categories, while crop farms are slightly more inclined to under-fertilise than pig farms but not at statistically significant levels. The difference between cattle farms and the other categories increases somewhat after the introduction of the nitrogen quota in 1994, indicating that the increase in under-

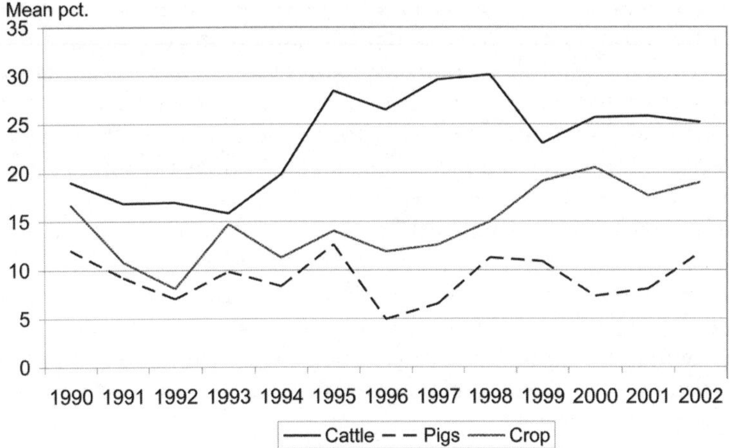

Figure 6.5 *Degree of under-fertilisation for different farm categories*

Note: Weighted means. Full sample. N varies from 128 farms in 1997 to 165 in 1990.

fertilisation noted in the descriptive analysis is driven largely by cattle farmers.

The findings lend only slight support to the hypothesis that degree of specialisation, hence degree of complexity, affects the inclination of farmers to deviate from optimal behaviour. As predicted, cattle farms deviate more from norms than do crop farms, but pig farms behave quite similarly to crop farms and thus break with expected patterns.

But findings vary for over-fertilisation and under-fertilisation, respectively. The livestock farms generally do over-fertilise more than crop farms, but differences are not large enough to be statistically significant. Furthermore, the findings for 1995–97 defy all expectations as pig farms and crop farms surpass cattle farms with regard to degree of over-fertilisation. For this period, the importance of complexity is expected to decline somewhat, as the nitrogen quota would tend to increase general attention to over-fertilisation. But the reversal of patterns is so complete as to suggest that explanatory factors other than differential complexity must be at play, not just a lessening of the effect of complexity. Finally, for the years 1998 to 2002 again there are no significant differences among the farm categories, although as expected cattle and pig farms do over-fertilise more than crop farms.

The analysis also confirms expectations that cattle farms under-fertilise more than crop farms, but the differences are statistically significant primarily for the period 1994–98. The fact that pig farms are less inclined to under-fertilise than crop farms obviously weakens the hypothesis that different degrees of complexity would lead to differences in under-fertilisation. The analysis suggests that other variables interfere with the relationship; variables on which pig farms and crop farms are more similar than they are with regard to complexity.

Generally, the analysis so far does not therefore point to farm category as a strong explanatory factor of variation in fertiliser practices.

Size

Several indicators of size might be used, but for the sake of simplicity, hectarage was chosen as the main indicator of size. Parallel analyses with number of fields or the livestock units do not change the findings.

Size is a dynamic measurement. The structural development of Danish agriculture during the 1990s has been characterised by an increasing concentration of land on fewer farms. This development is reflected in the dataset used here. Thus in 1990, the mean hectarage of a farm in the sample was 23 ha. By 2002 the mean had nearly doubled to 44 ha. For a more detailed view of the distribution across farm sizes, hectarage was divided into intervals. The increase in mean hectarage shows in a relative shift over the years from the small acreage intervals to the large intervals: see Table 6.4. Whereas in 1990 more than 70 per cent of farms had less than 30 hectares, by 2002 the share of farms in the smallest intervals had fallen to 50 per cent. Likewise, the share of farms with more than 100 hectares made up less than 1 per cent in the early years but amounted to 12 per cent by 2002.

Despite the general increase in size, the sample is dominated by what appears to be small and medium-sized farms, i.e. farms with less than 50 hectares. This pattern largely mirrors to a great extent the structural composition of the Danish agricultural sector as reported by Statistics Denmark. The structural development seen, all other things being equal, would work towards greater complexity.

Table 6.4 *Distribution by intervals of hectarage. Percentage of farms. Column per cent*

Ha	1990	2002
1–9.9	36	23
10–29.9	36	30
30–49.9	18	17
50–99.9	9	19
≥100	1	12
Total %	100	100
N	165	145

Note: N = farms.

Size and fertiliser patterns

Thus the general hypothesis is that the larger the farm, the greater the tendency to deviate from norms. The reasoning is that size increases the pressure on time and attention. But a larger farm may also have more hired help, which would reduce the effect of time pressure, and there is also an expectation that larger farms tend to be run more professionally, which would also interfere with the effect of size on complexity. Furthermore, the very small farms, often run by part-time farmers with little time on their hands, might deviate more from norms than larger farms. Unfortunately, number of employees and experience or a similar measure of professionalism represents a problem of omitted variables which cannot be controlled for in this analysis.

The prediction of a linear relationship between size and deviation is not confirmed. The smallest farms deviate significantly more from norms than any other group, which is not entirely unexpected. But there is no clear variation among the other size groups. The largest farms do tend to deviate more from norms than farms in the smaller size categories, but the differences are not statistically significant. Moreover, the other size categories follow each other quite closely except over a few years.

Looking at over-fertilising and under-fertilising separately does

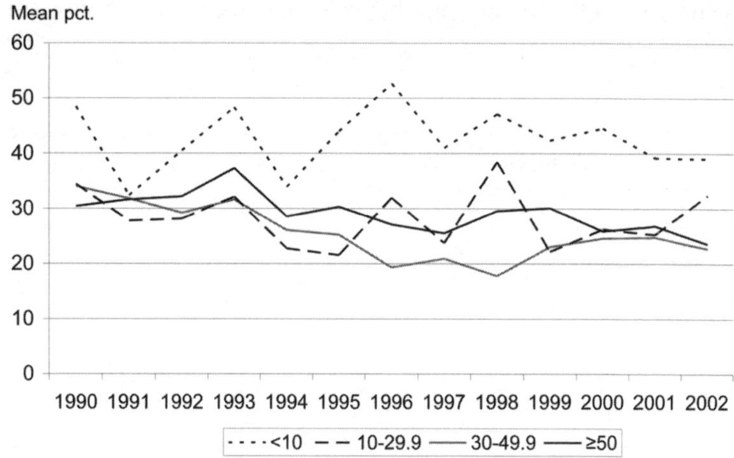

Figure 6.6   *Deviation from fertiliser norms by acreage intervals, over time. Means*

Note: Weighted numerical means. Full sample: N varies from 128 in 1997 to 165 in 1990.

soften this conclusion. Figure 6.7 presents over-fertilisation rates for each of the four hectarage intervals. The figure shows that larger farms are more likely to over-fertilise than smaller farms in the early years and again from 1999. Tests also show a positive and statistically significant relationship for over-fertilisation in the early years. This is in line with the hypothesis and also confirms that differences in complexity mattered more before the introduction of the quota.

During the years 1995 to 1998, on the other hand, the relationship between size and over-fertilisation almost reverses and shows large variations. It turns out that the small farms of 10 to 30 hectares are responsible for the leaps in 1996 and 1998 also seen in previous analyses. The differences are quite small, however, and not statistically significant.

For under-fertilisation there is no linear relationship between hectarage and degree of under-fertilisation. Except for the small-est farms, which consistently under-fertilise the most, the size groups switch relative positions intermittently, and differences are quite small. Correlation is negative, indicating that under-

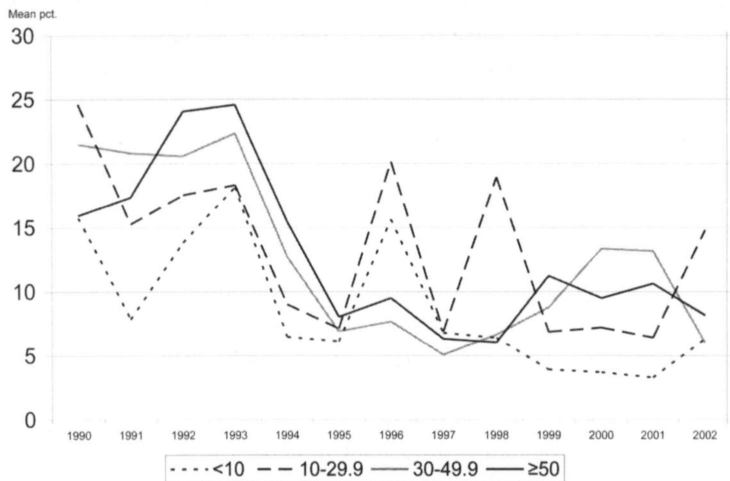

Figure 6.7   *Over-fertilisation by acreage intervals, over time. Means*

Note: Weighted means. Full sample: N varies from 128 in 1997 to 165 in 1990.

fertilisation decreases as size increases, but the relationship is not statistically significant.

Hence, when it comes to over-fertilisation the analysis offers some support for the proposition that deviation varies positively with size; although the differences are statistically significant only in the early years. But as it was also expected that the effect of size differences would become less significant after the quota took effect, this pattern is not inconsistent with the hypotheses. However, the pattern for the intermediate years again breaks with expectations and remains unexplained. As for under-fertilisation, the lack of differentiation between the size groups clearly refutes the hypothesis that hectarage increases deviation from optimal norms.

The analysis of the relationship between size and deviation, then, does not generally support the hypothesis that the greater the farm, the stronger the propensity for deviating from economically optimal fertiliser norms. But the analysis of over-fertilisation offers some qualifications to this conclusion. There is a positive and statistically significant relationship between size and over-fertilisation during the early years, exactly those years when the relationship would be expected to be stronger, as attention differentials due to complexity are unmitigated by the nitrogen quota. The pattern reverses for the intermediate years, for which there is no immediate explanation in the analytical framework; although small farms seem to cause the peak in over-fertilisation in 1996 and 1998. For under-fertilisation, hypotheses that size increases deviation are refuted quite consistently.

Complexity: manure

Fertiliser type is the final indicator of complexity. The expectation is that farms using manure are more likely to deviate from norms as manure involves more uncertainty with regard to its effect than artificial fertiliser and is generally more difficult to handle. However, there is a catch with regard to under-fertilisation. The more manure the farm needs to dispose of, the less the farm will be able to under-fertilise. Thus, while the analytical framework predicts a greater tendency to over-fertilise and under-fertilise on farms with large shares of manure, the fact that manure must be spread suggests that farms with manure will under-fertilise less than farms with little or no manure. These different effects on under-fertilisation are indistinguishable analytically.

The majority of the farms in the sample use manure as part of their fertiliser quota, although a sizable share of farms do not. In 1990, 55 per cent of the farms used some amount of manure as fertiliser. By 1993 that share had increased to 69 per cent, where it stayed for most of the remainder of the time series. Furthermore, the amount of manure used on farms increases over time from a mean of 41 kg per hectare in 1990 to almost 52 kg per hectare in 2002. This increase is a logical consequence of the regulatory demand for increased utilisation rates of nitrogen in manure and the increase in livestock units per farm. This measure offers a comparative standard among farms for the weight of manure and does not reflect the size of the farms as it is measured per hectare.

It follows also that an ever larger share of fertiliser derives from manure. Hence, among farms with manure, the mean *share* of nitrogen that derives from manure doubles over the period,

Table 6.5 *Manure, mean kg nitrogen per ha across farms*

Pct.	1990	2002
Mean	41.1	51.8
N*	91	100
N	165	145

Note: N = number of farms in total sample. Mean for farms with manure.
N* = number of farms with manure.

from 26 per cent in 1990 to 52 per cent in 2002. The rise in the use of manure implies that complexity for the sample as a whole has intensified throughout the period of study. All other things being equal, this should contribute to an increase in deviation from optimal fertilising.

The amount of manure varies among the different farm categories. Pig farms used more manure per hectare until 1999, at which point they are surpassed by cattle farms. In 2002, the average cattle farm spread 62 kg N through manure per ha while the pig farm spread only 50 kg N per ha. In 1990 the comparable numbers were 33 kg for cattle and 40 kg for pigs. In all likelihood, this development is due to the regulatory requirement to count manure deposited during grazing as part of the amount of nitrogen applied, which affects cattle farms primarily. Crop farms on average have rather little manure, but the crop farms that do use manure have about as much manure per hectare as pig farms and cattle farms.

The first analysis of the relationship is a simple comparison of farms with manure and farms not using manure. It shows that farms with manure do generally deviate more from fertiliser norms than farms without manure. However, the differences are statistically significant only for the early years. Separate analyses of over- and under-fertilisation reveal that differences reflect differences in over-fertilisation, whereas the degree of under-fertilisation is largely the same for the two groups. Farms with manure over-fertilise more than farms without manure almost every year. This confirms the hypothesis that uncertainty related to the use of manure increases over-fertilisation. For the intermediate years, 1995–98, the differences are too small to be statistically significant. This makes sense as regulatory changes aimed precisely to focus attention on over-fertilisation, so differences in this variable should decrease.

The tendency to deviate from fertiliser norms does not increase with the amount of manure, however: see Table 6.6. But this reflects contradictory tendencies for over- and under-fertilisation. Over-fertilisation does correlate positively with higher amounts of manure per hectare. Correlation is weaker for the years following the introduction of fertiliser norms, but increases again from 1999, when norms became economically sub-optimal. Under-fertilisation, on the other hand, tends to correlate negatively with level of manure, but the relationship is rarely statistically significant; although under-fertilisation decreases as levels of manure increase, which is almost inevitable given the regulatory set-up.

Overall, the analysis suggests that deviation from norms is affected by manure. Over-fertilisation increases the more manure a farm has; this is consistent with the prediction that uncertainty about the effect of manure would lead to more over-fertilisation. As for patterns in under-fertilisation, there are no differences between farms with manure and farms without manure.

Table 6.6 *Correlation between amount of manure and deviation, over- and under-fertilisation. Pearson's R*

Year	Deviation	Over-fertilising	Under-fertilising	N
1990	.075	.268***	-.211**	165
1991	.154	.412***	-.140	157
1992	.340***	.534***	-.128	147
1993	.319***	.452***	-.100	143
1994	.242**	.498***	-.110	138
1995	-.002	.175*	-.067	136
1996	-.185*	-.096	-.121	130
1997	-.053	.265**	-.150	128
1998	.067	.152	-.222**	155
1999	.124	.592***	-.115	155
2000	.104	.453***	-.151	151
2001	.111	.379***	-.101	147
2002	.214*	.309***	-.094	145

Note: Includes all farms, also those without manure. *** $p<.001$; **$p<.01$ and *$p<.05$.

While the findings confirm that manure affects the tendency to deviate from norms, the mixed patterns also suggest that the explanation does not rest purely on differences in complexity.

Over-fertilisation appears to be related to uncertainty regarding the effect of manure. Under-fertilisation may reflect a lack of attention to fertilising, perhaps a low priority being assigned to fertilising.

The intermediate years: omitted variable?

The analysis underscores the seeming abnormality of fertiliser patterns for the period 1995–98, but does not decisively offer an explanation for the findings. The break from usual patterns applies to size intervals as well as to farm categories and level of manure, indicating that a missing variable may drive over-fertilisation in these years. Bounded rationality theory would predict some fluctuation following changes in circumstances, such as fertiliser regulation, but if the fluctuations were to reflect erratic reactions to change alone, the effect should have been greatest in the more complex farms or, at the very least, uniform across different farm categories. Instead, the least complex farms show the largest fluctuations in these years.

One possible explanation for the differential patterns in over-fertilisation and under-fertilisation may be different crop profiles across farm types. Previous analysis has shown that grass crops are frequently under-fertilised (Grant *et al.*, 2000). The explanation offered is that norms for grass crops have been generous (Grant *et al.*, 2000: 40). This suggests that farmers may deviate from crop norms on certain crops because they do not consider fertiliser norms to reflect accurately the nitrogen needs of such crops. If this is generally the case, deviation from norms would indicate an attempt to optimise rather than inattention to norms. To attempt to come one step closer to an explanation the multi-variate analysis below will control for the effect of different crops on fertiliser patterns.

Multivariate analysis

Although the bivariate analyses have demonstrated only limited explanatory power of key variables, testing the variables against each other may yet uncover latent relationships. This calls for a multivariate analysis of the full model regarding the effect of complex circumstances on fertiliser behaviour. Multiple regression analysis enables testing of the overall explanatory power of the model as well as the effect of each of the explanatory variables while simultaneously controlling for the effect of the other variables (see, for instance, Agresti and Finlay, 1997; Gujarati, 2003). The basic model includes the independent variables farm category, size, and share of animal fertiliser. Farm category is included as a set of dummy variables, using cattle as the reference group.

The analysis controls also for the effect of crops. However, only some crops were included in the model. The specific crop categories were chosen based on their prevalence across farms and based on analyses of fields as to what crops were most often over- or under-fertilised. Thus, grass in rotation, permanent grass, spring cereal and root crops were selected.

Crops may interact with farm category. Such interaction would be in line with the theoretical prediction which claims that farms vary systematically in their fertiliser management, and therefore would fertilise different crops differently. Crops were calculated as share of fields with a certain crop. However, farm-level analysis indicates no systematic interaction between share of crops and farm category and therefore no interaction variables were included in the multivariate analysis.

Direct and indirect effects: the causal path

Farm category, size and amount of manure may affect the inclination to deviate from fertiliser norms directly. But farm category may also influence deviation indirectly, as farm categories vary by size, amount of manure and crop profiles. To analyse more precisely the effect of the set of variables, a path analysis is conducted, which allows for a test of causal relations among subsets of variables (see, for instance, Agresti and Finlay, 1997: 624). Figure 6.8 illustrates the causal model of the multivariate analyses, including direct as well as indirect effects.

The direct effect of each of these variables will be estimated using multivariate linear regression analysis, controlling for the effect of other independent variables. The indirect effects of farm category are estimated through separate regression analyses in which size, amount of manure and crop profiles serve as dependent variables and farm category as the independent. Finally, size measured in livestock units may indirectly affect deviation, if more livestock is related to the amount of manure. This is not

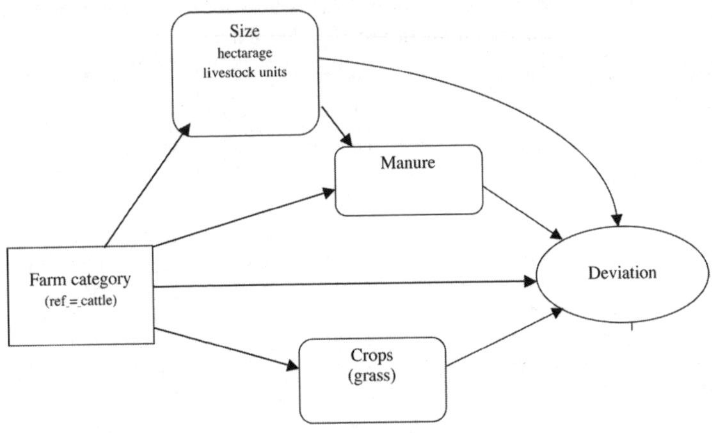

Figure 6.8   *Causal model of decision environment in relation to fertiliser practices*

given since manure is measured as mean amount per hectare, and a large livestock herd typically also implies a large area of land.

As for the dependent variable, the analysis so far indicates that different factors explain over-fertilisation and under-fertilisation, respectively. This suggests that the analysis should examine each of these dependent variables separately. Deviation as a combined tendency was examined but did not show any effects, and as the analysis yields no new insights it will not be included.

Over-fertilisation

Complexity measured as farm category, size, and livestock fertilisers does explain some of the over-fertilisation seen. Multiple regression analysis indicates that the combined complexity variables typically account for 20 per cent of the variation in over-fertilisation, although the R-square values vary quite considerably from year to year as shown in Table 6.7.

The variation in over-fertilisation found here is explained largely by the amount of manure per hectare the farmer has. Over-fertilisation increases when the farm uses a large amount of manure per hectare. On the other hand, farm size does not affect the tendency to over-fertilise. Thus, the findings above, which

Table 6.7   *Linear regression analysis (OLS), complexity on over-fertilisation. Unstandardised (B) coefficients*

Year	Size: hectarage	Manure, mean, kg/ha	Farm category (Reference = cattle)				R^2	N
			Pig	Poultry	Crop	Mixed		
1990	-.136	.256**	-2.530	-5.809	-7.348	-17.175	.095	165
1991	.068	.191***	-2.897	1.034	-10.781	-3.571	.217	157
1992	.036	.317***	.908	5.974	-6.999	-1.777	.314	147
1993	-.037	.281***	-1.676	-1.371	-3.819	-9.113	.220	143
1994	.048	.148***	1.669	1.330	-4.195	2.957	.268	138
1995	-.001	.054	4.717*	4.631*	-3.058	5.447	.115	136
1996	-.078	-.051	14.336*	11.209*	-11.120	11.214	.087	130
1997	-.028	.109***	2.670	5.024*	-1.729	1.687	.145	128
1998	-.154	.323	-12.213	-9.076	-15.257	-11.223	.035	155
1999	.026	.157***	1.471	.754	-3.389	.536	.380	155
2000	-.002	.184***	3.973	3.086	-3.835	-4.993	.230	151
2001	.019	.133***	-.255	-1.881	-2.808	-6.290	.154	147
2002	-.082	.305**	-9.426	-5.157	-2.609	-8.130	.114	145

Note: *** significant at $p < .001$, ** at $p < .01$ and * at $p < .05$.

show that size increased over-fertilisation in the years before the
nitrogen quota, disappear when other factors are controlled for.
An alternative analysis measured the effect of size in number of
livestock units, but this also has no effect independent of manure.
Farm category also does not generally affect over-fertilisation;
although pig farms and crop farms do over-fertilise significantly
more than cattle farms in the mid-1990s. At the same time the
relationship between manure and over-fertilisation is weaker for
the middle years, 1995–98. As previously discussed, the change in
pattern for these years is so remarkable that it requires explanations other than complexity.

Including control variables into the model does not alter the
picture. Only manure shows a statistically significant effect on
over-fertilisation, while different crops do not systematically
affect the tendency to over-fertilise. Farms with a higher share of
root crops were more likely to over-fertilise before the introduction of the fertiliser quota, but as of 1995 this relationship
disappeared. Root crop is a high-value crop; hence over-
fertilisation may reflect an insurance policy, so to speak, i.e.
giving extra fertiliser to ensure a good yield. The share of spring
cereal appears to explain some of the over-fertilisation that

occurred in the years 1995–97; this might indicate that farmers were uncertain about fertiliser norms for spring wheat. But these features do not decisively influence the overall conclusion that variation in over-fertilisation is not systematically due to differences in crop profiles.

Indirect effects

While the analysis has not demonstrated that farm categories vary systematically in their tendency to over-fertilise, farm category does affect over-fertilisation indirectly, i.e. through other variables.

Indirect effects are calculated as the product of the regression coefficients for each of the links in the causal chain; for instance, the effect of farm category on size multiplied by the effect of size on over-fertilisation. But as farm category is a categorical variable and such variables produce no independent regression coefficients, it is not possible to estimate quantitatively the combined effect of farm category with other variables. Instead the indirect effects of farm category may be assessed qualitatively. The indirect effect of farm category thus consists of the combined effect of all links in the causal path. Each link is estimated separately. Figure 6.9 indicates the findings of these analyses.

The dashed arrows from farm category to size and to manure indicate that crop farms are smaller than livestock farms and that they have less manure. They also have less grass. This implies that farm category would indirectly affect over-fertilisation through these variables. However, as manure is the only variable that affects over-fertilisation, the only indirect effect of farm category on over-fertilisation goes through amount of manure. This reflects the fact that crop farms have less manure and are therefore less prone to over-fertilise or that livestock farms are more likely to over-fertilise as they have more manure. As indicated by the grey arrow, size shows no direct effect on over-fertilisation and therefore also no indirect effect. This holds only for hectarage, however. Using number of livestock units as the size indicator produces another indirect effect in the model. More livestock increases the amount of manure, which in turn increases the tendency to over-fertilise. The combined effect of number of livestock and amount of manure explains approximately 16 per cent of variation in over-fertilisation.[6]

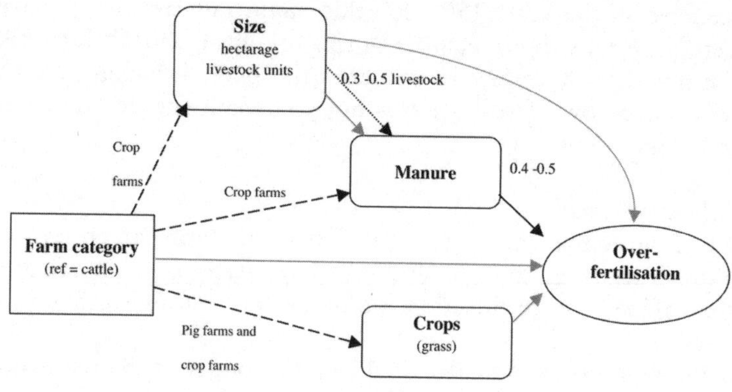

Figure 6.9 *Path analysis for over-fertilisation*

Note: Dashed: negative effect; grey: no effect; black: positive effect. Pig farms have more manure per hectare than cattle farms for the years 1993–96.

Generally, the path analysis underlines the conclusion that over-fertilisation is explained largely by livestock and manure, at least as concerns the variables used in this analysis.

This also leads to the overall conclusion that over-fertilisation is explained primarily by amount of manure the farm disposes of. Farm category does explain variation in over-fertilisation, but only indirectly through number of livestock units and amount of manure. This means that a lower tendency to over-fertilise for crop farms in comparison to cattle farms is explained predominantly by fewer livestock and less manure.

Under-fertilisation

Turning to under-fertilisation, it is necessary to amend the model. As indicated above, the tendency to under-fertilise is inevitably linked to the amount of manure that must be disposed of on the farm. This would mask any effect of complexity stemming from manure and under-fertilisation. Therefore, amount of manure will be excluded from the multivariate analysis. It is, however, included in the subsequent analysis as a control variable in order to clean out, as it were, the effect of amount of manure on under-fertilisation.

Complexity does affect the tendency to under-fertilise as the model including hectarage and farm category does explain some 25 per cent of the variation in under-fertilisation before 1995 and as much as 30 to 40 per cent in the mid-1990s (see Table 6.8).

Table 6.8 *Linear regression analysis (OLS), complexity on under-fertilisation. Unstandardised (B) coefficients*

Year	Size: hectarage	Farm category (Reference = cattle)				R^2	N
		Pig	Crop	Poultry	Mixed		
1990	-.257*	-6.068	-6.398	34.315**	1.910	.159	165
1991	-.142*	-7.304	-8.176*	37.174***	11.703*	.269	157
1992	-.203**	-8.007	-11.337	30.846**	7.225	.222	147
1993	-.090	-4.820	-2.290**	31.656**	14.163*	.120	143
1994	-.134*	-10.749**	-10.696	32.235***	7.409	.279	138
1995	-.038	-15.658**	-15.126**	49.472***	-11.066	.361	136
1996	-.098	-20.774***	-16.504***	46.489***	-11.568	.313	130
1997	-.129*	-21.590***	-19.746***	45.774**	-2.938	.428	128
1998	-.097*	-18.548***	-16.516***	33.892***	20.256	.416	155
1999	-.030	-12.140*	-4.557	29.213***	7.185	.176	155
2000	-.114*	-18.492**	-8.039	20.056*	5.497	.173	151
2001	-.091	-18.217**	-10.729*	22.896*	-.033	.182	147
2002	-.079	-13.467*	-8.765	3.112	-13.137	.068	145

Note: *** significant at p<.001, ** at p<.01 and * at p<.05.

The larger the farm the less likely it is to fertilise below norms, although the relationship is not strong enough to be statistically significant in many years.

As for farm category, they generally behave as expected, i.e. pig and crop farms are less inclined to under-fertilise than are cattle farms as the latter may be more pressed for time with their livestock. Finally, poultry farms quite consistently under-fertilise more than cattle farms. These have less manure and generally would be expected to pay less attention to field work.

But including control variables changes the findings: see Table 6.9. The primary change is that farm category no longer appears to explain any differences in the tendency to fertilise below norms. Only poultry farms retain an effect on under-fertilisation, whereas the differences between cattle farms and pig and crop farms, respectively, appear to be due to amount of manure as well as to the presence of grass fields. While a large amount of manure decreases the tendency to under-fertilise, a high share of grass fields increases the tendency to under-fertilise.

Including crop profiles boosts the explanatory value of the model, as R-square values jump by 20 percentage points, explaining as much as 68 per cent of variation in under-fertilisation in 1997. The explanatory value of the model, including control variables, is strongest for 1995–98 and weakest from 1999 onwards, although still around 37.

Indirect effects

Farm category also affects under-fertilisation indirectly through farm size and amount of manure, but also through the share of grass fields: see Figure 6.10. As a large amount of manure per hectare reduces the tendency to under-fertilise, livestock farms which have more manure are less likely to under-fertilise than crop farms. On the other hand, crop farms (and pig farms) also have fewer grass fields than cattle farms and the fewer grass fields the greater the tendency to under-fertilise.

Farm size affects under-fertilisation only when measured in livestock units instead of hectarage. Large livestock farms will be less likely to under-fertilise than small ones – which again is inevitable as farms with large amounts of manure must dispose of this.

The path analysis thus indicates that the two consistent predictors of under-fertilisation are share of grass fields, which increases under-fertilisation, and amount of manure, which reduces under-fertilisation. Farm category and size indirectly affect the tendency to under-fertilise as farm categories vary as to how many livestock units, how much manure and how many grass fields they have.

The effect of complex decision environments

The analysis of fertiliser patterns has examined the effect of complex decision environments on deviation from optimal decisions defined in terms of fertiliser norms. The expectation was that deviation from optimal fertiliser levels was more likely when decisions are complex, or when the circumstances in which decisions occur are complex. Hence, in this analysis complexity was

Table 6.9 *Regression analysis (OLS) of degree of under-fertilising. Explanatory model including control variables. Unstandardised regression coefficients. Year by year. Hectarage as size variable. (Reference = cattle)*

Year	Size: hectarage	Farm category (reference = cattle)				Manure mean kg/ha	Grass in rotation	Root crop	Permanent grass	Spring cereal	R^2	N
		Pig	Poultry	Crop	Mixed							
1990	-.184*	7.783	20.076*	-3.537	10.378	-.295***	38.166***	-13.066	44.664***	-3.200	.481	165
1991	-.071	2.245	24.989***	-4.067	13.869**	-.171***	17.688**	-12.264	43.529***	-4.881	.457	157
1992	-.136*	4.016	9.788	-4.501	8.802	-.13	27.761***	-4.530	53.336***	8.221	.437	147
1993	-.083	14.652	21.984*	11.601**	17.575**	-.113**	36.247***	-11.163	48.619***	-9.469	.500	143
1994	-.158**	-.171	19.203*	-5.004	9.002	-.098*	22.840**	-15.182	-1.624	.427	.398	138
1995	-.016	.697	41.089***	-2.065	-.490	-.093*	36.972***	-13.757	36.437***	-2.442	.589	136
1996	-.051	6.701	27.197**	-1.400	-3.130	-.156	44.251***	-8.733	52.372**	3.242	.579	130
1997	-.090	6.670	24.627**	-1.557	-.767	-.148*	46.691***	-4.922	38.212***	-3.017	.677	128
1998	-.041	-4.408	22.826***	-6.480	27.304***	-.158**	31.769***	-6.877	39.503***	-2.662	.553	155
1999	.033	7.681	17.731*	8.749	17.964	-.217**	54.348***	-4.576	48.215***	-6.404	.363	155
2000	-.078	-3.649	5.579	1.234	9.578	-.163**	26.849**	-18.947	49.399***	-20.314*	.370	151
2001	-.076	-11.142	9.072	-5.353	7.303	-.212**	22.218*	-42.437**	22.712	-30.377***	.371	147
2002	-.087	-1.126	-8.362	-4.972	-9.558	-.266***	33.547**	-34.220*	7.913	-16.032*	.234	145

Note: *** significant at p<.001, ** at p<.01 and * at p<.05.

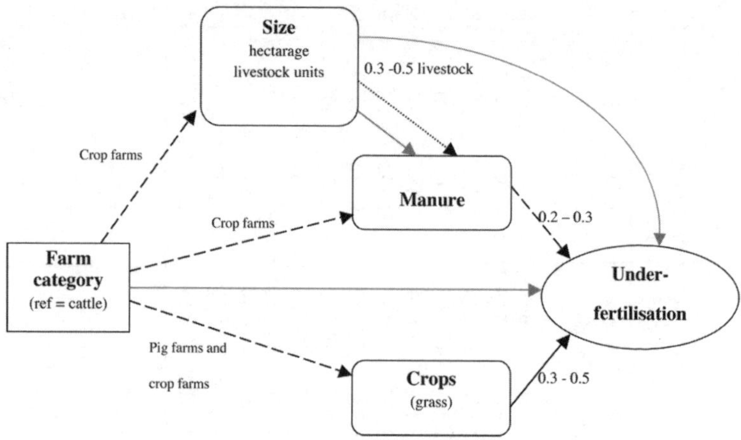

Figure 6.10   *Path analysis for under-fertilisation*

Note: Dashed: negative effect; grey: no effect; black: positive effect. Pig farms have more manure per hectare than cattle farms for the years 1993–96.

defined by farm category, by farm size, and by manure. It was assumed that livestock farmers face more competing claims on their attention and the same applies to large farms. Likewise, manure was assumed to increase complexity of fertilising as its effect is more uncertain. Finally, the analysis has studied the effect of institutional change on fertiliser decisions.

While theoretically, any deviation from norms is the relevant variable, the analysis examined also whether complexity might work differently on over- and under-fertilising, respectively. This was based on a notion that uncertainty may be more important for over-fertilising, whereas selective attention may work more strongly on under-fertilising. As it turned out that deviation typically reflected patterns in either over- or under-fertilisation, whichever sub-variable showed stronger trends, the discussion will focus on the findings for over-fertilisation and under-fertilisation only.

Complex decision environments: farm category, size and manure

As for fertilisation *above norms*, complexity variables do explain some behaviour, but typically only around 20 per cent. But only manure retains explanatory value, when all variables are tested in the same model. Overall, then, this analysis identifies one driver of over-fertilisation, namely amount of manure. A large amount of manure indicates a high level of fertiliser overall, but as discussed previously, regulation ensures that no farmer has more manure than he can use within his quota, so a large amount of manure does not automatically lead to over-fertilisation. Hence, the effect of manure shown here could stem from uncertainty regarding its effect, as expected. Expanding the model to include crops indicates that different crop patterns among farms may explain some over-fertilisation some years, but this yields no consistent pattern.

Analysing over time, there is a slight tendency for the complexity model to explain more over-fertilisation before the introduction of the fertiliser norms, reflected in slightly higher R^2-coefficients for the model. This indicates that complexity might have played a greater role before fertiliser norms forced attention on economically optimal fertiliser levels. Most of this effect again stems from differences in amounts of manure. Amount of manure thus played a greater role before regulatory changes forced farmers to utilise manure more efficiently. This could be interpreted either as an effect of uncertainty regarding manure or it could be interpreted as cost-cutting. In the latter case farmers would spread manure on fields close to the farm rather than incur the cost of transportation. This cannot be examined with the data available. The model explains least over-fertilisation in the years between 1995 and 1997. One possible explanation here might be inadequate adjustment to seasonal updates in fertiliser norms, which would fit with a bounded rationality explanation of selective attention.

As for under-fertilisation, the picture is more nuanced, but the conclusion largely the same. Amount of manure is inversely related to under-fertilisation. Thus, the variable suggests why farms do *not* under-fertilise, but in that sense does not explain what actually drives under-fertilisation. Hence, this finding does not substantiate the theoretical expectation that under-fertilisation would increase with increased complexity. But, as pointed out, this expectation is somewhat undercut by the fact that farms with large amounts of manure need to dispose of the manure and therefore logically will under-fertilise less.

What does appear to predict fairly well the tendency to under-fertilise is a high share of fields with grass in rotation. Fertiliser norms for grass in rotation are considered to be generous (Grant *et al.*, 2000), hence if farmers share this perception they may use less than the norms on their grass fields. The question is whether they reallocate the fertiliser saved on grass fields to other fields. The analysis does not support such a conclusion as farms with large shares of grass do not over-fertilise more than any other farms. In other words, the analysis indicates that farms with large shares of grass simply use less fertiliser than other farms. One interpretation might be that farms with large shares of grass fields pay less attention to fertilising. Another, of course, is that these farmers apply optimal levels of fertiliser. The analysis cannot definitively answer which of these explanations prevails.

Complexity variables explain more variation in the mid-1990s after introduction of fertiliser norms than they did before the regulatory change. The main expectation was that fertiliser norms would increase attention and therefore reduce the effect of complexity. On the other hand, uncertainty about exceeding the quota and the frequent regulatory changes might increase the effect of complexity. It would appear that the latter prediction prevails. Amount of manure, however, is the only complexity variable with explanatory power, yet this variable decreases the tendency to under-fertilise. Hence, complexity as defined here does not explain why under-fertilisation would increase after 1994. It is still possible that this increased tendency to under-fertilise occurs because farmers apply a safety margin in response to uncertainty about the norms. But in that case, variation in uncertainty would be explained by factors other than size and farm category.

Such an interpretation of uncertainty is not entirely supported by analysis. Over-fertilisation correlates negatively with under-fertilisation. In other words, farmers who are more likely to over-fertilise are less likely to under-fertilise. This pattern does not indicate that under-fertilisation represents a safety margin. These farms tend to use their fertiliser quotas, while other farms, which under-fertilise but do not over-fertilise, simply use less fertiliser. To put it simply, intense over-fertilisers and intense under-fertilisers are two different groups of farmers.

Based on the data available here, amount of manure appears to be the best predictor of over-fertilisation. This is in accordance with an interpretation that farmers who use manure over-fertilise at least in part due to uncertainty about the effect of manure. On the other hand, share of fields with grass in rotation seems to be the only predictor of under-fertilisation. Farms with many grass fields tend to use relatively less fertiliser. This could indicate a lack of attention to fertiliser, or it might simply reflect optimal fertiliser management as grass norms are considered high.

Institutional change

Hypotheses regarding changes in the institutional context fare somewhat better than hypotheses regarding complexity. Here, the main expectation is that the introduction of fertiliser norms increases attention to fertiliser levels, but that the patterns would oscillate in the first couple of years, as farmers adapt to the new regulation. The analysis shows that the degree of over-fertilisation drops markedly immediately after the norms are introduced, consistent with a notion that the regulation forces attention on over-fertilisation. Under-fertilisation *increases* just as clearly. This would be consistent with a hypothesis that farmers overreact to the new regulation. The analysis also confirms that deviations from norms tend to oscillate in the years following the changes in regulations. Perhaps the most important explanatory factor of these fluctuations is that farmers were slower to adapt to the updating of norms in the spring than to the norms themselves. This is also consistent with bounded rationality expectations. For the years after nitrogen norms were lowered, the pattern is less clear, but so were expectations. Under-fertilisation decreases, while over-fertilisation oscillates mildly. Altogether, these developments suggest that farmers rather quickly adjusted to the changing norms; nevertheless, adaptation was limited. Over- and under-fertilisation continued throughout the entire period, even if to a lesser degree after the regulatory norms were introduced than before.

The implications of findings for theoretical framework

Overall, the expectation that complex circumstances explain deviation from fertiliser norms receives only partial support from this analysis. This does not necessarily disprove the theoretical claim that complexity tends to increase deviation from optimal behaviour. Firstly, one may question the operationalisation of complexity as size. Size does affect the number of decisions and the competition for time facing the farmer. But large farms may also employ help, reducing the time pressure for the farmer. Secondly, there is a problem of omitted variables due to the data available. As the database includes no information about the farmer, such as age or education, which might affect the kinds of practices used, these factors cannot be controlled for. In line with this, the data do not allow for time-series analysis at the level of the individual. Therefore learning, which is an integral part of a bounded rationality framework, could also not be included in the analysis. Learning might reduce the effect of complex circumstances. Thirdly, the effect of the grass variable as well as early variations on root crop suggests that farmers may assess the norms and consciously decide to deviate from them. This suggests that the explanation for deviation is not necessarily a lack of attention to fertiliser, but rather a perception that some norms are not optimal. Furthermore, the fact that fertiliser patterns do not vary across farm category suggests that a common set of routines or standards guide fertiliser patterns.

So while the analysis does not offer strong support for the effect of complex circumstances on behaviour, it also does not support an outright rejection of the theoretical framework, as the fertiliser case appears to constitute a reasonably strong test of the framework. The effect of variations in complexity would be mitigated where farmers were well-trained professionals with a set of standard practices. Furthermore, the introduction of norms in 1994 reduced the effect of complexity, as they forced attention on economically optimal fertiliser levels. These factors suggest that one should perhaps not expect to see large differences due to factors such as size and farm category. The case may most accurately be thought of as a least likely test of bounded rationality.

Further, manure management is complex and characterised by uncertainty, requiring also technological considerations, and this variable does affect tendency to over-fertilise. Furthermore, the analysis also points to the explanatory power of the notions of maladaptive routines and delayed adjustment to changes in circumstances. Thus, it took the fertiliser quota to force attention on economically optimal levels of fertiliser; and while farmers did adapt to the quota, fertiliser patterns fluctuated considerably in the following years, perhaps in response to frequent changes in regulatory demands.

But a full assessment of the analytical framework requires further analysis. First of all, it remains to examine the effect of motivation on fertiliser behaviour, a variable included in the framework, but which could not be examined given the data available for quantitative analysis. Secondly, the qualitative analysis may also explore whether farmers even consider the norms to be economically optimal; if not, the question is whether deviation from norms actually represents optimising behaviour. Such a conclusion of course depends on how farmers actually arrive at the exact fertiliser levels when they do not follow the norms. Thus, thirdly, the qualitative analysis will examine whether farmers use particular heuristics or other simplifying decision mechanisms which may explain the pattern seen. It aims to uncover the decision processes by which farmers arrive at the fertiliser patterns.

Notes

1 For the sake of simplicity *manure* is used as a general term for animal fertiliser throughout this chapter.
2 This is not to be confused with a simplification of the overall enterprise of fertilising, as any farmer is quick to point out how much paperwork the regulation entails!
3 As mentioned, there is a break in the data series in 1998 when there was a substitution of one catchment area for a larger one. The deviation line denoted 'reduced sample' (Figure 6.1) includes only data from catchment areas that participate throughout the entire period. For this analysis over time only this subset of the data will be used to ensure that any developments over time are not simply a matter of a change in sample. But as the two curves illustrate, the difference between the full sample and the reduced sample is moderate.
4 A significance test is conventionally used to assess inference from a sample to a population. In this study, the LOOP data have been treated as population data rather than as sample data. Thomsen (1997) argues that significance tests may be used on such population data if one can reasonably assume that part of the variation in the data can be viewed as stochastic. That would appear to be a reasonable assumption here. Therefore, significance tests are used here to

examine the likelihood that differences in the data do indeed reflect systematic variation rather than arbitrary correlation.

5　In this section, diagrams showing development over time do not include mixed or poultry farms as they are too few.

6　Note that the coefficients indicated in the model are standardised regression coefficients, whereas Tables 6.7–6.9 report the unstandardised coefficients.

7

Information shortcuts and rules of thumb: how farmers make decisions on fertilisers

Decision processes provide the crucial link between environmental input and behaviour. An examination of the decision processes of farmers may therefore contribute to an explanation of why farmers do, or rather do not, follow fertiliser norms. Based on qualitative interviews, the analysis of farmers' decisions traces the decision processes in relation to fertilising, seeks to explain them, and sketches how they affect choice. Uncovering key elements of boundedly rational decision processes and examining how they affect fertiliser decisions serve to establish documentation for the role of decision processes outlined in the analytical model. Analytical focus will be on the objectives, the use of information and the decision rules that shape farmers' fertiliser management.

The analysis thus aims to fill in the gaps from the quantitative analysis by examining whether decision processes can account for the patterns in fertiliser behaviour seen in, but not explained by, the quantitative analysis. Furthermore, the enquiry into the role of motivation was explicitly left for the qualitative analysis. This part of the analysis then contributes to the test of the analytical framework. The analysis cannot answer conclusively the questions left unanswered by the quantitative analysis. The participants are different from those in the LOOP sample; they are too few for a precise test of variation, and they were interviewed long after the norms had been changed to sub-optimal, which in itself reduces variation, as seen in the previous chapter. But the study of decision processes offers the advantage of triangulation, i.e. improving the overall understanding of a phenomenon by attacking it from several methodological angles.

Theoretical expectations

The overriding concept in the bounded rationality framework is that decision-makers, both bound by and aided by their cognitive make-up, tend to employ simplifying decision mechanisms that differ significantly in character from the model of comprehensive decision-making implicit in the fully rational model. Generally, only if something attracts the attention of the decision-maker to a particular problem may the actor switch into a more comprehensive decision mode. Even so, the problem may be so complex or other things may compete for attention that the decision-maker cannot pay attention to all aspects of the decision and integrate them into an optimal decision. Instead, he attends to issues or problem dimensions one at a time. Selective attention applies to the objectives that will be pursued by the decision-maker, to the manner in which information is used and to the manner in which the final decision is arrived at. Restating the theoretical claims from Chapter 3 in the context of fertiliser management, the analysis is guided by the following expectations:

- Farmers have multiple objectives but attend to them sequentially. This implies that the farmer, contrary to the model of economic man, may not subsume all other objectives under the goal of profit-maximisation. Furthermore, objectives are typically stated in terms of aspiration levels rather than optimal utility.
- Use of information is selective and guided by the dominant objectives purposed by the farmer in relation to fertilising but also by social or professional norms about proper fertiliser behaviour.
- Decisions will be arrived at through standard operating procedures and heuristics rather than through synoptic calculation.

Interview data and analysis

The study included interviews with twenty farmers from most corners of Denmark. The respondents cover all agricultural branches and vary with regard to the size of the farm and the age of the farmer (see Appendix). The farmers were not selected with an eye to statistical representation but in order to ensure adequate range in the data to examine research questions.

The interviews revolved around a few basic questions, the answers to which form the backbone of the entire analysis. The central question asked the farmer to describe how he proceeded the last time he made decisions with regard to fertiliser, from planning through to application. Follow-up questions sought to ascertain the determining factors in the farmers' fertiliser planning, the objectives pursued, sources of information, how the objectives were weighted against each other, and how this was reflected in the decision. As far as possible, questions were asked in a form designed to prompt a description, although follow-up questions may have asked for more precise answers to ensure proper interpretation of the descriptive accounts. Another basic question asked the farmer to describe how the specific fertiliser decision compared with his fertiliser practice in general, while a third question asked about changes in fertiliser practices over time.

As for data analysis, the general procedure has been to look for relevant information throughout the entire interview about a specific concept. This implies that in addition to the directly elicited statements about, for instance, the objectives that guide fertiliser decisions, the descriptive accounts of fertiliser decisions were also included in the analysis of this question.

How farmers make decisions on fertilisers

It is a key claim of the analytical framework that deviations from optimal fertiliser norms may be explained by the character of the decision process; that is, deviations are more likely to occur when farmers employ a simple decision mode as conceptualised in the bounded rationality model. The first step of this analysis is to examine whether the features of bounded rationality are observable in the interview data, i.e. the incomplete trade-offs among multiple objectives, the selective use of information and the simplifying decision rules. The second step is to analyse whether such decision processes can explain deviation from optimal fertiliser patterns.

The questions left unanswered by the quantitative analysis of fertiliser patterns include analysis of the importance of motivation for fertiliser processes, which could not be examined with the quantitative data available. But the analysis also seeks to shed light on some of the unpredicted patterns, including the difference in over- and under-fertilising, respectively. Finally, the analysis examines the interview data for other explanations, such as perception of norms and the possibility that farmers take into consideration the cost of transporting manure.

The empirical question is how farmers determine the right amount of fertiliser for each field. But as the current regulatory scheme turned nitrogen into a truly scarce resource, farmers may approach this as a problem of how to allocate the quota among their crops and fields, knowing that they cannot apply an economically optimal level to every field. Because the interviews were conducted after fertiliser norms were reduced and thus no longer constituted the economic optimum, deviation from norms cannot be defined *a priori* as deviation from economically optimal behaviour. Such an assessment requires information about why farmers deviate from the norms.

The following sections divide the process into objectives, information use and choice, suggesting that these are neatly separable and causally related phases of decision processes. But, while these phases are analytically distinct they are not necessarily separable in an empirical context. Therefore, the analysis should not be read as linear, but rather as different elements or dimensions of decision processes which may all contribute to an explanation of outcome.

Objectives

Bounded rationality presumes intended rationality; hence, action is goal oriented, and decision processes are guided by objectives. But decision-makers do not easily cope with multiple objectives, let alone conflicting objectives, which require trade-offs. In this case, they tend to focus on one objective exclusively or one at a time, which from a neo-classical perspective leads to an outcome that is sub-optimal given their overall preference structure. Sub-optimality may even become a strategy for choice, as decision-makers settle for satisfactory goal achievement, forgoing optimal outcomes. Hence, in the present context, the focus of analysis is on the role of objectives in the decision process and the handling of trade-offs.

In terms of fertiliser levels, the nitrogen norm embodies an attempt to strike an economically optimal trade-off between increasing yield and controlling costs. The sub-optimal norm introduced in 1999 requires further trade-off with the objective of environmental protection. Which trade-offs and how much trading off is required depend on the objectives farmers pursue in their fertiliser decisions. Hence, the first questions to be examined in this section are what objectives are at play for the farmers and the extent to which they conflict. The second set of analyses then explores how the farmers mediate between multiple and perhaps conflicting objectives. Furthermore, the analysis seeks to determine whether aspiration levels can be identified in the interview data, or whether farmers do appear to aim for optimal utility. The expectation is that farmers will focus on one or a few objectives rather than try to integrate all objectives relevant for fertiliser decisions, and that farmers mediate among objectives by setting *acceptable* standards for goal achievement rather than *optimal* standards. The implications are, first of all, that the decision process will be shaped by the prioritised objective, which means the decision-maker will seek information selectively, and, secondly, that the final decision will be biased in the direction of this one objective – in other words the decision may not duly reflect all objectives pursued by the decision-maker.

To examine these questions, the farmers were asked directly about the objectives that guide their fertiliser practice. They were asked about the extent to which they perceived these objectives as conflicting. Finally, they were asked to recount in detail how they determine fertiliser levels, and these descriptions were probed for information on how they make trade-offs among different objectives.

Fertilising: multiple objectives, one dominant
Several types of objectives are at play in fertiliser management. The main ones are crop yield, efficient use of resources, economic return on field work, and environmental protection. The interviews show that farmers seek to achieve several objectives in their fertiliser management; in some cases these objectives are fairly compatible, in others somewhat conflicting. The objective of using resources efficiently may go well with an overall economic approach or even with environmental objectives. On the contrary, optimal yield may not always play well with a cost-cutting objective or even a profit objective.

The issue, then, is how farmers prioritise among such objectives, particularly when they collide. The interviews indicate a pattern of one objective dominating decisions; although other objectives are not completely ignored. Analysis of the farmers' descriptions of their fertiliser practices points to three overall modes of fertilising as defined by dominant objectives. The differences were discerned analytically by the extent to which the farmers talked about professional issues vs. economic issues, which professional issues they emphasised, the types of figures they cited (physical yield or cost, for instance), as well as by their stated objectives and descriptions of practices. It should be emphasised that all the farmers interviewed aim for high yields and all are concerned with the appearance of their fields; likewise, no farmer would completely ignore economic considerations. The difference lies in the extent to which each objective appears to motivate and direct their actions.

Some farmers prioritise production objectives. The objective that guides their fertiliser management is to promote the highest possible yield of crops. These farmers talk extensively of professional issues with regards to field management and fertiliser. They put considerable effort into fertilising and determining the best allocation of fertiliser across fields, seeking information and trying out new technologies. These farmers do not appear to consider search or transaction costs, as they typically have not tried to put numbers on them. Prioritising fertiliser among fields is guided by which crops need the fertiliser to thrive, and less by economic considerations. The quotes in Box 7.1 are evidence of this approach.

Good-looking fields are a source of pride and an important motivator for farming activities. Even though wheat prices at the time had been dropping to levels that did not necessarily sustain large costs of fertiliser, the value of an attractive field of wheat took precedence over economic calculations, as evidenced by quotes 2 and 3. This became even clearer as interviewee 3 shifted focus to pesticide use.

> He [the agricultural adviser] thinks we spray too much compared with many others. That could be the case. We have never made that calculation. Maybe the yields make up for it. It might be more economic not to apply pesticides and grow a little less, given the subsidies. But then again, the satisfaction I get from seeing a super crop out there, that is even greater...

Box 7.1.

Prioritised Objective: crop yield

Quote 1
Int: What aspects do you prioritise in your fertiliser planning,
 then; is it simply yield, or do costs also play a role?
IP: At the present time, when we are fertilising below [optimal]
 norms, it is yield, pure and simple.

Quote 2
Int: Now, when you shift fertiliser around, does that affect the
 your bottom line at all?
IP4: Well, if I were to put a number on it, it probably does not
 move many thousand kroner notes, it really doesn't. But it
 gives me a feeling of satisfaction to be looking at something
 that is developing well.

Quote 3
IP13: [Looking in a report from the advisory services.] It says
 here that there is a splendid yield ... that is probably what
 matters the most to us.
Int: Do you pay attention to the costs associated with all this?
 How important is that?
IP13: Well, he [the agricultural adviser] would probably say that I
 do not.

Other farmers are guided by a general attentiveness to effective
use of resources. These farmers are likely to be keen on getting the
most both out of animal manure and other fertiliser and to focus
on this. They tend to focus their effort perhaps less on moving
fertiliser between fields and more on finding the most efficient
application technologies or practices which ensure that plants
receive fertiliser when they can best absorb the nutrients.
Obviously, getting the most out of fertiliser also affects the physical and the economic yield from that field, but the operative goal
as expressed in the discourse among farmers with this focus is one
of not wasting resources. They make reference to economic gains,
but more as a general approach than in the form of precise calculations of costs and benefits, cf. quotes 4–6 in Box 7.2.

Box 7.2

Prioritised objective: efficient use of resources

Quote 4

IP3: A young farmer, today, he thinks about that [efficient utilisation
of manure] a lot. He does. Because if he can avoid buying fertiliser
altogether, that is a definite plus, both for him, economically, that
is, but also, you know, it's great to be able to grow just as much
and then not to have to buy that artificial fertiliser.

Int: So it is the professional challenge involved in it?

IP3: Yes, it is actually. It is. Now, I know several farmers who have
tried to inject [application method] their slurry, and they did not
have to buy any artificial fertilisers at all. And they have had just
as good results. So it has become a bit of a sport to be able to get
to that point. Partly a sport, and then it is an economic issue too.

Quote 5

IP11: It is important to be precise and to use resources optimally.
And we in Danish agriculture can be proud of that. We have
proven that we were able to reduce nitrogen levels. And we can
do the same with pesticides.

Int: But [efficient utilisation of manure] was that just kind of an
added bonus, or …?

Quote 6

IP10: No, it wasn't. We have always tried to utilise our slurry to
the greatest extent possible, because I thought it would be a
waste, since we had it, and then to use it poorly, and then to
have to spend money buying fertiliser. That was my starting
point. So we have always – have always tried to utilise the
slurry as well as we could.

Finally, some subsume objectives regarding fertiliser management under an overall objective of profitability. These farmers
pay attention to fertilising, but only until the point where the
effort begins to chip off the overall profitability: cf. quotes 7 and
8 in Box 7.3. Hence, they attempt to achieve high yield and/or
high utilisation of manure, but they include a clear transaction
cost perspective. The time and money spent on fertiliser is set off
against the economic pay-off.

Box 7.3

Prioritised objective: economic return

Quote 7

Int: Now you say that, earlier, one might have applied too much
fertiliser?

IP15: Well, no, I think looking at this curve for yield, one may
have gone all the way to here instead of to here [passing the
point of optimal marginal utility].

Int: But that would be a waste of money?

IP15: That's a waste of money. But back then – it depends on the
price of grain, you know. Back then, when grain brought in
150 DKK, everything paid. Today, we are probably all the way
down here with wheat prices of 68 DKK. In the end that is
actually what determines [fertiliser levels]. And this is why, the
fertiliser quota we have now, well we can probably live with it
Because the price is so low anyway. So our economically
optimal point is right here [pointing to a point farther down
the fertiliser demand curve].

Quote 8

IP17: I have noticed many of my colleagues who farm a considerable acreage, they use a huge amount of resources taking out
the sprayer for any little thing. And they use different kinds of
fertiliser for different things. But their input is enormous. Yet,
we all have to sell grain at a price of 70 or 80 DKK, right?
And they have to spend time, etc., every time they are out
driving in their fields, including wages for their employees, and
fuel and things. So in the end I think we can make more money
than they can.

These farmers also argue clearly in economic terms when they
describe how they allocate or reallocate fertiliser: see quote 8.
This farmer stated that while he does aim for the best yield possible, possible is defined by cost and income, and therefore he pays
less attention to fertilising than other farmers he knows.

Again, the analysis indicates that farmers tend to prioritise one
objective in their fertiliser management, but also that they do not
ignore other objectives entirely. Yield is important to nearly all of
those interviewed. But most are also impelled to pay attention to

the bottom line, and therefore inevitably must find ways to integrate these objectives also when they do not pull in the same direction.

Mediating among multiple objectives: aspiration levels
As predicted by the bounded rationality model, the analysis indicates that farmers make such trade-offs by setting aspiration levels for each objective. They define a satisfactory standard of achievement for a particular objective, but not an optimal one. This is particularly evident in weighing productivity objectives against economic objectivities. In general, yield-oriented farmers seem to have an aspiration level of improving their yield compared with some generalised version of past performance. Another example of an aspiration level is to aim for an optimal output on one choice crop and accepting whatever yield is possible within the nitrogen quota on other crops. A modified version of this is to opt for highest possible yield on the choice crop, but also setting a minimum standard for other crops. Interestingly, yield may also be measured in terms of the appearance of the field. Hence, a grass field should be dense, a wheat crop tall (and dense), dark green and evenly coloured – or such similar visual standards. Farmers who prioritise yield appear to set less specific aspiration levels for the economic outcome of production, but do seem to apply a standard where pecuniary costs are kept at a reasonable level expressed as 'we have to make a living from it as well' (IP14). The time they put into the work is not priced, however.

Aspiration levels typically derive from comparative standards or benchmarks. They compare their output with that of farmers in the area or generally through production statistics. In fact, the advisory service offers benchmark statistics tailored specifically to the farmer. Farmers may also compare this year's output to last year's, but year-to-year comparisons are difficult because conditions beyond their control make for fluctuations.

Farmers who focus more on the economic aspect of fertilising set their aspiration levels either in terms of a surplus, or they too compare with standard earnings for a given crop. In this case the aspiration yield for production is perhaps less specified, as in the best yield one can achieve, given the resources one is prepared to put into fertilising.

IP17: You know, if we put effort into the things we do, if we do a reasonable job, then I think it will be okay.

As far as resource use is concerned, the regulatory requirement of using a minimum proportion of the nitrogen in manure represents an aspiration level in and of itself, and most of the farmers seem to use it this way. Hence, only a few farmers are inclined to aim for higher utilisation rates than this. But again there is a trade-off with regard to the cost of achieving high utilisation. In this case the aspiration level, or the cost ceiling, appears to be that costs must stand in reasonable proportion to the extra yield.

Thus, the analysis shows that farmers do set aspiration levels, and these help mediate among conflicting objectives. Interestingly, aspiration levels seem more vaguely defined for the objective to which farmers give lower priority. The analysis also indicates that aspiration levels serve not only to help make trade-offs, but they also provide general guidance when objectives are hard to define in absolute terms, as is often the case, i.e. how much is 'optimal yield'? Thus farmers set aspiration levels based on comparisons with their own past performance or the performance of others with whom they find it relevant to compare themselves. This matches the predictions drawn from Cyert and March's *A Behavioural Theory of the Firm* (1963, 1992). The section on general decision strategies among farmers will explore the function of aspiration levels further.

Discussion

The analysis of objectives suggests first of all that fertilising is guided by multiple objectives, but that one type of objective tends to dominate the decisions of the individual farmer, confirming the theoretical prediction that decision-making is characterised by selective attention to objectives. Contrary to the assumption of neo-classical theory of businesses, farmers do not necessarily subsume other objectives under an overall profit-driven approach. Some farmers tend to focus on physical production yield. This does not imply that they completely ignore the economic aspects of their fertiliser decisions, but economic objectives are directly or indirectly downplayed as compared with crop yield. Some farmers explicitly state that high yield takes priority over other objectives; others say that cost and profit considerations are important, but their accounts of how they decide on fertiliser levels indicate that they pay more attention to information about yield. For instance, they may not know the cost of various fertiliser strategies or they make a qualitative assessment of it: see the following sections. In contrast, farmers who appear to keep an eye on profit will sacrifice high yield, if high yield does not bear the expenses involved. They apply a marginal value principle, although not necessarily a precise one.

The analysis of objectives further indicates that farmers make trade-offs in a qualitative manner, foregoing precise considerations or calculations as to optimal trade-offs. The interviews show that farmers set aspiration levels, which is in accordance with behavioural theories (Cyert and March, 1992). But what this analysis shows is that aspiration levels tend to be more specific for the dominant objective. If the farmer prioritises yield, the aspiration level will be set in terms of previous yields or yields of comparable farmers – or visual standards that indicate high yield. The aspiration level for the downplayed objective, economic yield in this case, is more likely stated in loose terms – such as 'not out of hand' or 'keep at a reasonable level'. Likewise, for profit-oriented farmers the aspiration level will be more specific for the economic yield of the crop than for the production yield.

The analysis of objectives offers only limited insight into the deviations from fertiliser norms. One would expect farmers whose fertiliser patterns are guided predominantly by physical yield to display a higher degree of over-fertilisation; although the inclination to over-fertilise is obviously tempered by the fertiliser quota. Farmers who focus on yields do seem to move their fertiliser around, giving prioritised crops as much as possible within the quota, but the interviews do not suggest large variation in over-fertilisation rates among the farmers. On the other hand, farmers who are very focused on cost considerations might evaluate different fertiliser strategies primarily from a cost savings perspective, emphasising to a lesser degree the effect on yield. One possible outcome of such an approach would be under-fertilisation, if low application costs are favoured over high fertiliser value of manure. The analysis so far does not support such a conclusion. For instance, the farmers interviewed typically do not include transportation cost as a decisive parameter in their decisions, much less a precisely calculated parameter. If they did, more under-fertilisation might occur.

Selective use of information

At the core of bounded rationality is a notion that the cognitive apparatus of decision-makers is overmatched by the amount of information flowing in their decision environment. This leads to an expectation that farmers are selective in their use of information and that they draw on stored knowledge and use simple information shortcuts. Attention may be directed by the objectives farmers prioritise in relation to fertiliser and by profession-wide models of what fertilising is about. Fertiliser regulation also to some extent directs attention, both by defining a maximum allowable amount of nitrogen, but also by augmenting the importance of efficient utilisation of manure. In other words, information search is framed by individual as well as collective professional and regulatory sources.

In order to examine the farmers' use of information, they were asked about the types of information they look for, when they will seek out information and when not, and how they decide whether to use information. The analysis furthermore draws on descriptive accounts of fertiliser planning.

This analysis focuses on the updating of information in relation to fertiliser planning. As for basic knowledge, most of the farmers interviewed have completed formal education programmes in agriculture and thus have received training in fertiliser management; although several of the interviewees received their training years before the fertiliser regulation was introduced. Thus, all the farmers in the study possess a repertoire of learned strategies for how to plan fertiliser, and this does shape their general approach. Much fertiliser planning consists of routines, where farmers tend to use their educational background and their own experience, and where they draw on information shortcuts, or heuristics, to generate knowledge for fertiliser decisions. Agricultural advisers are also typically involved in the initial planning of fertiliser application, in many cases drawing up a plan based on regulatory norms. But farmers seem to view these plans as a raw outline which ensures that they do not exceed the quota.

Frames for information search

Optimal fertiliser planning consists of balancing the costs of input with the income from output. Much of this information is embodied in the fertiliser norms, although the norms are now 10 per cent below economic optimum. But specific local conditions may affect the relationship between nitrogen input and crop yield. Also the norms do not include the cost of transporting fertiliser. Furthermore, different manure application techniques may affect both the effective fertiliser value of manure as well as the costs associated with fertilising. Hence, a full consideration of fertiliser management requires both agro-scientific information as well as economic information.

The farmers do use varied types of information, including information about appropriate fertiliser levels both before and during the season, about physical yield and determinants thereof, about nutrients in the soil and structural conditions in their fields, about methods and technologies that may improve the fertiliser value of manure, and about costs of various application strategies. They also indicate that information search is somewhat selective.

Objectives constitute one selection mechanism. For instance, farmers who prioritise high yield focus on information about methods that will help them boost yields, but appear less attentive to information about costs. They are able to cite production measures such as the amount of wheat per hectare, but they do not necessarily know offhand or at all how much they spend on fertiliser allocation or even their earnings from wheat. Farmers who are focused on utilising resources, particularly manure, look for information about the ability of different crops to take up manure, but they are also attentive to information about new application technologies. More economically oriented farmers focus on numbers such as the contribution margin.

The differences are relative, measured by what issues the farmer talks about in detail and what types of information come to mind more readily. But it does not mean that yield-oriented farmers use no economic information or vice versa. In fact, the analysis indicates a rather high degree of homogeneity in approaches taken with regard to information search across farmers. Professional norms about the fertiliser task as well as regulatory demands serve to narrow down differences.

Information sources: heuristics or measuring
Heuristics tend to dominate more precise measurements in the farmers' fertiliser planning as well as for follow-up in the field. Box 7.4 lists typical examples of such information shortcuts cited by the farmers.

Box 7.4: Information shortcuts

Experience and backward deduction

Quote 9
IP4: Neil Young ... – he has ties with farmers – and he had been
   talking to a farmer about the reasons for his [the farmer's]
   success – you know, why he was getting better even though he
   was getting older. Those two curves are not supposed to
   match. You are supposed to be able to do the most when you
   are young. But all he said was, 'I ain't getting young; I'm just
   getting used to my land.' It has to do with experience or
   something intuitive ... that is how it is for a lot of craftsmen.

Quote 10
Int: How do you know if it is working out?
IP3: Well, actually I go by the crop yield. So, if I have a high
   yield, I must be doing something right.

Quote 11
Int: How do you know what works?
IP12: You don't know until you have harvested some beets,
   really. In a way you have to do it several years in a row; nature
   is so varied and capricious that what is right one year is not
   necessarily right the next year.
Int: Do you collect information systematically, then?
IP12: No, I don't.

Visual cues

Quote 12
IP5: We never take our papers out to the man who is bringing
   out the fertiliser and tell him, give this amount and that,
   without first looking at the fields. That is, we always look at
   the fields.
Int: What do you look for?

IP5: The colour of the grass. Say, for instance, with grass for
   mowing, well, if it is really pale then it needs a really good
   plastering, and if it is nice and dark, then it doesn't need very
   much.

Quote 13
IP3: Well, grass needs to be really dense. It should be like a
   carpet. And if it isn't the first time you mow, then you can be
   absolutely sure that it will never give topnotch yield that year.

Quote 14
IP19: There should be no light stripes in the field, and there
   should be no stripes where the crop is tilting, and the crop
   should stand nice and even everywhere.

The most commonly cited source of knowledge in fertiliser
planning among the farmers interviewed was experience, and
specifically familiarity with their fields. Hence, farmers will reallocate fertiliser compared with fertiliser norms, because their
experience tells them that this field needs extra fertiliser, while
that field can do with less. This is expressed in quote 9. This
approach may be described as 'knowing your fields'.

Another approach may be labelled 'looking at your fields' as
farmers cite frequent use of visual cues to judge the effect of
fertiliser levels applied. As expressed in quotes 12 to 14, visual
cues include colour and density of the crop and are used throughout the growing season as farmers examine whether to adjust the
fertiliser plan.

While experience features as a key source of information, the
form in which information from previous years is incorporated in
the planning process varies from the impression-based to meticu-
lous registration of practices and outcomes. Some adjust their
fertiliser management a little from year to year in response to
their past experience. If fertiliser practices have led to a successful
crop, the practice will be repeated; if the crop turned out poorly
the farmer will change his approach, cf. quote 10.

Some farmers do look for precise information. One farmer
conducts tests on the animal manure to get accurate information
about the actual, not standardised, content of nitrogen in manure.

Some go so far as to conduct parallel experiments on their fields as a way to obtain comparative information about different practices controlling for annual weather changes. Some measure protein levels in the crop in order to assess fertiliser levels.

> Int: Do you keep that kind of information in your head, or do you keep records?

> IP1: Gradually, you come to know that information. In the beginning you write it down. We make notes on everything we do in the field, we do. With fertiliser … I cannot remember how much fertiliser I have applied, so with that I check either my field plan or check my computer, I keep records in both, and then I go back and check – how much did we give to that field and how much did we apply to malt barley, and how did it produce. Are we going down or up and what are the protein levels? So that is how we use the information.

Generally, however, farmers use less precise indicators and some consider precise measurements to be a waste of effort given the unpredictable fluctuations in weather and other natural conditions: see quote 11 above.

Information shortcuts substitute for precise knowledge, for instance, on the optimal nitrogen requirement of the crop throughout the growing season and the effect on yield, which are not measurable until the time of harvest. Hence the cues may represent the best available knowledge. The uniformity and frequency with which these visual cues are used indicate that they represent professionally learned strategies. Furthermore, farmers generally seem to prefer such cues over more precise information. They compared favourably the value of looking at their fields with the more research-based knowledge presented by the advisers, sometimes mildly put down as 'desk expertise'. Only a few farmers seem to find it worthwhile to apply precise measuring techniques to get information about nitrogen levels in the soil or in manure.

This is not to say that farmers do not use information produced by the agricultural advisers. In fact, the agricultural community seems to draw on a common pool of knowledge, which is disseminated through the education system, through the advisory service, through the agricultural associations, and through professional networks in general. This knowledge is, in other words, part of a store of knowledge on which the farmer can draw, and he does not have to seek it out specifically.

The use of experience and professional norms appears to have affected fertiliser practices even more before the introduction of the regulatory norms, which have considerably restricted the room for manoeuvre of farmers. While some farmers said they knew of or used the recommended norms before the regulation was introduced, the farmers interviewed said they used to rely to an even greater extent on their experience and on visual cues to judge whether crops needed more fertiliser. But with a cap on nitrogen, they may not be able to follow previous routines and perceptions of optimal levels. Furthermore, they have to plan ahead more thoroughly, which reduces the possibilities for mid-season adjustments, even if the crops appear to need more fertiliser.

Updating information: when does it happen and when does it not?

Routines characterise much of the information search described so far, but farmers are prompted to update or seek out new information. This is typically problem driven, i.e. when farmers are prompted by a specific problem or a desire to improve upon a specific practice. Performance under par provides impetus for looking for information and new solutions.

> IP18: The joy of having a field which yields a nice crop, that is big, compared to, you know, if it is really disastrous, right. Because then you begin ... what did you do wrong or what went wrong. Is it too wet or too dry, or did you not start it well enough? And then you have to try to take that into account the next year – what did we do wrong?

New tasks or new problems also prompt information search. Hence, the regulatory changes in the fertiliser area in recent years have stimulated a considerable search for information. In this case, farmers are looking particularly for information about how to improve the use of manure.

Fear of making mistakes may also prompt use of information. Hence, many farmers draw on their advisers for fertiliser planning more than they used to in order to avoid costly errors, and now that EU subsidies are tied also to regulatory compliance. Likewise, one farmer began to monitor carefully his stock of manure after he had run out of fertiliser the previous year.

These examples reflect negative motivation for information search. But information search may also be motivated by a general interest in new solutions and the promise of progress. Farmers with a general interest in boosting their yields or their manure utilisation rates may also seek information. Several of the farmers had participated in experimental study programmes under the auspices of the agricultural advisory services.

Problem-driven information search appears to be a conditional relation, though only if the farmer is confident that he can affect the outcome, i.e. actually do something with the information, will he seek to update information. Farmers who feel they have too little room for manoeuvre due to physical or regulative restrictions appear to be less motivated to pay attention to information about fertiliser.

> Int: Do you consult anyone about fertiliser management?
>
> IP12: No, except I go to these meetings on crop production. It is so tightly regulated all this about nitrogen requirements … so I do not make many changes to my strategies.

Uncertainty may also reduce the impetus for information search, as reflected in those who refer to the unpredictability of field work.

> IP4: It may very well be that the outcome would have been better if I had done some things differently; you will never know … Then you should have run two experiments out in the field, but that is not of much use, because then you find out what you should have done, but what good does that do, because the next year the situation is completely different.

Finally, time would be an obvious limiting circumstance on information search, but not one that was pointed out as a major issue. A part-time farmer pointed out that he did not look much for new methods, because he could not afford to waste his time on an unproven technology; likewise, a farmer indicated that if pressed for time he would be more inclined to go by fertiliser norms and spend less time assessing the field.

In short, farmers are likely to seek new information when they face failure, encounter a new problem, or entertain the promise of progress. On the other hand, farmers are less inclined to look for information when they have little confidence that they can significantly affect the outcome of decisions.

Discussion

The analysis confirms the expectation that the use of information is selective, typically shaped by routines and heuristics. Much information used for fertiliser planning is stored; it reflects the knowledge and experience of the farmer as to what works on his fields, or it reflects professional conventions and practised rules about how to achieve high yields or efficient use of fertiliser and it relies on visual cues about outcomes which are also professionally defined.

Much of the time such information search is rather efficient and targeted, but there is an inherent risk of bias in using information shortcuts. For instance, the use of visual cues may represent what has been termed an overconfidence bias (Klayman *et al.*, 1999; Shefrin, 2002), which refers to overestimating the quality of one's information. A few farmers volunteered examples to illustrate this point. They mentioned that measurements of yield at harvest time often deviated considerably from the expectations they had formed based on visual cues. And the farmer who had conducted extensive testing of nutrients in his soil, indicated how surprised he was to discover that the actual levels differed significantly from the expectations he had formed based on visual cues. Hence, he generally rejected visual cues as a reliable source of information.

Likewise, experience may turn into a confirmatory bias where information that does not fit one's own experience is filtered out. Several expressed mixed confidence in the information they received from their advisers, and a few indicated that they were more likely to listen to the adviser when the information supplied squared with their own beliefs. Also, farmers who had participated in fertiliser experiments appeared to have more confidence in the fertiliser norms than farmers who had not. The former had seen firsthand how a change in practices might bring about the same yields with less fertiliser, while the latter seemed to doubt research results because they held to a different belief, i.e. that high yields require high levels of fertiliser.

Generally, routine-bound information search as seen in this study may undervalue or overlook new information that could improve practices. But farmers in these interviews do appear to seek out new information fairly actively, which is not to say that the information always forms their practices. The analysis indicates that farmers seek new information mostly when they perceive a problem, for instance when their yields are lower than expected. In fact, the introduction of the fertiliser norms and their lowering did increase significantly the interest in new information about fertiliser practices, as fertiliser became a scarce resource and a requirement for utilisation of the nitrogen in manure created new challenges.

Overall, the widely shared pool of knowledge about fertiliser practices and the institutionalised dissemination of information across the agricultural community appear to ensure a fairly high level and continuous updating of information. The main difference lies in differential weighting of different sources of information and different indicators.

As for deviations from fertiliser norms, these follow directly from the use of experience and visual cues as sources of information, simply because farmers believe they can do better than the fertiliser norms. But at the same time introduction of the fertiliser norms have narrowed the scope of deviation from optimal fertiliser levels *measured in terms of fertiliser norms*. Their introduction forced farmers to abandon routines and incorporate recent information into their fertiliser management. In that sense they provided a corrective of the course set by previous routines.

Decision rules and choice

Economic models assume that farmers choose that level of fertiliser which offers the highest level of marginal return, calculating marginal cost of fertilisers to marginal earnings on output. Bounded rationality theory predicts that farmers are more likely to decide by simple decision mechanisms, such as rules of thumb, and that they will satisfice rather than optimise. In terms of outcome, the expectation is that less attention to the process and pronounced use of routines and simple decision rules are more likely to result in deviation from optimal fertiliser levels.

The analysis of choice thus examines how farmers arrive at actual fertiliser levels and the presence and role of simple decision strategies in this process. Specifically, the analysis looks at how farmers deal with inevitable trade-offs. The analysis builds particularly on the descriptive accounts farmers gave of their fertiliser practice. As for studying the effect of the process on the tendency to deviate from fertiliser norms, the analysis is confronted with the problem that the norms no longer represent optimal fertiliser levels for each crop. This implies that the decision output can be assessed only qualitatively and the effect of the process may be assessed only indirectly.

Fertiliser allocation

Glossing over many nuances, three alternative principles for allocation of fertiliser can be identified among the farmers interviewed. One principle is to give crops the highest level of fertiliser possible; this principle is typically related to a general impulse to achieve the highest yields possible. Another principle is to give optimal fertiliser to high-value crops and distribute the remainder of the quota more or less evenly among the rest of the fields. This reflects a mix of economic and productivity considerations. And the final principle is to allocate fertiliser based on optimal distribution of manure, meaning that manure is spread where it will be used most efficiently. The second principle, which may be called strategic optimising, explicitly breaks with the fertiliser norms at their current sub-optimal levels. The other two principles do not necessarily lead to deviation from norms. But as it turns out, nearly all farmers interviewed, regardless of overall allocation principles, do stray from the norms. They either distribute fertiliser unevenly within the fields, or they redistribute fertiliser among fields compared with the norm allocation, or both. Typically, redistribution is in the order of 10–20 per cent of the fertiliser norm. The next section analyses how they arrive at these particular levels.

How to decide on fertiliser levels

As a general rule the farmers interviewed do not calculate in great detail optimal levels of fertiliser, as in comparing cost of input to value of output. The level of precision in decision modes varies considerably, but simple decision rules, or heuristics, are evident in most of the descriptions. Box 7.5 draws up the range of decision strategies evident in the data and discusses how they may impact fertiliser patterns.

Box 7.5

Standard operating procedures

Quote 15
IP2: Well, we pretty well know the level, having worked each field for many years. We know what level we are at. And that is what we base our fertiliser management on.
Int: So you basically follow last year's plan for a particular crop in a particular field?
IP2: Yes, the plans for the last five years, in principle. Because we know how much we have grown the last five years for each field.

Anchors

Quote 16
IP8: It may not be accurate, but it is probably optimal. Why would they tell us otherwise? Whether it is one crop or the other that can use the fertiliser, the experiments do show that. That much you have to believe – that it makes some difference that we conduct all these experiments.

Quote 17
Int: So it is sort of a little more or a little less than the [fertiliser] norm?
IP3: Yes. That is, the norm always serves as a benchmark. Because I can't take it out of thin air. Because then I am just as much at a loss as you are.

Quote 18
IP20: And then we spread the fertiliser based on the high-value crops that I mentioned; that is, seeds and sugar beets, and some on the rapeseed, and then the cereals get what is left.

Saving for a rainy day

Quote 19
We do try to keep a small buffer of artificial fertiliser. And if we think something looks all wrong – it might be that we have ploughed the slurry in the sandy fields and have applied only 25 kg nitrogen on top, but it has rained so much that the slurry – or the nitrogen – has penetrated deeper into the ground. Then we can buy and sprinkle once more and still stay within our quota. And this is the kind of stuff we fiddle around with.

Farmers clearly follow routines and standard operating procedures in their fertiliser planning. One way to determine this year's fertiliser plans is to use the plans from previous years with necessary adjustments, including crop rotation. Some stick to the same basic plan, but they may adjust levels somewhat based on observations in the field. They know how their fields respond to different crops and different levels of fertiliser and apply amounts accordingly, as expressed in quote 15. As indicated in the quote, standard operating procedures do not necessarily imply a lack of attention or reflection. Routines rely on evidence and may also be updated. It is, in other words, a measured reliance on routines.

The dominant feature of fertiliser decisions is adjusting from a baseline. In the behavioural economics literature this is referred to as anchoring, that is the decision is determined in part by the value of the baseline (Tversky and Kahneman, 1974).

The fertiliser norm constitutes an obvious anchor. The norms guide fertiliser allocation. The analysis indicates that norms are used when time is scarce or when the farmer weighs the effort to reconsider the norms against the expected benefits. If for some reason the farmer is pressed for time, the norm-based plan represents a simple and time-saving approach to fertilising. Even though the farmers generally consider the norms to be at sub-optimal levels, some use them as the best standard there is: see for example quote 16.

More commonly, farmers use the norm as a baseline from which to reallocate fertiliser among fields, as illustrated by quote 17. Different rules guide this reallocation. In some cases, more fertiliser is moved towards the crops that offer the highest economic return; high-value crops such as sugar beets and grass seed. In other cases, the reallocation is argued in productivity terms. Fertiliser is moved toward the crops most in need of extra fertiliser. For instance, there is a widespread perception that nitrogen norms for wheat are too low to produce wheat of a competitive quality, so some farmers redistribute nitrogen to their wheat fields.

Finally, some farmers as a rule reserve some fertiliser so that they have a little on hand in case certain crops do not develop as planned (see quote 19). Looking over the fields, those crops which do not measure up to colour or density standards may get an extra dose. Likewise, fertiliser levels may be adjusted within individual fields, passing a tough spot in a lower gear or passing it twice.

Calculations

The farmers interviewed typically do not subject fertiliser allocation to detailed calculation. The task is one of getting the most fertiliser value out of the nitrogen quota, and it is a widespread perception that this makes sense economically, but few actually carry out the calculation. The following response to the question of economic assessment is quite typical:

> Int: Do you always apply a little extra when you are allowed to? Or do you undertake an economic evaluation?

> IP9: I always apply it all, because I know that it can always take more.

As pointed out, farmers will move fertiliser to high-value crops, but this is typically done by common-sense argumentation rather than by calculation. Only a few indicate that they base their decisions on calculation of the earnings on each crop. If at all, earnings tend to be assessed for crop production as a whole.

The cost of transporting manure is rarely included in the calculations. Transportation cost may enter into the choice between two application technologies, but cost of transportation is not included in a calculation as to whether it is worth taking fertiliser to, say, a distant field. The only example of a farmer who used transportation cost as a parameter was one who said that he took only the lighter, artificial fertilisers to far-lying fields. Cutting down on fertiliser on a field simply due to distance appeared to be out of the question.

Qualitative trade-offs and aspiration levels

Moving fertiliser around in the manner described requires some trade-offs, either between different crops or between yield and cost. The interviews indicate that farmers typically do this in the manner predicted by the bounded rationality model. They make trade-offs, but they do so in a qualitative manner, and they tend to be loaded toward one objective, ignoring or downplaying other aspects of the decision. Hence, the farmer quoted below assesses fertiliser needs differently from his adviser, because he focuses solely on yields, whereas the adviser includes also economic aspects in the calculation:

> Int: How do you know that you are doing it right?
>
> IP19: That is just basic knowledge. I think, I kind of argued with [my adviser] about this just the other day. I think overall the fields get 10 kg less than they need. But he says I don't have any more to give. And that I am not under-fertilised. You know it has to do with these norms for optimal fertilising, and what is economically optimal, and when you hit that point – and that is where I think we still come up short by about 10 kg, but [the adviser] says that the level is not completely wrong given the prices we get today. There is no room for much more, and you won't get much out of it, he says. We don't quite agree about that.
>
> Int: How do you know that he is mistaken?
>
> IP19: I don't think my crop yields measure up to what they should.

This farmer copes with trade-offs by prioritising one objective. Another way to cope with trade-offs is to optimise fertiliser on a few crops. This may well be optimal, but as the trade-off is made qualitatively rather than quantitatively, the jury is out. In fact, this may be considered a good example of a lexicographic strategy, as the decision is based on a good outcome for a single dimension of the decision rather than a calculation of optimal pay-off.

Furthermore, expectations about yields seem to be based on aspiration levels. While farmers aim for the highest possible yield they appear to be satisfied as long as yield does not drop below the previous year's yield, or at least some multi-year average yield. Several of the farmers also acknowledged that they compare their fields to those of other farmers and as long as they match or do just a little better, they are satisfied.

> Int: And yield, do you measure that just in relation to the yield of previous years or do you compare with the fields of your neighbours?
>
> IP3: ... I have an adviser who comes around every other month, and he knows what other farmers are growing. Last year he was quite impressed. So that is nice.

Possible consequences of a simple versus a comprehensive strategy

Traces of bounded rationality as conceptualised in simple decision modes are abundant in the farmers' accounts of fertiliser decisions. Fertiliser management is to some extent routine-based, following the same general procedure from year to year, but routines are updated in response to convincing new research findings. Choice of strategies is passed through the filter of experience of the farmer, and heuristics such as anchors or benchmark values typically substitute for precise calculation. To deal with difficult trade-offs farmers make qualitative rather than quantitative trade-offs, and the trade-off is typically loaded toward one alternative or objective. Alternatively, the choice follows a lexicographic strategy of assessing one objective at a time. Furthermore, objectives are assessed against aspiration levels such as the yield of comparable farmers. It is not possible to categorise each farmer as using a simple or a comprehensive decision mode. Rather fertiliser decisions represent a mix of strategies; although some are more inclined to calculate, whereas others are more inclined to rely solely on rules of thumb.

However, the simple decision modes may well be adaptive in the sense that they bring about optimal fertiliser plans, given the quota constraint. But the farmers who rely primarily on heuristics and employ few precise data cannot know whether their expectations are sustained. The risk of decision biases is intrinsic to this decision mode, and the analysis points to a few potential errors as measured against a fully rational decision. The greatest risk is that optimal yield in the field comes at too high a price, resulting in a sub-optimal economic outcome. This may happen if farmers focus on the sub-objective of high yield and ignore the costs associated with bringing in these high yields. For instance, falling wheat prices in the years prior to the interviews[1] did not yet seem to have made a great impact on fertiliser practices. At least farmers in the interviews, with a few exceptions, seemed to put considerable effort into keeping up yield and quality in their wheat fields; although wheat appeared to be turning into a low-value crop, economically.

Likewise, many farmers appear to put considerable effort into outguessing the fertiliser norms, confident that they can do better.

However, much less effort is put into actually measuring the effect of the effort. The imprecision of the causal model of fertiliser effect and weather-related uncertainty easily explain why farmers are hesitant to measure yields too precisely. But there is an inevitable risk that decisions are based on wishful thinking when not controlled precisely. On the other hand, using the norm as a baseline and adjusting by just a few percentage points would reduce the risk of making major errors; although an optimal strategy given sub-optimal norms would be to calculate the pay-off from various combinations of fertiliser levels across fields.

It is noteworthy that the farmers who are more inclined to use precise information and employ cost–benefit calculations in their decision-making in the end come up with quite similar fertiliser plans as those more prone to the simple decision strategies. Most farmers appear to redistribute some amount of fertiliser among their fields. It is possible that there would be a greater effect of decision mode on fertiliser pattern without the restricting effect of the fertiliser regulation. Farmers do not have as much latitude as they used to.

While fertiliser patterns may not differ much among the farmers interviewed, this analysis has substantiated that farmers differ with regard to decision processes. To complete the analysis of the theoretical framework the following section will examine factors that may stimulate different strategies, looking particularly at the role of motivation.

Possible determinants of decision mode

Motivation
Strength of motivation was identified as a trigger of comprehensive decision mode. One hypothesis was that crop farmers would be more attentive to fertilising, because more of their income derived from field work. The interviews do not confirm this expectation. Crop farmers do not appear to employ a more comprehensive decision mode than livestock farmers. And livestock farmers do not necessarily put less effort into fertilising than crop farmers. In fact, several livestock farmers explicitly said they preferred field work to work in the stables and spent more time outside than inside. This finding then confirms and to some

extent explains the finding from the quantitative analysis that crop farmers and livestock farmers do not differ significantly in their tendency to deviate from fertiliser norms. Livestock farmers do find the necessary time to fertilise, and they do so because the task of fertilising holds professional satisfaction. Some livestock farmers, however, stated a rule of thumb, which said that time and resources should be allocated among activities in proportion to the income generated from each activity.

The farmers interviewed generally had only vague notions of the degree to which fertiliser management affected their bottom lines. One estimated that it would be in the order of 2–3 per cent of his overall earnings, but farmers typically had not made the calculation. In fact, when asked about the importance of fertiliser for the bottom line, farmers often explained instead the importance of fertiliser in professional agricultural terms.

> IP3: Of course, fertiliser management is something which occupies farmers quite a bit. There is no denying that. It's partly because we have at our disposal only the approved amount. So it must be allocated accurately. There is no mercy at all.

This quote also indicates what *does* seem to be an important source of motivation among the farmers interviewed: professional pride. Farmers care about yield also as a signature of their professional ability. And good-looking fields are an obvious marker of professionalism since, as one farmer pointed out, they are more visible than the accounts.

> IP14: Well, I prioritise that a field looks good, when what you have brought out is spread evenly ... Because everything is revealed when the nitrogen norms are no higher than they are ... it is revealing, when it has not been placed properly. And then you get these stripes. So that is probably what I prioritise the highest that the field looks good, when it is turning green.

One farmer spoke at length about his failure to harvest 13 hectares of grain a few years ago. Due to mechanical failure he had postponed the harvest of these last hectares for a day, but the next day a three-week rain set in, and the crop rotted in the field. This cost him nearly 100,000 DKK, but he seemed more preoccupied with the blow to his professional pride.

> IP19: That one stung, professionally.

> Int. Why? What is the professional aspect of failing to bring it in?

> IP19: That was poor farming practice. That was a misjudgement on my part, you know.

Other farmers talked with equal intensity about errors they had made.

> IP16: And then I'm careful ... I must say, that is also due to experience, I am careful not to bring fertiliser out too late. You see, normally we do three rounds ... and once I got behind, I spread it, and then we had no rain afterwards. And then, when it begins to lose colour, let me tell you, that is really bad.

Again, the issue is not necessarily that the mistake cost the farmer a large sum of money, typically, he has not calculated this, but it is the chink in professional identity that motivates. The interview data thus may be interpreted as a substantiation of North's hypothesis that the degree of motivation is related to how important the task is for the decision-maker's sense of identity. First of all, one might argue that fertilising is important in part because it lays open for all to see the skills of the farmer. Furthermore, if a farmer's professional identity has been threatened because he made a mistake that reflects poorly on his competence, he is more motivated to pay attention to similar activities in the future.

Do decision processes explain deviation from fertiliser norms?

This concluding section will discuss whether the deviations from fertiliser norms can be explained by boundedly rational decision processes. The data merely permit an indicative conclusion, however. Firstly, the interviews were conducted at a time when fertiliser norms were 10 per cent below economic optimum, which changes the fertiliser task. Secondly, because the decision processes uncovered cannot be neatly dichotomised but cover rather a spectrum of decision-making strategies, the data do not lend themselves to a test of the linear relationship between an independent and a dependent variable. These qualifiers aside, the analysis does offer some insights with regard to the role of the decision process and also goes part way to an explanation of the fertiliser patterns seen in the previous chapter.

Elements of simple decision processes

The simple hypothesis pursued in this analysis is that farmers who are less attentive to decisions and use a simple decision mode are more likely to deviate from optimal fertiliser levels. Hence the first question is how to perceive the decision processes described in interviews. The analysis has uncovered a range of decision strategies, varying in their degree of simplicity or comprehension. But the following traits of boundedly rational decision processes are evident in the interviews.

Farmers appear to differ in their *modus operandi*; they typically state several objectives for their fertiliser management, but in their descriptive accounts of fertiliser management they tend to emphasise one objective over others. Three main leitmotifs can be identified: productivity-optimising, resource-optimising, and profit-optimising. Without claiming that farmers guided by the first two objectives pay no attention to economic issues, they do tend to prioritise either yield or degree of utilisation of manure and make only imprecise trade-offs with costs. Farmers who profit-optimise are more inclined to make the trade-offs under an overall earnings, or profit, approach, in some instances actually calculating the trade-off.

Information use is also selective; it is partly directed by the main objective. If fertilising is a matter of achieving the highest possible yield across all crops or in a few choice crops, information search will be directed toward indicators of yield and methods to improve the effect of fertiliser; if fertiliser management focuses on the best possible use of manure, information search targets application techniques and indicators of nitrogen value in manure, etc. If the focus is on economics, the farmer will look for economic indicators such as cost and earnings. While such a pattern appears, it is also clear that there is a high degree of homogeneity in the agricultural community. Farmers draw on a pool of shared knowledge about fertiliser practices and this pool is continuously maintained. This may mitigate the difference in information search, although information may weigh differently in the final decision. But it still allows for the use of information shortcuts, such as the colour of a crop, rather than precise measurement of yield.

Finally, the decision regarding fertiliser allocation is also guided by routines and by simple decision heuristics such as anchors. The fertiliser quota has forced farmers to make trade-offs among crops or among yield and cost, and they do so in a qualitative manner, attending to objectives lexicographically and by setting aspiration levels. Obviously, fertilising practices as well as all other farming activities have always been subject to trade-offs. But with the quota, trade-offs have become an unavoidable constraint. Examples of aspiration levels are average yields for comparable farmers, fields that measure up to those of the other farmers in the community in terms of colour and density, or putting in a reasonable effort. The interviews also include efforts to make more precise calculations, but these are generally considered difficult to carry out because of the uncertainty of predicting the effect of fertiliser on yield.

Overall, the analysis shows that farmers deviate from fertiliser norms because they attempt to outdo the norms. They believe in their own experience and, very concretely, they believe their own eyes, and they do what they think usually works. And for some, the value of a beautiful field of wheat or a high yield carries more weight than how much the fields contribute to the bottom line. They pursue objectives other than or in addition to profit-optimising.

Yet the deviations from norms described by the farmers are of a relatively minor order of up to 20 per cent. The analysis of decision processes also offers some possible explanations for this. Firstly, the regulatory norm and the nitrogen quota do serve to anchor fertiliser levels, framing the decision as allocation of a fertiliser quota around the norms, and as such make explicit the necessary trade-offs: over-fertilisation of one field inevitably leads to less fertiliser for another. Secondly, while some farmers aim for high yields they are not ready to ignore cost considerations entirely. And according to the farmers interviewed, the cost of fertiliser has become relatively more important, forcing more attention on fertiliser than was necessary in the early 1990s. Thirdly, the analysis makes clear the importance of institutional learning. The agricultural community shares a store of fertiliser strategies, and the advisory system and the peer network system that operates in Danish agriculture ensure that these are continuously updated. In addition to the regulation of fertiliser norms, this system has also worked to improve knowledge about good fertiliser practice.

Farmers deviate, but could it be optimal?
So farmers deviate from norms, but two circumstances suggest that deviations from fertiliser norms could represent efforts to optimise fertiliser use.

Firstly, fertiliser norms by design are now below the level required for economically optimal fertilising. Furthermore, farmers perceive the norms as too crude in the sense that they do not take into account the great variability within fields caused by natural topography, soil quality, and similar differentiating circumstances. If norms are not optimal, moving fertiliser around may be.

Secondly, some farmers argue that the nitrogen quota makes the cost of fertiliser invariant, thus irrelevant. The decision is not whether to buy more or less fertiliser, but simply how to allocate the maximum allowable amount. In this sense there is no economic calculation involved in fertiliser management, some argue.

Moving fertiliser around, then, implies intention to optimise. But the operative word is intention. The analysis of decision processes indicates that farmers move fertiliser around based on rules of thumb and selective information rather on than precise information; hence, they do not know whether their decisions are in fact optimal. Without marginal calculations in economic terms of yield gains on one field versus yield losses on another, the deviations from norms may be at least as imprecise or crude as fertilising based on the norms. Furthermore, while the cost of fertiliser itself may not vary, the costs of application and the amount of labour used for detailed applications do vary, but this is typically not calculated or, if so, it is calculated in a rather rudimentary manner. The time required for detailed fertiliser management is typically not priced either.

What is more, the interviews indicate that farmers also relied on simple decision rules both when fertiliser norms were economically optimal and before the regulation was introduced at all. This suggests that deviations from fertiliser norms cannot be explained solely with reference to sub-optimal norms or invariant costs. Obviously, interviews conducted in 2005 are a rather unreliable source of information about the whats and whys of fertiliser management in 1990, but taking, as indicators, the personal accounts of the farmers who farmed also before the introduction of norms, heuristics appear to have played an even greater role in determining nitrogen levels when farmers were unrestricted by fertiliser norms. A common rule of thumb before introduction of regulatory norms, frequently mentioned by farmers, was to apply enough fertiliser so that crops would grow right up to the point of lodging, but not so much that the crop would actually lodge, which would make it difficult to harvest: a trial-and-error approach.

> IP18: I've always said that cereal should have [fertiliser] right up until the point ... right before it falls over. Now, if it lies down entirely when we get too much water, that means it has had too much fertiliser. If it manages to just stay upright then you have hit the optimal.

A few said that they used the recommended norms as an anchor and adjusted, typically upwards. Likewise, some would use a fertiliser plan from their agricultural adviser and again adjust levels upwards; in the words of one farmer, 'we thought we could get higher yields from adding a bit more' (IP16). Whether or not this extra yield materialised and how it compared with prices was not calculated. These decision rules generally led to significantly higher levels of fertiliser, by the accounts of the farmers themselves.

Acknowledging that they had fertilised well above economically optimal levels, farmers said that fertiliser was cheap so it did not matter. Now, they say, fertiliser is more expensive, which has also served to focus their attention on fertiliser management. This would tend to support an argument that businesses operate well within the margin of profit, also known as 'slack' in the economic literature – until forced by external pressure, whether economic or regulatory, to pay closer attention to their use of resources.

On a final note, the fines do not appear to figure in economic calculations. Farmers are aware of the fines but appear to consider them in a qualitative manner: as something to avoid. Keeping in mind that this would be a sensitive subject, the interviews offered no indications that farmers had entertained the idea of exceeding the quota and paying the fine.

Optimising – but not necessarily optimising profit
The analysis, however, also points to an alternative explanation of deviation from norms. Some farmers seem more tuned in to physi-

cal yield than to economic yield. They put considerable effort into moving fertiliser around and are therefore less likely to fertilise according to norms. And the simple decision rules they use seem to support a yield-optimising decision more than they support a profit-optimising strategy. Clearly, this is not a case of inadequate attention to fertiliser, although it does indicate perhaps inadequate attention to economic indicators. The interviews here point to a non-economic source of motivation: many farmers derive considerable professional satisfaction from having good-looking fields, defined as fields with a tall, strong, uniform-looking crop, which convey high yield and good craftsmanship. The motivation seems to be intrinsic as well as extrinsic. The farmer derives personal satisfaction from being a competent professional.[2] But such good-looking fields also signal professional merit to other farmers and thus affect the standing of the farmer in his professional community. Hence, farmers, typically with a self-mocking smile, said that they would look at the fields of other farmers as they drive by, both to evaluate their own performance as well as that of the other farmer. Thus, it would appear that farmers are guided by a set of professional norms about what makes a good farmer, passed on through family, education, and professional networks. These norms embody both performance standards and means by which to achieve objectives. As such one might argue that they reflect a fusion or at least an overlap of the logics of consequence and appropriateness. But the analysis has also confirmed the expectation that professional norms serving in this heuristic capacity may lead to fully rational as well as boundedly rational behaviour.

Farmers, who are driven more by economic outcome, measure professional success in different terms than those driven by yield. This does not imply that their behaviour is not affected by professional norms. First, high income also confers professional merit. But more importantly with regard to fertiliser patterns, economically motivated farmers also use the professionally learned decision rules, such as visual cues, as these do represent information efficient strategies. So they reason in similar ways, but they assess the effort against the output and therefore may put less effort into fertiliser decisions. Given the institutional context of fertiliser norms the difference in behaviour then is limited. In a different institutional context, for instance regulation by economic incentives, greater variation is conceivable.

Conclusion

In conclusion, the analysis has shown that farmers in the main follow a set of process rules rather than use marginal calculation when they plan fertiliser levels. These rules appear to spring from a set of personal and professional routines, i.e. stemming from a general idea about how much fertiliser their crops need, they use visual cues to judge the necessary adjustments from year to year. These decision processes then do provide some explanation for the deviations from fertiliser norms. The fact that the rules stem from professional routines may also help explain why the quantitative analysis showed little variation across such differences as farm category. Livestock farmers know and use the visual cues as well as crop farmers do.

But simple decision rules do not provide a full explanation. The analysis shows that farmers deviate from fertiliser norms because they think they can get a higher yield by applying their own knowledge and standards. In other words, they do not consider the norms to be accurate assessments of fertiliser needs. This is obviously the case now that norms are below economically optimal levels. But farmers say they would also move fertiliser around within the quota if norms were economically optimal.

Does this imply that deviating from norms is economically optimal, then? It might be, but the decision processes are not. Farmers to varying degrees optimise on yield, rather than on earnings, i.e. they do not typically calculate the cost of such optimising. There is a general rule that prioritising some crops must not take too much away from other crops, while some do tend to give optimal levels to high-value crops. But typically this is carried out by way of qualitative reasoning rather than calculation, and generally costs of transporting fertiliser or of labour are not included.

The analysis of decision processes suggests that professional pride is an important motivator for farmers and that this affects their fertiliser decisions. They are more attentive to production objectives than to overall economic objectives. Farmers, again some more than others, are driven by professional ambitions, and high yields are a hallmark of craftsmanship; because there is a professional rule that says that a good-looking field is an indicator of high yield, a tall, dense crop of healthy colour becomes an indicator of professional merit. Professional considerations might be less likely to outweigh stringent economic ones if fertiliser costs weighed heavily in the overall budgets of the farmers.

Finally, the analysis offers a few clues to the patterns of over- and under-fertilising seen in the previous chapter. Over-fertilisation appears to follow from yield optimising, as one would expect. It is not a matter of lack of attention. The picture is again less clear on under-fertilising, since farmers interviewed generally use their entire quota. Most of them indicate that they under-fertilise only to compensate for over-fertilisation on other fields. But some do indicate that they are keen not to use more fertiliser than necessary, so they may not use their entire quota.

Notes

1 Prices have begun increasing again.
2 This point also became clear during a discussion with a group of farmers about the findings of the present study. One farmer repeatedly expressed deep-seated frustrations about the difficulty of keeping up a good crop of wheat due to the low nitrogen norms. Later on in the conversation, he said that he had sold off some land the previous day and had banked nearly 30 million DKK. The money he could make on improved wheat yield would have been negligible in comparison, but he seemed to care at least as deeply about the loss of production as the windfall from the sale of his land.

8
Optimising or satisficing: when and what

The analysis of farmers' decisions on fertiliser pointed to objectives and decision rules as key factors in explaining fertiliser behaviour, whereas differential attention did not seem to make a considerable difference. But the case of fertilising represents a particular context in which regulation has both increased attention to fertilising and has also considerably constrained the paths of behaviour. The institutional context may have shaped these decisions to make them atypical. A comparison with other types of decisions may serve to examine whether dynamics uncovered in decision processes of fertiliser apply more generally to farmers' decision-making. Other types of decisions include what might be termed management tasks, such as feeding strategies for livestock and pest control in crop cultivation, as well as larger, discrete decisions, such as purchase of farming equipment and investment in land. These decisions vary as to the frequency with which the decision comes up, the amount of money involved, and the rigidity of the decision, i.e. the ease with which the decision may be changed.

The chapter first examines, comparatively, the decision processes involved in these types of decisions. The analysis builds on accounts by the farmers as to how they go about different types of decisions but also evaluates statements as to how they perceive different types of decisions and differences and similarities among them. Subsequently, the chapter draws up features of decision-making that are common across decision types, highlighting the role of different objectives, spread of information, the handling of trade-offs and the role of motivation for the farmer's attention to different decisions.

To explore whether the findings hold beyond the agricultural sector, the chapter briefly discusses how the findings of this study might explain responses to incentive-based environmental policies in other sectors.

Pest control and livestock feeding strategies

Pest control and livestock feeding strategies differ from fertilising in that the tasks occur more frequently, feedback on the effect of different courses of action is more immediate, and in that these activities typically involve more money for the farmer.

Even so, like fertilising, pest control strategies embody uncertainty as to the timing and the dose, which affects decisions. Spraying too late or too little may ruin the crop or at least reduce yield, while on the other hand premature or unnecessary application of pesticides embodies waste of an expensive resource.

Farmers apply one of two general strategies. Some are quite cost-conscious in their approach. They will aim for precision, which means spraying only problem areas rather than entire fields and also waiting for the moment when spraying is most opportune. This involves a fair amount of monitoring of the fields and subscribing to an online advisory service which alerts the farmer when conditions warrant treatment of specific crops. Some farmers may abstain from treatment if the costs are not borne out by crop prices.

> IP7 wife: We get nothing for our grain ...

> IP7 husband: ... so we have to calculate all the time. Does it pay? They just wrote in the [farmers' trade paper]; drop the spraying of mildew. But we've known that for 30 years.

The other prevalent strategy is driven by aversion to risk; for many farmers the risk of losing a crop or a part of it to fungi or pests leads to a strategy expressed in the heuristic, 'better safe than sorry'. As one farmer said: 'If you get behind just one day on mildew, then you can quickly lose an entire field. There you have to be ... well, rather one day ahead than one day behind' (IP13). Such preventive decision rules may help explain why farmers have been considerably less responsive to the pesticide tax than predicted by economic models (Christensen *et al.*, 2007);

although farmers in this and other studies assert that they are cost-conscious in their decisions on pest control.

While losing an entire field would be costly, the approach also reflects a general quest for high yields as well as the professional pride that comes from having nice-looking fields. A field with evidence of weeds is scoffed at because it indicates sloppy farming.

> Int: Generally around here, if farmers compare themselves with other farmers, what would you be looking at?
>
> IP14: That would be how well you apply pesticides.
>
> Int: That is the most important thing?
>
> IP14: Yes, all things considered. That you don't have a bunch of weeds just dangling in the field.
>
> Int: But is it because weeds affect yield or because it's considered to be slovenly work?
>
> IP14: It's both. If you are going to spend the money spraying you may as well do a good job.

For livestock farmers, decisions regarding feeding strategies require much attention. Feed represents a significant expense, but types of feed and amounts also affect the production outcome in terms of the weight gain of the animals as well as their robustness. Generally the farmers attempt to balance the desire for high yield with a need to keep down costs. Numbers figure prominently in these decisions. Farmers follow the effect of strategies, using precise indicators; for instance, measuring the effect of feeding strategies on milk production or livestock growth rates. And they adjust their strategies based on this information. At the same time, economic calculations frequently form decisions. A dairy farmer, for instance, changed his feeding based on the cost of different types of feed.

For both decision domains, farmers vary as to how they prioritise production yield in relation to economic considerations. But economic calculation does seem to enter the picture much more regularly than is the case with fertilisers. For pest control and feeding, decision processes exhibit more traits of economic optimising and comprehensive decision-making than do fertiliser decision processes. This is evident in the greater use of precise indicators and the greater tendency to attempt to calculate marginal utility of decisions, trading off costs and benefits.

Even so, the processes also show simple decision mechanisms indicative of bounded rationality, such as the use of trial-and-error decision-making. A farmer may be offered a certain pesticide and try it out, or he may try new feeding strategies. When consequences of different strategies are uncertain, trying out one approach is one way to discover whether something works without committing large resources to making the decision. When feedback is quick, trial-and-error may be a simple and cost-effective approach to decision-making as adjustments can be made in time to prevent failure.

Investments and other strategic decisions

Decisions that involve large investments, be it in new production facilities, land or the other decisions that affect the future direction of the farm, differ from fertilising, pest control and feeding in that they tend be of a discrete nature and difficult to change. They also typically involve large sums of money. They also involve strong conflicts among multiple objectives, as strategic decisions concern both the economic future of the farm but also professional interests and lifestyle. And once taken, the decision tends to bind the farmer to his choice, including the trade-off among different objectives. It goes without saying that economic goals play a role in the decisions of all farmers interviewed. After all, farms are businesses. But farmers differ as to the extent to which future income guides their decisions. Economic survival is a bottom line condition for all decision-making, but while some use an economic yardstick for all strategic decisions, others organise such decisions around lifestyle criteria.

Strategic decision processes do seem to rely on extensive information gathering, including consultation with the agricultural advisers. Such decisions also typically involve a much more comprehensive decision process, as one would expect when a farmer considers locking himself into 30–year debts.

A typical decision process is illustrated by the case of a farmer who was considering switching from dairy cows to pig production. Among the criteria he considered was the dwindling profitability of dairy production at the time, how to use the existing buildings of the farm, what types of livestock production he would find agreeable from an animal welfare point of view, and what type of production would lend itself to reasonable working hours. He approached the decision piecemeal, considering one criteria at a time. Hence he settled first on a preference for feeding pig production, based on working hours and the fact that he could use existing buildings. In the second step he decided on a so-called deep litter stable system, because he thought it best in terms of animal welfare. At this point the economic calculation entered the picture.

> IP4: Well, I had the financial adviser out here. So we estimated a [price] we thought we could get for a pig like that. And that was of course based on history, what other people had made. And then we set a floor with regard to the [price], how far down we thought the price might go in the worst case. And we set that at 9 DKK (per kg), that is how far down we thought the price could go. But then, I remember, my mother, she was serving coffee and listening in, and then she said, 'Well, what are you going to do, if it drops down to 8 DKK?' 'Well, then everything stops. It has never been down to 8 DKK for an entire year.' You'd better believe, it did [go down].

Within a year the price did in fact tumble to 6 DKK per kg, i.e. two-thirds of his floor estimate.

While the decision process is comprehensive, in the end the choice exhibits clear traits of satisficing. Rather than trading parameters off against each other, the farmer approaches it in a lexicographic manner, choosing first the production form, then the production technology. Finally, he applies an aspiration level: if the economic calculation were to show pig production as being feasible, he would make this choice. Feasibility is judged by making an assumption of a floor price, which is based on back-casting (what other people had experienced) rather than forecasting (what factors might determine future prices).

Another example also indicates that while the consideration of alternatives may be comprehensive, the actual choice appears somewhat intuitive. One farmer describes how he decided to build a new cow stable.

> IP9: Well, we spent all winter ... drawing different designs for a cowshed. I think I must have drawn 10 different cowshed designs. And different floor plans. And I had the advisers look them over

and give their opinions. And I am well aware that if we ask our livestock adviser, then he is going to tell us to build that cowshed because that is his job ... And we were talking back and forth about it a lot. Finally, we ended up asking for some bids on construction of the cowshed. So we got the bids and we had them adjusted so they fitted the price, too. The final decision was taken one day when the builder we were thinking of using came around. He was here, and then he says, 'Now, you have to make a decision because we can be ready to begin shortly.' I think that was on a Thursday or a Friday, and then I said, 'Well, I'll sign then, and then let's begin.'

This example is quite typical. Farmers examine many aspects of a decision and may take considerable time doing so, sometimes years, but when something prompts them to make a final choice, the decision appears intuitive. Often, the farmers could not explain exactly what made them go one way or the other. Clearly, as in the case above, economic considerations played a role, but often in the form of a baseline condition. Calculations were used to prove the feasibility of the decision, but in the end other considerations seemed to determine the final choice.

Purchases of equipment also provide many examples of how decision rules are mixed, as farmers include elements of calculation and combine them with qualitative assessments. Typically, the farmer defines ahead of time the capacity he needs as well as other criteria that are important, including a rough price estimate. But, to offer a mild caricature, in the moment of decision the economically optimal purchase seems to give way to a single criterion of bigger-is-better. Often the farmer ends up buying equipment with larger capacity than he had anticipated. Typically, the farmer argues that in the end the price difference is so small that they might as well, and he may throw in the argument that a larger tractor or harvesting machine is an investment for the future, in case he were to buy more land. This is of course a valid argument, but typically appears as a *post-facto* justification not subjected to calculation. Similar processes have been found in other studies, which have shown that such reasoning has led to an equipment–land spiral, and that farmers typically have too much capacity (Jacobsen, 1994). Jacobsen also found that farmers typically overestimate the maintenance cost on equipment and underestimate overall equipment expenses, leading them to replace machinery before it is economically optimal. The present study cannot confirm this in terms of precise numbers, but the interviews in general do confirm that farmers seem to apply a qualitative standard as to when maintenance costs warrant replacement.

Again, while these decision processes reflect traits of comprehensive decisions, they are less precise and the outcome less predictable than the fully rational model would have it. Parallel consideration of several decision criteria or alternatives may still result in a choice process that is essentially lexicographic, i.e. chosen by one criterion rather than weighting several against each other.

Regret and risk

Even strategic choices may be forced upon the farmer, offering little time for a comprehensive decision process. This is typically the case when land or a neighbouring farm is put on the market. One farmer said that about half of his bigger decisions were guided by calculations of proper price; the other half were driven by a need to act.

> IP20: This other half, often you have to strike when the opportunity presents itself, and then you must do the calculation afterwards. You can walk around and fantasise and make a few calculations and think through all of it, but then sometimes something pops up from the outside which forces you to make a decision here and now.

One factor that seems to make a difference as to whether farmers stop or jump in that situation is the experience of regret over a previous decision. Particularly, farmers who regret previously having forgone an opportunity may be quick to jump. This is in line with experimental studies which have shown that fear of regret may influence, or bias, decisions (Larrick, 1993; Shefrin, 2002).

Whether the decision mode is 'deliberate and jump' or 'jump and deliberate', risk aversion affects the qualitative assessment of alternatives. Farmers who are well-established economically tend to avoid decision alternatives that would jeopardise all they have earned, whereas farmers who are starting out are more inclined or are forced to take risks to get established. Risk-averse farmers may invest interest accrued, or other such measure of surplus, but would not touch the principal.

> Int. Are you saying that you don't put in enough money to risk capsizing?
>
> IP17: Yes, I don't. And I think it has to do with having saved up that capital which has allowed me … well, when it is your own money, then you don't want to lose it. But if I had started out as a 23–year-old and had borrowed 10 million DKK or 15, as some do in the bank or the mortgage company, well then I think you are more inclined to go full steam ahead, and then it's make or break. And there, I've never been all that inclined to let it break. I'd rather make less money and then also invest less.

This is a clear example of an endowment effect often found in behavioural studies, which show that people take bigger risks with money they have won in a lottery than with money they have saved from income (see, for instance, Thaler *et al.*, 1992). Interestingly, established farmers, such as IP17 and IP20, appear quick to jump at opportunities, but this reflects not a greater risk propensity but rather that they have worked up a considerable surplus which allows them to put money on the line without taking from the principal.

Across decision domains there is ample evidence of attempts to optimise, but also clear evidence of bounded rationality. The comparison suggests different patterns among different types of decisions.

Management decisions such as those on feeding strategies or pest control are economically significant, and they are more often subjected to economic calculation than appeared to be the case for fertiliser decisions. For instance, farmers consider cost of feed in their decisions on feeding strategies. They often use more precise numbers in these decisions, partly because these are available, but also because feedback on the effect of different strategies is more immediate, which reduces uncertainty about outcomes. Not everything is calculated, however. Much occurs through trial-and-error, but as farmers pay close attention to the outcomes and adjust strategies as needed, even trial-and-error in such situations may represent an efficient decision strategy.

In comparison, fertiliser decisions seemed to use neither calculation nor pure satisficing strategies, but relied instead primarily

Table 8.1 *Features of decision processes by domain*

	Pest control	Feeding strategies	Strategic decisions: purchase of machinery or land, long-term development
Objectives	Yield Avoid losses in crops	Production yield Economic yield	Multiple objectives
Information	Visual inspection Adviser, information materials Alerts	Measuring Follow-up Adviser, information materials	Adviser Written information Talking to others
Decision mode	Heuristic: sooner rather than later Cost-benefit calculation	Heuristic: trial-and-error Cost–benefit calculation	Sequential consideration of alternatives Cost–benefit calculation Aspiration levels Qualitative trade-offs
Overall approach	Simplifying but approaching optimising	Approaching optimising with few simple decision rules	Satisficing

on anchor values, i.e. the norms plus adjustments, and on trial-and-error based on visual cues. The comparison with feeding and pesticide decisions suggests that the possibility of delayed feedback leads to uncertainty about the outcome of the fertiliser decision, which reduces the motivation to use precision strategies. Numbers also figure in purchase of equipment, such as tractors, but typically other goals such as capacity or comfort determine the final choice when prices were not too far off the mark, given aspiration levels.

Thus, cost–benefit calculations are more often undertaken when numbers are available, when the calculation is not too complex, and when outcomes are reasonably predictable. Likewise, a mix of calculation and satisficing may be used when goals of quality and price conflict.

Generally, strategic decisions are largely comprehensive in their information search and information processing; yet when it comes to the actual choice, the decisions show clear marks of bounded rationality. The decision tends to be lexicographic, i.e. it is broken down into partial decisions in order to reduce the complexity involved in assessing alternatives simultaneously and making a conscious trade-off. Often economic calculations enter the picture but they do so as the final step and economic criteria tend to represent an aspiration level. Typically, the aspiration level holds that the decision must break even or even a little better, but alternatives are rarely assessed in terms of which option will actually yield the greatest economic outcome. In this sense the decision processes tend to resemble satisficing. This reflects the difficulty of navigating among multiple important and at times conflicting objectives.

The comparison suggests that uncertainty, particularly when consequences reach far out in time, and conflicting objectives are more likely to cause elements of simple decision-making than is complexity of the task itself.

Bounded rationality across decision domains

Compared with fertiliser decisions farmers do have more latitude in other decision domains. This leads to greater variation in decision strategies. It does not necessarily lead to more precision, however. There is clear evidence of attempts to optimise, but simple decision strategies show through just as clearly. This section draws up decision features which cut across decision domains and which may represent evidence of bounded rationality.

Objectives and values

The analysis of fertiliser management indicated that farmers tend to focus selectively on different objectives. Analysing decision processes more broadly shows distinct approaches to farm management, reflecting different motivating forces or values. Analytically one may distinguish among farmers who aim to optimise on production and farmers who are more oriented toward the overall economic picture; although farmers probably would be located along a continuum between the approaches rather than in either category. In fact, the continuum might even be expanded into a triangle, as a few farmers seem to be driven predominantly by a resource utilisation or cost-cutting perspective.

Some dairy farmers illustrate well the drive to optimise production. To produce and sell milk, a farmer must buy a quota, which then constitutes the upper boundary of his production. Several of the farmers interviewed were doing so well with their cows that they produced considerably above their quota. Hence, they would have to buy a larger quota or scale down production, which implied a lower production standard. The latter option seemed to figure only theoretically. The farmer below increased the share of high-powered feed to his cows and noticed with great satisfaction that their milk production increased. But he was now pushing, or exceeding, his milk quota, resulting in the following consideration.

> IP3: The milk quota runs from April to April and I have to do what I can to stay within it. At this point I have to hold back a little. At the moment, I produce an excess of 300 litres of milk a day. So I either have to slaughter some cows or give some cows a long resting period before they are back at it. So that will probably be the outcome. Because I have purchased more [milk quota] for next year. I have purchased 116 tonnes so that I can produce a little more. We'll see. It's mostly to keep up the number of cows I have. I would like that.

The farmer had not calculated whether he would be better off with the smaller number of cows, but average prices from that year indicate that his decision to buy milk quota is not justified just on the face of these. One kilo of milk quota at the time when he was buying the quota went for a price between 3.25 DKK and 3.70 DKK, and there are other production costs. Yet the standard price paid to farmers per kg milk, at the time, was 2.36 DKK (Mejeriforeningen, 2009). Subsidies may improve the final calculation. This indicates that the farmer is driven to a large extent by a professional ethos.

Others lean more toward a business ethos, focusing to a greater degree on economic optimising; that is, assessing all activities against their contribution to the bottom line, as modelled in economic man. Asked what motivates his decisions the farmer expressed this attitude.

> IP17: To always have in the back of my mind that what we do has to be profitable ... I'll be damned if my employees spend their time sweeping the floor of the tractor. They need to earn some money.

> Int: So it's time to switch to other activities as soon as what you are doing is of marginal importance?

> IP17: That's it. I'm very focused on that. And probably much more so than my colleagues in general.

This does not mean that professionally motivated farmers ignore economic aspects of decisions, or that profit-motivated farmers do not care about professional competency. The distinction reflects the extent to which production optima are considered against overall economic outcome. Those motivated by professional achievement tend to aim for high production value across the board, tend not to calculate the value of their work, and to measure instead their work by output.

Farmers motivated primarily by profitability appear to have a business orientation in general: they are likely to also be involved in other types of investments or business activities, be it farms in Eastern Europe, windmills, or entrepreneurial projects. Finally, as for resource optimising, some farmers do appear to be subject to economic pressure that is forcing them to pay attention to cutting costs, perhaps focusing less on opportunities to make money, while others again appear to act simply out of a moral *habitus* of making the best use of resources.

However, the analysis indicates that there may be a difference between what might be considered daily management decisions and decisions regarding issues about the overall direction of the farm, such as investments in land and production facilities. It is possible to optimise economically in the management decisions, yet apply a different yardstick to larger, more strategic decisions, such as land purchases. Economics surely play a role in the decisions of all farmers interviewed, but the weight assigned to economic objectives varies among farmers. While some apply an economic yardstick to all decisions, others form their strategic decisions around professional aspirations or lifestyle criteria, lest this compromises economic survival.

Professional orientation is reflected in production optimisation; the farmer derives satisfaction from performance in the field or in the barn, such as the farmer who had to buy a larger milk quota cited above. Lifestyle-oriented farmers tend to emphasise community relations and they may rather sacrifice economic gain than compromise their standing in the community. Hence, one crop farmer has chosen not to use manure, because he does not want to jeopardise relations with his neighbours. Another emphasised that he would never want to engage in competition over land if it implied conflicts with his neighbours.

The implication is that policy incentives will be filtered – for larger investments one should expect the general value structure to affect the choices of farmers. For lower-level management decisions, economic considerations may play a greater role, but even decisions on fertiliser and pesticide also reflect the specific objectives pursued by the farmer. Most likely these objectives also link to the overall value structures. Economic incentives are more likely to work directly and predictably on those farmers who are firmly business oriented.

Learning from others

The farming community is well organised, as is the dissemination of information through advisers, study groups, and written information sources such as trade magazines. This works toward homogenising knowledge and cultivates standard operating procedures. It also implies that ideas tend to spread in a trend-like manner.

A farmer may hear of a particular technology from a neighbour or an adviser, and this idea then frames his consideration of different strategies; the first idea forms a benchmark against which all others are considered. Likewise, technologies that have gained status in farming circles as the state-of-the-art solution to a given problem will be explored first. For instance, in the case of fertiliser application a technology that injects fertiliser into the soil has captured the position as state-of-the-art with regard to natural fertiliser utilisation, which all but ensures that farmers will at least consider the technology if they are looking to increase their utilisation of animal manure. Likewise, deep litter stables were introduced at one point as a way to achieve better animal welfare. Within a few years many farmers were switching to these stables, only to discover that they caused new problems. Deep litter stable systems were then replaced by a wave of new barn systems, addressing the problems associated with the deep litter stables.

Even overall strategies seem to follow this pattern to some extent. Currently, the mantra in agriculture is to 'grow or wither'. This is how consultants frame the choice among future paths, according to farmers interviewed. Generally, farmers accept this premise for strategic decisions. Yet a few scrutinised the assumptions in the context of their own farms and against their overall values and opted instead for different paths.

The way alternatives travel through the agricultural community evokes the concept of information cascades; that is, the dynamic whereby decision-makers look to those who move first for clues about what to do (Jones, 2001: 114). As shown, such agenda setters may be a reputable farmer or a trusted adviser. The example with the deep litter system above shows the risk inherent in such social or professional learning – it tends to magnify small mistakes if many farmers follow the first mover and if it turns out that the first mover was wrong. On the other hand it is a force which may efficiently be used for the dissemination of new ideas.

Yet the first mover, including the adviser, may be less influential if the suggested solution is dissonant with other considerations or preferences of the farmer. For instance, farmers typically express less confidence than normal in their adviser when the adviser suggests that fertiliser norms are adequate. Following fertiliser norms would imply that the farmer does not aim for optimal yield. Likewise, farmers who value having a smaller farm are sceptical of the reasoning of the advisory services that only big farms will make it in the future, while others subscribe wholeheartedly to this scenario. In both cases, the difference does not lie in the actual choice, which would simply indicate preferences. It lies in the degree of consideration the alternative receives. Farmers appear more likely to question the assumptions of new alternatives if they involve a conflict with their overriding objectives, as in a growth strategy when one prefers a manageable farm. This provides a filter against the information cascade.

Either way, jumping on the bandwagon or considering solutions in a biased manner contrasts with the fully rational model which assumes parallel consideration of alternatives.

Skirting trade-offs

Decision areas may be more or less amenable to synoptic decision processes, but across the board trade-offs represent a key barrier to the full implementation of rational decision processes. When farmers attempt to compare different alternatives across key criteria, the pattern is not generally one of subordinating other criteria to a profit calculus. Rather, decision processes manifest obvious traits of simple decision strategies.

One feature is the sequential consideration of alternatives. Farmers break decisions down and consider one aspect at a time in a lexicographic manner rather than in parallel, as in the example of the farmer above who switched from dairy cow to pig production.

Farmers satisfice. They set an aspiration level for how a given technology or strategy should perform and may pick the choice which meets this aspiration level without checking whether even better strategies exist. Aspiration levels often concern economic decision criteria. Economic objectives may be set at break-even point or as a minimum level of earnings. If that criterion is met, other criteria often determine the outcome. Decisions typically are not defined in terms of economic optima. This is particularly evident in purchases of equipment and strategic investment choices. This partly reflects motivation other than economic gain, but also uncertainty about exact outcomes. This suggests that aspiration levels serve not only to avoid trade-offs, but they also help decision-making when it is difficult to form precise expectations about outcomes.

Trial-and-error also represents a strategy for avoiding a direct trade-off. Instead of applying a synoptic comparison of different technologies, the farmer may simply decide by trying one of the options out on all or some of his fields. If the technology lives up to the promises by virtue of which it was chosen it passes the first test. But in many cases there are additional standards to meet: in the course of trying out the technology farmers may discover unforeseen side effects. For instance, some farmers tried and rejected the injection technology, when it turned out that the heavy machinery caused structural damage to their soils. But second alternatives may not be searched for or considered until the first alternative has been rejected. Likewise, a farmer may be offered a certain pesticide and try it out. If it performs satisfactorily, he will use it. Uncertainty seems to pave the way for this approach. When the consequences of different strategies are uncertain, trying out one strategy is one way to discover whether something works. This works particularly if it can be tried out without a full-scale investment. For instance, one farmer tried fertiliser injection in one crop and found that he had the worst yield in that crop ever. The following year he scaled down the trial to just part of the crop. Others also conduct parallel experiments to see what works.

Thus trial-and-error decisions also bear the marks of satisficing. One alternative is tried, and if it passes aspiration levels on important parameters it will be chosen. Clearly, the trial-and-error rule leads to sequential consideration of alternatives. This could be an efficient way to minimise uncertainty about outcome and to overcome the inability to make trade-offs. But it also means that the farmer may never consider the best alternative if his trial starts with an inferior one.

Attention and motivation

Finally, the study shows that a higher degree of motivation will increase the attention allocated to a decision or task. In other words, attention is selective. Granted, interview data are at best a flawed source of information on attention, as they can uncover only decisions to which farmers actually do pay attention. Nonetheless the descriptions of decision processes do offer some insights as to differential attention foci.

Firstly, the interviews highlight the role of motivation. According to North (see, for instance, Denzau and North, 2000), motivation would be determined by the degree to which the actor's identity is determined by the outcome of the decision and the degree to which the actor is confident that the actions taken affect the outcome. Additionally, a straightforward economic expectation would be that motivation is determined by the significance of the decision for the economic performance of the business. The study shows that all of these factors matter.

To take the economic argument first: the level of risk involved affects the time spent considering the decision. Hence, farmers spend more time considering large investments than regular management decisions about feeding strategies. Likewise, farmers say they pay more attention to pest control than to fertilising, because pest control is more important for the bottom line. This does not imply, however, that strategic decisions in the end are more optimal by an economic standard, because they are also more complex and require more trade-offs, as argued above. But risk differs not only among decision types but also among farmers. Established farmers generally, though not in all cases, appear to spend less time considering decisions than farmers just starting out. This may be due to the fact that established farmers tend not to risk everything when they make decisions, cf. the discussion of the endowment effect.

Furthermore, true to North's prediction the interviews also indicate that the importance of the task for the identity of the farmer affects the level of attention. This was also shown in the analysis of fertiliser decisions. Hence, farmers who see themselves as farmers first and foremost tend to pay much attention to those aspects that indicate professional ability, such as good-looking fields or high yield. Farmers who tend to see themselves as much as businessmen are more attentive to investment opportunities and to the bottom line. In fact, farmers differ as to how they choose to compare themselves with other farmers – whether they look at profit or whether they compare by yield.

Finally, the degree of uncertainty appeared to affect the level of attention. Farmers who emphasised the unpredictability of farming, particularly of field work, were less inclined to evaluate systematically their practices and to include such lessons into future decisions. On the other hand, farmers would pay more attention to areas that lend themselves to clear feedback of actions, such as feeding. While the general picture is that uncertainty leads to less precision and attention, some do take the opposite approach. They seek to compensate for uncertainty by using systematic measuring and data gathering.

In conclusion, then, motivation does seem to make a difference for the amount of attention to and the precision of the decision process, but the analysis does not allow for a firm conclusion as to how differential attention affects outcome.

Conclusion: decision processes

The previous chapter suggested that fertiliser decisions were in some measure affected by the fact that farmers might be pursuing non-profit goals more vigorously than they pursue profit, and that they could afford to do so because fertiliser decisions would not break their budgets. This chapter has analysed other decisions in order to examine whether different patterns hold for other types of decisions, including decisions involving large sums of money such as land acquisition.

The analysis has pointed to some differences. Farmers do appear more inclined to apply numbers and cost–benefit calculations to decisions regarding feeding or investing in equipment. The comparative analysis suggests some conditions under which farmers will employ more precise calculations in the decision process, and also how these more comprehensive analyses are used. It goes without saying that it must be possible to assign a monetary value to the alternatives; in the instances cited throughout it was possible to undertake simple budget-like calculations, because a money value could be assigned to some of the dimensions of each alternative. A further condition seems to be that the calculation includes only those few dimensions that can be measured in money values in a very simple way, i.e. with low transaction costs. Also, when decisions are characterised by greater uncertainty, the value of precise calculation may be doubted. Finally, the economic importance of the decision also does seem to make a difference. Whether or not the outcome of the calculation determines the choice of alternative depends on what other goals are at play and how they rank compared with the economic calculation.

But the analysis also suggests that some of the features characterising fertiliser decisions represent general characteristics of decision-making.

Firstly, the analysis indicates that some farmers are generally more focused on production goals than on economic goals. Again, this should be interpreted in relative terms. No farmer ignores economic considerations altogether, but some may make economically sub-optimal decisions because they are driven by professional considerations. They measure their success by how much milk is produced per cow or how many kilos of wheat per hectare. Furthermore, the analysis indicates that farmers may have several motivation structures, depending on the level of the decision. Lower-level management decisions may be subject to profit-optimising, whereas strategic decisions such as the future of the farm may be subject to lifestyle criteria as well – or vice versa.

Secondly, the analysis of use of information and generation of alternatives again shows that while farmers are inclined to select information based on their problem frame, there is an efficient dissemination of information throughout the agricultural community which does ensure a rather continuous updating of information. On the other hand, this tight-knit professional community also embodies a risk of setting off information cascades where particular solutions are considered, and considered first, because agenda setters make it a preferred option. And due to satisficing, the first alternative on the agenda may become the only alternative if it is considered adequate. A more parallel, or comprehensive, consideration of alternatives might have produced a better solution for the individual farmer. However, there is wide variation from farmer to farmer and from decision to decision in this respect.

Thirdly, the analysis of the actual decisions shows marked similarities to satisficing, understood in the broadest sense. Hence, farmers apply lexicographic choice strategies and make trade-offs in a qualitative manner. This is not to say that economic considerations do not figure in decisions; they do. More precisely, perhaps, they figure more frequently in daily management decisions than in overall business decisions. But economic objectives seem to be stated in terms of a baseline; hence, farmers check whether a particular choice can break even, and if so, the final decision is made based on other criteria. The economic goal, then, is set as an aspiration level.

The analysis indicates that such aspiration levels and qualitative trade-offs are more likely when trade-offs are difficult. This is in line with the bounded rationality framework. But the analysis indicates that aspiration levels are also a response to uncertainty. Farmers are less inclined to apply precise decision criteria and calculation when the outcome of a decision cannot be predicted with any degree of certainty.

Finally, the analysis indicates that motivation is important for the degree of attention farmers pay to a given decision or task. Economic significance does make a difference; farmers will generally consider carefully decisions with a large amount of money and risk involved. But attention is also affected by the importance of the task for the identity of the farmer. Hence, farmers who see themselves primarily as farmers are very attentive to production issues, while farmers who describe themselves also as businessmen keep a closer eye on the accounts or profit opportunities.

Importantly, uncertainty may play a role for attention; if the farmer does not think he can affect or predict the outcome of a decision he may be more likely to consider the decision quickly. This indicates that farmers do not necessarily operate at the margin of error; slack may arise if the decision does not involve large sums, but also if the farmer is preoccupied with goals other than profit or reneges on deliberation due to uncertainty.

Overall, however, the analysis also indicates that farmers intend to optimise. They just do not necessarily intend to optimise profit.

Environmental taxation in industry

The question is whether the patterns of decision-making found here are restricted to the agricultural sector. Are farms too unusual as a case for the findings to be applied to other sectors or types of actors? Farms are considerably smaller as organisations than most industrial businesses. This might simplify organisational structure but not necessarily decision-making, as the farmer cannot as easily compartmentalise; the farmer must integrate all aspects of the business. From a behavioural and cognitive perspective individual and organisational decision processes are quite comparable. And the analysis has shown that uncertainty about outcomes and conflicting objectives increase the inclination to use simple decision strategies; these are circumstances facing businesses regardless of size.

But to explore whether and how the findings might apply to other environmental policy fields, we will briefly consider how bounded rationality might play out in industry's response to energy and waste taxation, respectively, and review the available knowledge of the effect of these taxes in Scandinavia from this perspective. This draws on available evaluations of these taxes.

Energy taxes

All the Scandinavian countries have environmental tax systems targeting energy consumption and air pollution (Speck *et al.*, 2006). Taxes are levied on fuels, electricity and heat supply for industry and households as well as on fuels for transportation. Generally, the tax regimes consist of energy taxes, CO_2 taxes and sulphur taxes. The taxes aim to lower CO_2 emissions, which can be brought about both through lower energy consumption and through substitution with less carbon-intensive sources of fuel. Ex-post evaluations of carbon-energy taxes generally focus on taxes levied on industrial responses (Speck *et al.*, 2006).

Companies may respond to carbon-energy taxes in two ways, and indeed taxes aim for both. First, they may lower their energy consumption on an ongoing basis, changing procedures much in the way a household would be turning off lights or lowering temperatures. Secondly, they may invest in alternatives to carbon fuels and in energy-saving technology used in production as well as non-production related activities. The former change would resemble management decisions in farming, i.e. it relates to ongoing decisions and to routines. The latter represent discrete decisions such as investments in new equipment.

When it comes to a change in routines, the role of motivation for attention suggests that the response of a given company would depend on the importance of energy costs to the business. The larger the energy costs the more complete the response. By implication, if a company does not use much energy it would take a relatively large incentive, i.e. a high tax rate, for the incentive to break through and change routine decision-making. Such businesses may not even pay attention to a price change caused by taxes.

Another factor that may affect the impact of a tax on energy-consuming routines is whether the required behavioural changes interfere with professional norms for a job well done – as lower fertiliser levels interfere with the farmer's quest for beautiful, high-yielding fields. This cannot be ascertained independently of the context, i.e. the particular business sector or process, but conceivably many types of businesses could reduce energy-consuming habits without compromising the quality of their core activities. As for households, however, energy consumption may be closely related to lifestyle issues. In fact, transportation has proven to be quite price inelastic (Speck *et al.*, 2006), indicating precisely that households do not respond smoothly to a change in fuel prices by driving less.

Some changes in energy consumption require investments in new equipment. Whether or not such a decision is even entertained would again depend on the size of the incentive relative to the impact of energy consumption in the business. But once a business considers such investments, the decision might take on the traditional features of a marginal utility calculation. The question is whether the investment would conflict with other objectives, in which case the economic incentive might be subordinated to other objectives.

The effect of tax incentives on energy use and CO_2 emissions
A review of the carbon-energy taxation offers some insight into responses. Generally, the taxes implemented have been effective. Across countries and sectors, growth-adjusted energy use and CO_2 emissions have declined since the taxes were introduced (Speck *et al.*, 2006). But evaluations also show indications that industries have not responded as efficiently as intended. Typically, reductions in CO_2 emissions directly attributable to carbon-energy taxation are in the order of 2–3 per cent for the decade, although these estimates vary. With total emission reductions of up to around 25 per cent (Denmark) and 19 per cent (Sweden), tax incentives account for a relatively small share of the effect. Yet Enevoldsen (2005) in a comprehensive and

sophisticated analysis finds that the Danish energy tax regime caused a reduction of as much as 9–11 per cent in CO_2 emissions between 1990 and 2000. However, major change did not begin until 1996, when the tax rate was tripled (Enevoldsen, 2005). Prior to that, the tax incentive was too weak to cause reductions in energy use. Several studies across the Nordic countries conclude that the first tax regimes were too low to prompt energy savings. It did not help that large shares of energy use were spared from the full burden of taxation due to refund schemes for energy-intensive companies. Furthermore, the tax regimes were seen as too complicated with too many differentiations to have the proper incentive effect.

This could be interpreted as the tax not being large enough to affect economic optimum calculations and therefore optimising businesses not having really been motivated to adjust energy consumption to any great extent; but it could also fit with the bounded rationality prediction that the economic incentive must be large enough to gain attention and prompt changes in routines, and this could generate a greater incentive than would be prompted by a strict calculation of marginal utility or economic modelling.

The review also shows that tax incentives work through their attention-drawing function as much as through their price signal. Hence, some studies found that taxes focus industry's *attention* on the cost-effectiveness of environmental abatement and energy savings, regardless of the pre-tax cost-effectiveness of abatement (ECON, 1997, cited in Speck *et al.*, 2006). Taxes provide the jolt to cut slack.

These evaluations do not offer precise enough data to assess whether industries responded in an economically optimal manner; typically policy objectives are not defined in precise figures against which responses can be measured. But the response does offer glimpses of bounded rationality. Hence, it took a rather large and sudden increase in tax rates to prompt a response, and some companies in interview studies indicated that they did not necessarily respond to the tax in terms of how it affected their marginal cost considerations, but in a more qualitative manner, focusing attention on energy savings.

Waste taxation
A study of the Danish waste taxation scheme also shows traits that fit with some aspects of boundedly rational decision processes.

The tax was introduced in 1987 in order to curb generation of waste and increase recycling. Originally the waste tax was 40 DKK per tonne, but throughout the 1990s taxes were increased and differentiated so that by 1996, at the time of evaluation, rates were DKK 195 for landfill and DKK 160 per tonne of waste delivered for incineration (Andersen, 2000b).

The tax was to some extent successful, but not entirely in the way foreseen. The volume of waste was reduced by 26 per cent by 1996, but this reduction reflected an 8 per cent *increase* in waste from commerce and industry, while most of the reduction involved the heavier components of household waste as well as construction waste and mixed waste.

Follow-up interviews showed that only waste-intensive companies, including construction companies, paid attention to the tax. And indeed the tax had the greatest impact on these businesses. For other companies, the incentive was not sufficient to cut through routines and standard operating procedures (Andersen, 2000c). Specifically, the authors point to the organisational structure of companies as a barrier, as waste bills were paid by office workers in a routine manner, while those who were responsible for handling the waste were not exposed to the tax incentive. Such a finding is in line with behavioural studies of organisations, which show that organisational structure determines the distribution of attention and inattention. It also mirrors one of the findings of farmers' decision-making: the possibility for feedback is a conditioning factor in how decision-makers integrate economic incentives into their decisions. Those who handle waste were not seeing the costs involved or the potential savings and therefore did not pay attention to its minimisation.

9
Conclusion: money *also* matters

A story from one of the interviews, partly recounted in the previous chapter, aptly sums up one conclusion to this analysis on decision-making among farmers.

It is the story of one of the dairy farmers, who had planned his fertiliser allocation in order to get the highest possible yields in maize, because maize was an important source of feed for his cows. And high quality feed was one of the most important tools in his effort to increase milk production in his cows. He was successful; to his explicit satisfaction, maize yields and milk production both increased considerably. But there was a catch. Cows were actually producing more milk than allowed under his milk quota. As a consequence, he bought a larger milk quota. The reasoning was not so much that he needed the earnings from the milk, because these were probably less than the cost of the quota, but that he would be able to retain the same number of cows in his herd.

The point is not that this farmer does not optimise, but that he appears to optimise on production as much as or more than on profit. Economic incentives matter, but farmers are professionals driven also by professional standards of merit and demerit – although to varying degrees and with different interpretations. The story also indicates that decision-makers may optimise on each area of operation, yet the end result may not be economically optimal. As such, the example matches Cyert and March's behavioural theory of the firm (1992), which showed that organisations tend to lose sight of the overall objectives as each department optimises according to its own goals. It is possible that a detailed calculation of the final outcome of all of the decisions would have turned out to have been economically optimal, but the farmer above did not undertake detailed calculation and instead reasoned with a mixture of calculation and qualitative considerations. The last point of the story then is that much decision-making relies on simple decision rules, which may or may not lead to optimal outcomes.

This concluding chapter summarises and discusses the findings of the study of farmers' decision-making and assesses the implications for the rational model of behaviour and for incentive-based public policies.

Explaining fertiliser behaviour

The study has examined whether deviation from economically optimal norms is caused by the interaction of a complex decision environment and boundedly rational, or simple, decision processes. Each of these will be examined in turn.

Decision environment

The claim in the bounded rationality framework is that deviations from optimal decisions are more likely to occur in a complex decision context. Complexity is defined by the character of the problem itself, by the abundance and fluidity of information, by uncertainty about outcomes of decisions, and by multiple and conflicting goals; and the effect of these circumstances is amplified when decisions are made under pressure of time. The point in terms of information is that information overload is at least as threatening to achieving fully rational decisions as is a lack of information. Based on the variables available in the LOOP database, complexity was thus defined by farm size, as farm size might increase the complexity of the task itself as well as the general time pressure; and by farm category, as crop farms and livestock farms differ with regard to their focus on field work, and perhaps also with regard to conflicts between goals. Finally, manure was seen as a complicating factor as farmers may be more uncertain about the effect of manure than about the effect of artificial fertilisers.

The analysis only partially substantiated the expectation that complex circumstances explain deviations from optimal behaviour. Farms with a large amount of manure per hectare are indeed more likely to over-fertilise. This is consistent with an interpretation of uncertainty. Farmers are uncertain about the fertiliser effects of manure and this may cause them to apply larger amounts of manure on some fields to be sure to get the highest yield possible.

However, neither of the other indicators of complexity, size or farm category, appear to explain why farmers deviate from fertiliser norms. Size is in any case an ambiguous variable as size may also connote more employees or the resources to hire external help, both of which could pull towards simplification. Hence, the fact that size does not show the predicted effect is not entirely damaging to the framework. It is, however, more surprising that farm categories do not vary in their tendency to deviate. The fact that crop farmers specialise in field work, that their incomes depend on field work, and that they do not have to use animal manure all point in the same direction: crop farmers would pay more attention to fertilising, and they would be experts in this area. Likewise, differences in the labour intensity of different types of livestock production suggest that farm category might also differ in relation to deviation from optimal norms. But the analysis showed that farm categories do not differ at statistically significant levels – or rather it shows that the extent to which they differ is largely explained by differences in the amount of manure.

The analysis of decision processes did not specifically address the effect of complexity; the small number of interview subjects does not allow for a study of systematic variation. Yet a few insights from the interview analysis may provide some clues as to how to interpret the mostly negative findings regarding variation in decision environments. By and large this part of the study confirms that fertiliser practices do not vary by farm size or by farm category. Because fertiliser management is planned once a year, time constraints are not generally considered a major obstacle for the planning process; this would serve to reduce the importance of complexity differentials. Moreover, the regulatory norms and computer management tools tend to standardise the overall approach to fertiliser management, which cuts across both size and farm category. Finally, it turned out that livestock farmers are generally as interested in field work as are crop farmers. Hence, in this regard, the analysis suggests that there is no attention differential between different categories of farmers.

Thus, while farmers do differ in their tendencies to deviate from fertiliser norms, different degrees of complexity in the decision environment do not provide a strong explanation for these differences, with the important exception that differences in amounts of manure do seem to explain much over-fertilisation.

Institutional change

As for the effect of changes in the institutional context, the analysis does show oscillating adaptation to the fertiliser norms, particularly during the mid-1990s when regulatory changes were frequent. This is consistent with the expectation that agents update information disproportionately and react with delay to changes. It is particularly interesting that while farmers did react to the introduction of the binding norms the first year, they appear to have been slower to adapt to the requirement to adjust fertiliser plans to the spring update of the fertiliser norms. The binding norms constituted a major regulatory change, while the regulation requiring the spring update represented a smaller change, comparatively speaking. It is possible that this regulatory change became lost, so to speak, in the many regulatory changes on fertiliser management that came into effect during these years.

Decision processes

Decision processes represent another source of deviation from optimal behaviour in bounded rationality. The study therefore examined whether fertiliser management reflected simple decision processes. This implies that farmers would not necessarily subordinate all decisions to a profit-maximising objective, that objectives would generally be stated in terms of aspiration levels, i.e. acceptable outcomes. Hence, the final choice would reflect a qualitative trade-off among goals, prioritising one over the other. Information search and evaluation would be selective and would be guided by simple decision rules as well as by professional or social norms.

All of these traits were evident in fertiliser decisions, but so were traits of the comprehensive decision processes embedded in the economic model. The material does not allow for a dichotomisation of farmers by decision mode, but indicates instead various intermediate forms. Generally, however, the decision processes do resemble satisficing in the broadest sense of the concept.

Thus, farmers do state several objectives for their fertiliser management, including high yields, nice-looking fields and low costs. But the descriptive accounts of fertiliser decisions indicate that each tends to emphasise one objective over another, and more to the point that he does so in a qualitative manner. Some are more likely to pay attention to yield, i.e. they appear to optimise on production; a few focus on cost-cutting and optimal use of resources, and some keep their eye on the bottom line, that is they profit optimise. The difference among farmers lies in the relative weighting of these objectives. Neo-classical economics predicts that all would profit-optimise.

One way that farmers make trade-offs among goals is to set aspiration levels; hence, the objective may be stated as a yield or economic surplus at least as high as last year's or at least on a par with comparable farmers. If a farmer is keen to achieve high yields, he may consider whether the costs are prohibitive, but he may not take on the marginal calculation of comparing income from extra yield to the costs incurred in order to bring about that extra unit of yield.

The use of simple decision heuristics is widespread, both in the use of information as well as in the manner in which the actual choice comes about. As already indicated, trade-offs are made in a lexicographic manner, i.e. considering one aspect at a time; fertiliser levels are established using the fertiliser norms as an anchor value or using past levels in the same manner; farmers use visual cues to evaluate the need for adjustments, and they have professional norms such as density and uniform colour for how to judge the quality of their fertiliser management. The ubiquitous references to these rules suggest that they are professionally learned rules that have been passed on through education, through the advisory services and through peer networks.

Overall, the analysis indicates that decision processes do bear the marks of simple decision modes. The question is whether these decision processes can explain deviation from optimal fertiliser norms. Answering this question is complicated by the fact that the interviews were conducted at a time when the fertiliser norms were below the economic optimum, but the analysis does suggest several elements of an answer. Firstly, the simple decision mode does *not* result from a lack of attention to fertiliser management. In fact, the farmers interviewed seem to put considerable effort into fertilising, although of course there is variation. But deviations from norms do not reflect a lack of attention to norms. Secondly, deviation from norms occurs because some farmers consider the fertiliser norms in relation to physical optima rather than in relation to economic optima. Thirdly, farmers also deviate from fertiliser norms because they consider the norms to be imprecise in concrete contexts, or simply inadequate. This means that the character of decision processes does not provide a strong explanation for *why* farmers deviate from fertiliser norms.

This said, some farmers do use simple decision mechanisms and rather intuitive decision strategies in their decisions to reallocate fertiliser, which may explain some deviation from optimal levels. Specific practices appear to be shaped in large measure by professional routines about how to judge fertiliser needs, and how and when to adjust norms. This suggests also that decisions are driven by personal or social norms, which hold that the quality of fertiliser and, by extension, the professional proficiency of the farmer, may be judged among other things by the look of his fields. These norms compete with the regulatory norms of proper fertiliser levels, and farmers have to negotiate these different sets of norms.

In that sense, decision processes do contribute to an explanation of the fertiliser patterns seen.

Motivation

The study also analysed the role of motivation as a catalyst for how decisions transpire, i.e. whether a simple or comprehensive decision process is applied. The analysis does not substantiate the expectation that the relative economic importance of fertiliser decisions leads to different degrees of motivation, at least not when comparing livestock and crop farmers, where the latter presumably depend more on field work for their income. Many livestock farmers appear to put just as much effort into fertilising as do crop farmers. But generally the farmers answer in quite imprecise terms when asked about the economic importance of fertiliser decisions. One interpretation would be that fertiliser generally does not cost enough to really affect the bottom line; hence, these decisions are not important economically, although several farmers point out that fertiliser has become more expensive in recent years.

Instead, the analysis suggests that the degree of motivation is affected by how important the fertiliser task is for the decision-maker's sense of identity. Field work seems to be an integral part of being a farmer, and quality fertilising, reflected in high yields and good-looking fields, is a hallmark of craftsmanship.

This would explain why farmers do pay attention to fertilisation even if economically it does not make a great difference in terms of earnings. But this also reveals a paradox. It appears that deviation from norms actually indicates a high degree of attention to fertilisation, as deviation implies that farmers are trying to optimise their fertiliser quota. This contradicts the bounded rationality notion of the role of attention, which would predict more deviation with a low level of attention. The explanation again lies with motivation, but, in this instance, with the substance of motivation. Farmers are motivated not only by profit, as stated, but also by professional pride.

Optimising, but not necessarily profit-optimising
The study of fertiliser behaviour indicates that farmers intend to optimise and that they generally pay considerable attention to fertiliser management. But the analysis suggests also that farmers do not necessarily optimise economically. Contrary to theoretical expectations, deviations from optimal management cannot be explained by the decision context as measured by the indicators size and farm category. However, the analysis does offer uncertainty as a plausible explanation for deviation from optimal fertiliser levels.

But two other factors serve to explain deviations. One is that (some) farmers are motivated by achieving high physical yields and focus more on this than on the economic outcome of fertiliser management. This is perhaps underscored by the difficulty, and hence the inherent uncertainty, of forecasting with any precision the economic outcome of such decisions. But it is also possible that physical yield takes precedence only as long as fertiliser decisions have relatively little economic consequence for the overall economic yield of the farm. Motivation, then, appears to be an important determinant of decisions. Motivation relates both to what decision-makers are motivated by, but also to the degree of motivation.

The other explanatory factor is that farmers use a set of simplifying decision rules which seem to reflect standard operating procedures of the agricultural profession. These rules specify how to judge the need for fertiliser and thus serve as a corrective to fertiliser norms. But they are not precision tools; neither are the indicators by which farmers evaluate the outcome of fertiliser decisions. But fertiliser norms and decision rules also serve to keep deviations from norms within relatively narrow margins. This may have helped to constrain the effect of circumstances.

Alternative interpretations of the findings

Some might argue that farmers do indeed optimise fertiliser management. A previous study indicated that farmers may have refrained from fertilising far-lying fields because they considered the costs of transporting manure, whereas the fertiliser norms do not include this cost (Miljøstyrelsen, 1999). The interview study does not support such an interpretation. Farmers generally stated that they needed to use all of their fertiliser and did not consider the cost of transporting manure. A few indicated that transportation cost did affect how they allocated manure and artificial fertilisers, respectively, but transportation cost did not affect whether a field received fertiliser or not. The LOOP data showed that some farmers did not use their entire fertiliser quota, which raises the question as to whether these farmers do consider transportation costs. While the data do not allow for a conclusion on this issue, the fact is that these farmers have to allocate their manure, which is more expensive to spread, while they forgo artificial fertilisers, which are cheaper to transport. This would not be strong evidence for a transportation cost argument, therefore.

Another argument is that farmers do in fact optimise, because fertiliser norms are too crude and hence not optimal in the specific context. This is a weighty argument, but as outlined, farmers arrive at these corrected fertiliser levels by way of simplifying decision rules; hence, it is not possible to ascertain whether these new levels are indeed optimal. Farmers typically have not made the calculations. Hence, it does not seem to affect decisions to deviate from norms whether such reallocation in fact does improve the economic outcome of field work.

On a different level one might object that a realistic economic model of rationality would not expect farmers to optimise on every single decision on the farm; rather, it would expect farmers to optimise profit and therefore to focus on those decisions or areas of operation that carry the greatest economic weight. The analysis shows quite clearly that farmers do invest time and attention in the area of fertilising, and that they do intend to optimise. So this objection is less relevant here. In fact, one might argue that farmers would pay less attention to fertiliser practices if they kept a close eye on the bottom line, but professional satisfaction seems to compete with economic incentives.

Evidence of simple decision processes: when and how

This study contributes to a deeper understanding of decision processes, particularly when and how simple decision mechanisms play out. These findings also have implications for the use of incentive-based public policies.

Farmers were asked how they go about other types of decisions, distinguishing between frequent management decisions such as pest control and decisions related to livestock, and more infrequent decisions of greater economic magnitude.

Some of the features found in fertiliser decisions seem to apply more generally to farmers' decision processes. There are indications that farmers deal with objectives in a sequential manner, that they pay selective attention to information, that they consider decision alternatives one at a time rather than in parallel, that they set aspiration levels and do so by comparing their performance to that of previous years or to their peers, and that trade-offs are typically carried out in a qualitative manner. Economic criteria are important but not necessarily dominant, and perhaps less so than assumed in neo-classical models.

However, the analysis also exposes variations among different types of decisions, which may be explored for a more precise understanding of decision processes.

Management decisions such as pest control or feeding strategies appear to be subject to economic calculation more often than other decisions. Perhaps more importantly, these decisions are also evaluated with greater precision.

Purchases of equipment are typically subject to some level of comprehensive decision process, assessing various criteria against each other, but economic criteria do not necessarily determine the final choice. These purchases are often undertaken when the farmer has some room in the budget, i.e. if it has been a good year, which may explain why features such as comfort or capacity may sometimes lead farmers to spend more than they had set as a target in the first place. Likewise, *land acquisition or business development* decisions typically imply a lengthy consideration phase, in which the farmer assesses different criteria against each other in a comprehensive manner. But the actual choice often appears to be made quite suddenly, in some cases almost intuitively. Calculations are undertaken in the consideration phase, and these calculations do provide a foundation for the decision in the sense that farmers ask whether the acquisition or investment will break even or not, not necessarily whether it will improve their earnings or profit margin. But if this criterion is fulfilled, farmers may decide by criteria such as lifestyle, working conditions, or perceptions of what it takes to ensure a healthy farm in the long run. However, well-established farmers appear more risk-averse than more newly established farmers. Established farmers describe more of an incremental strategy whereby they are willing to risk an amount that constitutes a surplus or a reserve. This confirms many experimental studies of risk behaviour.

Based on these descriptions, it is possible to draw up some specifications regarding decision processes. Firstly, one may draw the rather obvious conclusion that in order to make precise calculations, figures must be available. Hence, it is possible to calculate cost and benefits of feeding strategies with some degree of precision. This may also explain why Jacobsen (1994) found that farmers approximated the fully rational ideal in purchasing decisions on fertiliser, foodstuffs, etc. Prices are available; they provide an anchor from which the farmer can or cannot try to bargain, and the farmer knows how to calculate in a simple way how these costs will figure into his overall economic picture. Secondly, it appears to be important that feedback is more immediate in these decision areas. Farmers know quite quickly how livestock respond to new feeding strategies, and they can also tell whether their pest control is effective. Feedback from fertiliser decisions is less clear. So, when feedback is immediate and precise, uncertainty is reduced and farmers appear more inclined to apply precise decision processes as well. This is in line also with Öhlmér's study, which showed that farmers were more likely to evaluate their decisions ex-post if the decision outcome could still be influenced (Öhlmér *et al.*, 1998).

Thirdly, when decisions have considerable economic reach, decision-makers do attempt a comprehensive decision strategy. But the difficulty of making trade-offs among different criteria in a quantitative manner and the effect of uncertainty about decision outcomes tend to lead to satisficing or lexicographic decision strategies, i.e. alternatives are assessed against aspiration levels, trade-offs are made in a qualitative manner and the choice is one that is acceptable on the most important parameters, but not necessarily economically optimal.

Finally, this study indicates that farmers typically do juggle different types of objectives. Economic criteria seem to weigh more into decisions when economic indicators are readily available, and when decisions may threaten the economic safety of the farm. When that is not the case, other types of motivation, in this case professional satisfaction, appear to drive decisions to a considerable degree.

Relevance of the study

The question is whether insights about farmers' decision processes bear any relevance to other cases. Farms are businesses. Like any other business enterprise they are expected to optimise profits. In economic terms they may be fairly large businesses, but as organisations they are quite small. Hence, in this respect they most resemble small businesses. This might simplify organisational structure but not necessarily decision-making, as the farmer cannot as easily compartmentalise; the farmer must integrate all aspects of the business. From a behavioural and cognitive perspective individual and organisational decision processes are quite comparable. And the analysis has shown that uncertainty about outcomes and conflicting objectives increase the inclination to use simple decision strategies; these are circumstances facing businesses regardless of size.

At the same time, more than most other types of business, perhaps, farming is a lifestyle. Farmers live where they work, although this is also beginning to change, particularly with large pig farms. But generally farms do differ from other businesses in this respect. While a farmer may include lifestyle considerations in his strategic decisions, a publicly owned company may apply economic criteria to a greater extent. Yet this applies primarily to strategic decisions; when it comes to management decisions farmers are not necessarily that different from other businesses.

Hence, other types of businesses are also run and manned by professionals, and the study indicates that professional satisfaction is an important driver of decisions. Professionalism also shows through in the decision rules farmers apply, which seem to be learned and passed on through the agricultural community. This implies that the findings of this analysis are relevant at least for businesses and organisations in which professionals constitute a central group of employees, including public bureaucracies.

Implications for theory development and economic modelling

The analysis indicates that bounded rationality in the form of simplifying decision mechanisms is evident outside the laboratories of cognitive psychologists and behavioural economists. It suggests furthermore that these simple decision mechanisms are quite common; also in large-scale decisions of some economic importance to the decision-maker. These mechanisms appear more likely to come into play when there is a lack of precise information or some aspects of a decision cannot easily be quantified. But uncertainty about the outcomes of decisions also seems to play an important role. Contrary to neo-classical economic theory, which assumes that decision-makers apply probability rules to determine the likelihood of various outcomes, the decision processes studied here suggest rather that decision-makers will apply a qualitative decision mode and decide by standard rules rather than by expected outcomes, when uncertainty is pronounced.

The analysis also suggests that the role of economic motivation in rational actor theory could be modified. Even businesses may pursue objectives other than or in addition to profit. As one farmer put it, facetiously perhaps, 'money *also* matters', but economic considerations do not necessarily constitute the one overarching principle to which all other criteria are subordinated. Instead, economic criteria often take the form of an aspiration level, for instance stated in terms of break-even, or a minimum level, or for expenses not exceeding a certain level. Rational choice theorists and economists as well would argue that rational theories allow for this. Choices based on criteria other than profit simply reflect different preference structures. So-called thin rational models make no assumptions about agents' preferences and therefore may easily accommodate lifestyle-based preferences or the professional satisfaction of growing a strong crop. But this reverts to the claim of Simon and other scholars in the bounded rationality tradition, who insist that objectives must be established empirically. Besides, the theoretical insight of thin-rational theory has yet to spill over into economic modelling of the firm, which still tends to assume profit optimisation. Some behavioural economists have begun to model firms with varied preferences (Foss, 2001a). The findings of the present study indicate the merit of developing such models. However, it also indicates the difficulty of modelling bounded rationality, when boundedly rational outcomes cannot be uniquely identified.

Scholars within the rational choice tradition, and particularly within economics, may also argue that individual level biases or deviations from optimal behaviour may not matter because errors will cancel each other out or constitute random error at the aggregate level. But as the interviews indicated, it is just as likely that reasoning errors or biases will be amplified at the aggregate level due to information cascades, i.e. a general tendency to follow social rules or cues. This may happen both in the marketplace and in organisations.

Institutions can play into decision-making in two ways. Appropriately designed, institutions may narrow the margin of error; the fertiliser norms may serve as an example of this. But institutions, such as ill-adaptive decision rules or social norms, may set off a motion in the direction away from economically optimal behaviour (Fehr and Tyran, 2005).

As for the bounded rationality perspective, the analysis suggests that the model may be made more precise by distinguishing between different types of decisions, based on availability of precise information as well as the level of uncertainty involved. But it also suggests distinguishing between types of actors, be it individuals, businesses or organisations, defined by likely motivation structures and potential professional decision rules. This analysis has demonstrated the difficulty of conducting precise testing of decision processes, because even simple decision mechanisms can lead to optimal decisions, but it has also proved the value of studying decision processes and assessing them against a rational standard.

Implications for the use of incentive-based policies

Fertiliser regulation is not an example of market-based regulation, quite the contrary. But the case nonetheless offers insight into economic incentives to the extent that the fertiliser norms indicate at least roughly the level of fertiliser that an economically optimising farmer would settle on with or without norms.

The analysis does indicate that farmers are responsive to economic incentives, but perhaps to a lesser degree than assumed in neo-classical environmental economics. Environmental economic models do not assume that everyone is equally responsive to economic incentives, but that the differences stem from different cost functions with regard to abatement costs. Hence, those who can reduce pollution at the lowest marginal cost will respond more to the incentives.

But the study of farmers suggests another source of differences in response: some actors optimise on criteria other than profit. This implies that farmers would be less responsive to economic incentives, such as an environmental tax on nitrogen. In fact, pesticide taxes have been much less effective than predicted by ex-ante evaluations which claimed that farmers could reduce the use of pesticide without noticeable economic losses (Christensen *et al.*, 2007).

It is quite conceivable, then, that incentive-based policies would be less effective in any organisation or setting in which motivations other than economic values have a prominent hold, such as organisations with a high share of professionals. In fact, the findings here match studies of professionals, for instance in the medical sector. These have shown that professional norms, where such exist, regulate behaviour more strongly than economic incentives (Goodrick and Salancik, 1996; Andersen and

Blegvad, 2002). Where such norms do not exist, economic incentives are more likely to work as predicted by economic theory.

Furthermore, individual and organisational decision processes may interfere with seamless adaptation to economic incentives. For behavioural changes which require changes in routines, competition for attention will affect the response to incentives, as will the ease with which the incentive can be integrated into the economic calculations. Thus it may not be enough that the costs arising from an environmental tax can be calculated if a change in behaviour requires changes in processes which cannot as easily be assessed economically. Where incentive policies aim to promote investments in new technologies, the study indicates that the effect of the incentive will depend in part on the certainty with which the costs and benefits can be ascertained and, again, on potentially conflicting policy goals.

Both factors imply that economic incentives in order to bring about a targeted effect may have to be larger than a marginal economic calculation would suggest. Large economic incentives may overcome attention deficits, and they diminish the importance of conflicting goals as the economic importance of the decision increases.

However, if economic incentives must be set at a rate much higher than economically optimal considerations dictate, the economic incentive approach, which usually comes out as the most cost-effective regulation form in comparative analyses, may lose at least some of its comparative edge over command-and-control regulation. However, if actors respond less to the incentive than anticipated, the cost per reduced unit of pollution increases.

It is conceivable that other market-based instruments would work differently. Emission trading schemes make for quite visible price signals, as emission permits literally must be bought. This system differs somewhat from environmental taxation, where the tax is an integral part of the price of an input factor. Hence, a trading scheme may force attention on the price mechanism more effectively. It might also make clearer the trade-off between higher production and emissions on the one side and costs on the other. Thus, the incentive structure in a trading scheme could be more compatible with attention deficits and different motivation structures. As for farmers, the answer may be positive with regard to the attention factor. But the story which introduces this chapter would seem to indicate that motivation is more important. The milk quota could be likened to an emission quota, and as the story indicates, even a high price on this production quota does not necessarily force economic criteria to the forefront of the farmers' decision criteria.

Thus, choice and design of incentive-based policies must build on a proper understanding of the particular motivation structures of those who are to respond to the incentive. In some cases, this may imply that the incentive needs to be designed in accordance with broader motivations than economic incentives; in other cases it may mean that different policies altogether are better. This requires consideration of the character of the targeted group rather than blanket approaches.

Furthermore, policy preparation might also benefit from knowledge of the decision processes and the decision rules applied by different actors in relevant decision domains. It is possible to adapt the incentive to these, but also to seek to shape decision rules such as professional norms through education systems and professional organisations. In fact, the fertiliser norms also serve in this capacity. They provide an anchoring value, which has ensured smaller deviation from optimal behaviour.

Appendix
List of features of the farmers interviewed for the qualitative analysis

IP no.	Farm category	Size	Farmer's age and no. of years of ownership
1	Crop production	Cultivates 236 ha, owns 263 ha	Age 57 Farmed or owned since 1971, family farm
2	Feeding pigs	6,000 pigs 168 ha	Age 48 Leased or owned since 1983
3	Dairy	150 LU 144 ha	Age 34 Gradual takeover of farm since 1998
4	Feeding pigs Cattle	70 LU pigs 14 LU cattle 70 ha	Age 39 Owned since 1998, family farm
5	Dairy	27 LU 50 ha, owns 24 ha	Age 40 Owned since 1993
6	Feeding pigs Mink	220 LU pigs; 30 LU mink 225 ha	Age 50 Owned since 1970s Married couple, ages 65 and 60
7	Dairy	42 yearlings 33 ha	Owned since 1969, family farm
8	Feeding pigs	5,000 pigs; 35 horses (20 LU) 110 ha, owns 95 ha	Age mid-50s Gradual takeover of family farm between 1975 and 1982
9	Dairy	165 LU 100 ha	Age 51 Owned since 1981

IP no.	Farm category	Size	Farmer's age and no. of years of ownership
10	Pigs	250 sows 70 ha	Age 54 Owned since 1977, bought from relatives
11	Dairy	About 100 dairy cows and heifers 85 ha	Age 47 Owned since 1987, family farm
12	Pigs	120 sows with annual production of 2,600 feeding pigs 100 ha, owns 78 ha	Age 39 Owned since 1991, family farm
13	Feeding pigs	7,500 pigs 235 ha, owns 185 ha; and 70 ha of forest	Age 41 Owned since 1993
14	Dairy cattle	160 dairy cows (120 LU) 94 ha, owns 61 ha	Age 45 Owned since 1988
15	Pigs (mostly handled by employee) Crop production	160 sows, producing 3,000 feeding pigs 200 ha	Age 41 Leased or owned since 1983
16	Crop production Various investments	400 ha, owns 347 ha	Age 60 Owned since 1968
17	Mink Crop production	600 ha, owns 50 ha	Age 44 Farmer since 1988, bought farm in 1999
18	Pigs	180 sows (130 LU) 87 ha	Age 37 Co-owns with father since 1998
19	Crop production Part-time	50 ha	Age 37 Owned since 1993, family farm
20	Pigs	115 sows 350 ha, owns 160 ha with partner; rest leased	Age 54 Partnership, farmer since 1973

Notes: LU= livestock units; ha= hectare. 'Family farm' means that the farmer is at least second generation on the farm.

References

Agosto, Denise E. (2002). 'Bounded rationality and satisficing in young people's we-based decision making', *Journal of the American Society for Information Science and Technology*, 53116–27.

Agresti, Alan and Finlay, Barbara (1997). *Statistical Methods for the Social Sciences*. Upper Saddle River: Prentice Hall.

Alchian, Armen A. (1950). 'Uncertainty, evolution and economic theory', *Journal of Political Economy*, 58 (3), 211–221.

Andersen, Hans E., Berg, Peter, Blicher-Mathiesen, Gitte, Jensen, Pia G., Kronvang, Brian and Schwærter, Rikke C. (1994). 'Landover-vågningsoplande', *Vandmiljøplanens Overvågningsprogram 1993*. Danmarks Miljøunder-søgelser, Faglig Rapport fra DMU Nr. 120.

Andersen, J.M. *et al.* (2003). *Vandmiljø 2003. Tilstand og Udvikling – Faglig Sammenfatning*. Faglig Rapport fra DMU Nr. 471.

Andersen, J.M. *et al.* (2004). *Aquatic Environment 2003. State and Trends – Technical Summary*. NERI Technical Report No. 500. National Environmental Research Institute. Copenhagen: Ministry of the Environment.

Andersen, J.M. *et al.* (2005). *Aquatic Environment 2004. State and Trends – Technical Summary*. NERI Technical Report No. 561. National Environmental Research Institute. Copenhagen: Ministry of the Environment.

Andersen, Lotte Bøgh (2005). *Offentligt Ansattes Strategier*. Ph.d.-afhandling ved institut for statskundskab. Aarhus: Politica.

Andersen, Lotte Bøgh and Blegvad, M. (2002). *Private or Public Service Provision? Economic and Professional Incentives in Danish Dental Care for Children*. Aarhus: Department of Political Science, University of Aarhus.

Andersen, Mikael Skou (2000a). 'Designing and introducing green taxes: institutional dimensions', in M.S. Andersen and R. Sprenger (eds),

Market-based Instruments for Environmental Management. Cheltenham: Edward Elgar.

Andersen, Mikael Skou (2000b). The Danish waste tax: the role of institutions for the implementation and effectiveness of economic instruments', in M.S. Andersen and R. Sprenger (eds), Market-based Instruments for Environmental Management. Cheltenham: Edward Elgar.

Andersen, Mikael Skou (2000c). 'Effektiviteten af grønne afgifter og betydningen af institutioner', in *Stok eller Gulerod. Virkemidler i Miljøpolitikken.* Nyhedsbrev for Det Strategiske Miljøforskning-sprogram, Nr. 45.

Andersen, Mikael Skou and Hansen, Michael W. (1991). *Vandmiljøplanen: Fra Forhandling til Symbol.* Harlev: Niche.

Anker, Helle T. (1996). *Miljøretlig Regulering på Landbrugsområdet – Særligt om Handlingsplaner og Konsekvensvurderinger.* København: Jurist – og Øko-nomforbundets Forlag.

Arnott, David (2006). 'Cognitive biases and decision support systems development: a design science approach', *Information Systems Journal*, 16, 55–78.

Arrow, Kenneth (1986). 'Rationality of self and others in an economic system', *The Journal of Business*, 59 (4, 2): *The Behavioural Foundations of Economic Theory* S385–399.

Atkinson, Paul, Coffey, Amanda and Delamont, Sara (2003). *Key Themes in Qualitative Research – Continuities and Change.* Walnut Creek: Altamira Press.

Babbie, Earl (1989). *The Practice of Social Research.* Belmont: Wadsworth Publishing Co.

Baumgartner, Frank R. and Jones, Bryan D. (1993). *Agendas and Instability in American Politics.* Chicago: University of Chicago Press.

Becker, Gary (1976). 'The economic approach to human behavior', reprinted in Jon Elster (ed.) (1986), *Rational Choice.* New York: New York University Press.

Begg, David, Fischer, S. and Dornbusch, R. (1984). *Economics.* Maidenhead: McGraw-Hill Book Company.

Bendor, Jonathan (2001). 'Bounded rationality', in *International Encyclopedia of the Social and Behavioral Sciences.* Elsevier Science Ltd. Available at: www.sciencedirect.com (accessed 3 May 2009).

Bendor, Jonathan (2003). 'Herbert A. Simon: political scientist', in *Annual Review of Political Science*, 6, 433–471.

Bettman, James, Luce, Mary Frances and Payne, John (1998). 'Constructive consumer choice processes', *The Journal of Consumer Research*, 25 (3), 187–217.

Bjørner, Thomas Bue *et al.* (2002). *The Effect of the Nordic Swan Label on Consumers' Choice.* Copenhagen: AKF-forlaget.

Borgers, Tilman (1996). 'On the relevance of learning and evolution to economic theory', *The Economic Journal*, 106 (438), 1374–1385.

Boyne, George A., Farrell, Catherine, Law, Jennifer, Powell, Martin and Walker, Richard M. (2003). *Evaluating Public Management Reform*. Buckingham: Open University Press.

Browne, Eric (1991). 'Coalition theory', in *Blackwell Encyclopedia of Political Science*. Oxford: Blackwell Publishers.

Bruun, Finn (1997). 'New public management: diskussionstemaer og spændinger', *Politica*, 29 (3), 237–243.

Buchanan, James M. and Tullock, Gordon (1965). *The Calculus of Consent*. Ann Arbor: The University of Michigan Press.

Camerer, Colin and Thaler, Richard (1995). 'Anomalies: ultimatums, dictators and manners', *The Journal of Economic Perspectives*, 9 (2), 209–219.

Christensen, Jørgen G. (2003a). 'Normer og incitamenter i offentlig virksomhed', *Distinktion*, 7, 91–103. Aarhus: Institut for Statskundskab.

Christensen, Jørgen G. (2003b). *Velfærdsstatens Institutioner*. Aarhus: Magtudredningen and Aarhus Universitetsforlag.

Christensen, Jørgen G. (2003c). 'Pay and perquisites for executives', in *Handbook of Public Administration*. London: Sage Publications.

Christensen, Tove, Pedersen, Anders B. and Nielsen, Helle Ø. (2007). 'Analyse af virkemidlers effektivitet i pesticidpolitikken. Notat fra projektet: EUs landbrugsordninger og pesticidpolitikken', København: FOI.

Coffey, Amanda and Atkinson, Paul (1996). *Making Sense of Qualitative Data – Complementary Research Strategies*. London: Sage Publications.

Cohen, J.W. (1988). *Statistical Power Analysis for the Behavioural Sciences*. Hillsdale, N.J.: Lawrence Erlsbaum Associates.

Conlisk, John (1996). 'Why bounded rationality?', *Journal of Economic Literature*, 34, 669–700.

Cosmides, Leda and Tooby, John (1994). 'Better than rational: evolutionary psychology and the invisible hand', *The American Economic Review*, 84 (2) 327–332. Papers and Proceedings of the Hundred and Sixth Annual Meeting of the American Economic Association.

Cyert, Richard M. and March, James G. (1992). *A Behavioural Theory of the Firm*. Cambridge: Blackwell Business.

Danish Environmental Protection Agency (2000). *Aquatic Environment 1999. State of the Danish Aquatic Environment*. Environmental Investigations No. 3, 2000. Copenhagen: Danish Environmental Protection Agency.

Danish Farmers' Unions (2002). *Agriculture in Denmark 2002*. Cophagen: Landboforeningerne.

Danmarks Miljøundersøgelser (DMU) and Danmarks Jordbrugsforskning (DJF) (2000). *Vandmiljøplan II: Midtvejsevaluering*. Miljøministeriet.

Denzau, Arthur T. and North, Douglass C. (2000). 'Shared mental models: ideologies and institutions', in Arthur Lupia, Mathew D. McCubbins, and Samuel L. Popkin (eds). *Elements of Reason. Cognition, Choice and the Bounds of Rationality*. Cambridge: Cambridge University Press.

Dequech, David (2001). 'Bounded rationality, uncertainty and Institutions', *Journal of Economic Issues*, XXXV (4), 911–929.

Douma, Sytse and Schreuder, Hein (1998). *Economic Approaches to Organizations*. London: Prentice Hall.

Downs, Anthony (1957). *An Economic Theory of Democracy*. New York: Harper and Row.

Dyner, Isaac and Franco, Carlos Jaime (2004). 'Consumers' bounded rationality: the case of competitive energy markets', *Systems Research and Behavioral Science*, 21, 373–389.

Eggertsson, Thrainn (1990). *Economic Behaviour and Institutions*. New York: Cambridge University Press.

Elster, Jon (1986). 'Introduction', in Jon Elster (ed.), *Rational Choice*. New York: New York University Press.

Enevoldsen, Martin (2005). *The Theory of Environmental Agreements and Taxes: CO_2 Policy Performance in Comparative Perspective*. Cheltenham: Edward Elgar Publishing.

European Environment Agency (2002). *Environmental Signals 2002. Benchmarking the Millennium*. Environmental Assessment Report No. 9. Copenhagen: EEA. Available at: www.eea.europa.eu /publications/environmental_assessment_report_2002_9 (accessed 1 September 2007).

European Environment Agency (2005). *Market-based Instruments for Environmental Policy in Europe*. EEA Technical Report No. 8/2005. Copenhagen: EEA. Available at: www.eea.europa.eu /publications/technical_report_2005_8 (accessed 3 May 2009).

Fehr, Ernst and Tyran, Jean-Robert (2005). 'Individual irrationality and aggregate outcomes', *Journal of Economic Perspectives*, 19(4), 43–66.

Ferejohn, John (1991). 'Rationality and interpretation', in K.R. Monroe, *The Economic Approach to Politics*. New York: HarperCollins.

Fiorina, M.P. (2001). 'Rational choice in politics', in *International Encyclopaedia of the Social and Behavioral Sciences*. Elsevier Science Ltd. Available at: www.sciencedirect.com (accessed 3 May 2009).

Fishburn, P. (2001). 'Utility and subjective probability: contemporary theories', in *International Encyclopaedia of the Social and Behavioural Sciences*. Elsevier Science Ltd. Available at:

www.sciencedirect.com (accessed 3 May 2009).

Flaherty, Karen and Pappas, James M. (2004). 'Job selection among sales people: a bounded rationality perspective', *Industrial Marketing Management*, 33, 325–332.

Foss, Nicolai J. (2001a). *From 'Thin' to 'Think' Bounded Rationality in the Economics of Organization: An Explorative Discussion*. Working Paper, revised draft 10, January 2001. Copenhagen: Copenhagen Business School.

Foss, Nicolai, J. (2001b). 'Simon's grand theme and the economics of organization', *Journal of Management and Governance*, 5, 216–223.

Fox, John (1991). *Regression Diagnostics*. No. 79 in the series, Quantitative Applications in the Social Sciences. London: Sage Publications.

Frey, B. and Oberholzer-Gee, F. (1997). 'The cost of price incentives: an empirical analysis of crowding-out', *American Economic Review*, 87, 746–755.

Friedman, J. (1996). 'Introduction: economic approaches to politics', in J. Friedman (ed.), *The Rational Choice Controversy*. New Haven: Yale University Press.

Friedman, Milton (1953). 'Introduction', in *Essays in Positive Economics*. Chicago: University of Chicago Press.

Friedrichs, Jürgen and Opp, Karl-Dieter (2002). 'Rational behaviour in everyday situations', *European Sociological Review*, 18 (4), 401–415.

Gertner, Jon (2003). 'The futile pursuit of happiness', *New York Times*, 7 September. Available at: www.nytimes.com/2003/09/07/magazine /the-futile-pursuit-of-happiness.html?sec=health (accessed 3 May 2009).

Gigerenzer, Gerd (1996). 'On narrow norms and vague heuristics: a reply to Kahneman and Tversky', *Psychological Review*, 103 (3), 592–596.

Gigerenzer, Gerd (2001). 'The adaptive toolbox', in G. Gigerenzer and R. Selten (eds) (2001), *Bounded Rationality – The Adaptive Toolbox*. Cambridge: MIT Press.

Gigerenzer, Gerd, Czerlinski, J., and Martignon, L. (1999). 'How good are fast and frugal heuristics?', in *Decision Science and Technology*, reprinted in T. Gilovich, D. Griffin and D. Kahneman (eds), (2002) *Heuristics and Biases: The Psychology of Intuitive Judgment*. New York: Cambridge University Press.

Gigerenzer, Gerd and Selten, Reinhard (2001). 'Rethinking rationality', in G. Gigerenzer and R. Selten (eds), *Bounded Rationality – The Adaptive Toolbox*. Cambridge: MIT Press.

Glaser, B.G. and Strauss, A. (1968). *The Discovery of Grounded Theory*. London: Weidenfeld and Nicholson.

Goldstein, William M. and Hogarth, Robin, M. (1997). 'Judgment and decision research: some historical context', in M. Goldstein and R.M. Hogarth (eds), *Research on Judgment and Decision-making*. New York: Cambridge University Press.

Goodrick, Elisabeth and Salancik, Gerald (1996). 'Organizational discretion in responding to institutional practices: hospitals and cesarian births', *Administrative Science Quarterly*, 41, 1–28.

Grant, Ruth, Blicher-Mathiesen, Gitte, Andersen, Hans E., Berg, Peter, Friberg, Nikolai, Kronvang, Brian, Bak, Jesper and Rasmussen, P. (1993). *Landovervågningsoplande. Vandmiljøplanens Overvågningsprogram 1992.* Danmarks Miljøundersøgelser, Faglig Rapport fra DMU Nr. 87.

Grant, Ruth, Blicher-Mathiesen, Gitte, Andersen, Hans E., Berg, Peter, Jensen, Pia G. and Laubel, Anker R. (1995). *Landovervågningsoplande. Vandmiljø-planens Overvågningsprogram 1994.* Danmarks Miljøundersøgelser, Faglig Rapport fra DMU Nr. 141.

Grant, Ruth, Jensen, Pia G., Andersen, Hans E., Laubel, Anker Rode, Deibjerg, Christian, Rasmussen, Henrik and Rasmussen, Per (1996). *Landovervågningsoplande. Vandmiljøplanens Overvågningsprogram 1995.* Danmarks Miljøundersøgelser, Faglig Rapport fra DMU Nr. 175.

Grant, Ruth, Blicher-Mathiesen, Gitte, Andersen, H.E., Laubel, Anker Rode, Jensen, Pia G. and Rasmussen, Per (1997). *Landovervågningsoplande. Vandmiljø-planens Overvågningsprogram 1996.* Danmarks Miljøundersøgelser, Faglig Rapport fra DMU Nr. 210.

Grant, Ruth, Blicher-Mathiesen, Gitte, Andersen, H.E., Laubel, Anker Rode, Paulsen, Irene, Jensen, Pia G. and Rasmussen, Per (1998). *Landovervågningsoplande. Vandmiljøplanens Overvågningsprogram 1997.* Danmarks Miljøunder-søgelser, Faglig Rapport fra DMU Nr. 252.

Grant, Ruth, Blicher-Mathiesen, Gitte, Jørgensen, Ole J., Kloppenborg-Skrumsager, Birgitte, Kronvang, Brian, Jensen, Pia G., Pedersen, Marianne and Rasmussen, Per (2000). *Landovervågningsoplande 1999. NOVA 2003.* Danmarks Miljøundersøgelser, Faglig Rapport fra DMU Nr. 334.

Grant, Ruth, Blicher-Mathiesen, Gitte, Paulsen, Irene, Jørgensen, Jørgen O., Laubel, Anker R., Jensen, Pia G., Pedersen, Marianne and Rasmussen, Per (2001). *Landovervågningsoplande 2000. NOVA 2003.* Danmarks Miljøundersøgelser, Faglig Rapport fra DMU Nr. 376. Available at: www.dmu.dk/Udgivelser/Faglige+rapporter/Nr.+100-199/ (accessed 3 May 2009).

Grant, Ruth, Blicher-Mathiesen, Gitte, Andersen, H.E., Jensen, Pia G., Pedersen, Marianne and Rasmussen, Per (2002). *Landovervågningsoplande 2001. NOVA 2003.* Danmarks Miljøundersøgelser,

Faglig Rapport fra DMU Nr. 420. Available at: www.dmu.dk /Udgivelser/Faglige+rapporter/Nr.+100-199/ (accessed 3 May 2009).

Grant, Ruth and Waagepetersen, Jesper (2003). *Vandmiljøplan II – slutevaluering*. December 1993. Danmarks Miljøundersøgelser.

Green, Donald P. and Shapiro, Ian (1994). *Pathologies of Rational Choice Theory*. New Haven: Yale University Press.

Gregory, Robert and Christensen, Jørgen G. (2004). 'Similar ends, differing means: contractualism and civil service reform in Denmark and New Zealand', *Governance: An International Journal of Policy, Administration and Institutions*, 17 (1), 59–82.

Gujarati, Damodar N. (2003). *Basic Econometrics*. New York: McGraw-Hill.

Haas, Reinhard and Schipper, L. (1998). 'Residential energy demand in OECD countries and the role of irreversible efficiency improvements', *Energy Economics*, 20, 421–442.

Hall, Peter A. and Taylor, Rosemary (1996). 'Political science and the three new institutionalisms', *Political Studies*, 44, 936–957.

Hansen, Ejvind (1990). 'Overgødskning med kvælstof i dansk landbrug', *Ugeskrift for jordbrug*, Hæfte 35–36, 567–569.

Hansen, Lars G. and Christensen, Jan (2000). *Incentive Regulation of Agricultural Nitrogen Loss: the Case of Danish Pig Farms*. Publication No. 38, Copenhagen: Institute of Local Government Studies.

Hansen, Trine Bille (1997). 'The willingness-to-pay for the Royal Theatre in Copenhagen as a public good', *Journal of Cultural Economics*, 21, 1–28.

Hardin, Garrett (1968). 'The tragedy of the commons', *Science*, 162 (December), 1243–8.

Hasler, Berit (1998). *Styring af Kvælstofanvendelsen i Landbruget*. Ph.d.-afhandling, Danmarks Miljøundersøgelser. Afdeling for Systemanalyse.

Hastie, R. (2001). 'Problems for judgment and decision making', *Annual Review of Psychology*, 52, 653–683.

Hellevik, Ottar (1977). *Forskningsmetode i sociologi og statsvitenskap*. Oslo: Universitetsforlaget.

Hood, Christopher (1991). 'A public management for all seasons?', *Public Administration*, 69, 3–19.

Jacobsen, Brian H. (1994). *Landmænds Beslutningsadfærd. Empirisk Undersøgelse af Landmænds Økonomiske Beslutninger på Kort, Mellemlangt og Langt Sigt*. Ph.d.-afhandling. København: Den Kgl. Veterinær- og Landbohøjskole.

Jones, Bryan (1999). 'Bounded rationality', *Annual Review of Political Science*, 2, 297–321.

Jones, Bryan (2001). *Politics and the Architecture of Choice: Bounded*

Rationality and Governance. Chicago: University of Chicago Press.

Jones, Bryan D. (2002). 'Bounded rationality and public Policy: Herbert A. Simon and the decisional foundation of collective choice', *Policy Sciences*, 35, 269–284.

Jones, Bryan D., Baumgartner, Frank R. and True, James L. (1996). 'The shape of change: punctuations and stability in U.S. budgeting, 1947–94', Paper presented at the Midwest Political Science Association, Chicago, Illinois.

Kahneman, Daniel (2002). *Maps of Bounded Rationality: A Perspective on Intuitive Judgment and Choice*, Nobel Prize Lecture, 8 December, in Stockholm. Available at: http://nobelprize.org/economics/laureates/2002/kahneman-lecture.html (accessed 3 December 2003).

Kahneman, Daniel, Slovic, Paul and Tversky, Amos (eds) (1982). *Judgement Under Uncertainty: Heuristics and Biases*. Cambridge: Cambridge University Press.

Kahneman, Daniel and Tversky, Amos (1979). 'Prospect theory: an analysis of decision under risk', *Econometrica*, 47, (2), 263–291.

Kahneman, Daniel and Tversky, Amos (1996). 'On the reality of cognitive illusions', *Psychological Review*, 103 (3), 582–591.

Kato, Junko (1996). 'Institutions and rationality in politics. Three varieties of neo-institutionalists', *British Journal of Political Science*, 26, (4), 553–582.

Kettl, Donald F. (1997). 'The global revolution in public management: driving themes, missing links', *Journal of Policy Analysis and Management*, 16 (3), 446–462.

King, Gary, Keohane, Robert O. and Verba, Sidney (1994). *Designing Social Inquiry: Scientific Inference in Qualitative Research*. Princeton, N.J.: Princeton University Press.

Klayman, Joshua, Soll, Jack, Gonzales-Vallejo, Claudia and Barlas, Sema (1999). 'Overconfidence: it depends on how, what and whom you ask', *Organizational Behavior and Human Decision Processes*, 79 (3), 216–247.

Knudsen, Leif (2000). *Faktuelle tal til den aktuelle miljødebat*. Available at: www.lr.dk/planteavl/informationsserier/nyheder/lpnyhed24miljoedebat bilag.htm (accessed 4 April 2005).

Kolstad, Charles D. (2000). *Environmental Economics*. Oxford: Oxford University Press.

Kreiner, Kristian and Augier, Mie (2005). 'Valg, vane og vision – en introduktion', in March, James, *Valg, Vane og Vision – Perspektiver på Aspiration og Adfærd*. Gylling: Forlaget Samfundslitteratur.

Kvale, Steinar (1988). 'The 1000 page question', *Phenomenology & Pedagogy*, 6, (2), 90–106, reprinted in Fog, Jette and Kvale, Steinar (eds) (1992), *Artikler om Interviews*. Aarhus: Center for Kvalitativ

Metodeudvikling, Aarhus Universitet.

Kvale, Steinar (1989). 'To validate is to question', in Kvale, S. (ed.), *Issues of Validity in Qualitative Research*, reprinted in Fog, Jette and Kvale, Steinar (eds) (1992), *Artikler om Interviews*. Aarhus: Center for Kvalitativ Metodeudvikling, Aarhus Universitet.

Kvale, Steinar (1992a). 'The qualitative research interview: a phenomenological and a hermeneutical mode of understanding', *Journal of Phenomenological Psychology*, 14(2), reprinted in Fog, Jette and Kvale, Steinar (eds) (1992), *Artikler om Interviews*. Aarhus: Center for Kvalitativ Metodeudvikling, Aarhus Universitet.

Kvale, Steinar (1992b). 'Om tolkning af kvalitative forskningsinterview', in Fog, Jette and Kvale, Steinar (eds) (1992), *Artikler om Interviews*. Aarhus: Center for Kvalitativ Metodeudvikling, Aarhus Universitet.

Landbrugsministeriet (1991). *Bæredygtigt Landbrug*. En teknisk redegørelse 1991. (Foreløbigt tryk). Landbrugsministeriet.

Landbrugsrådet (2004). *Agriculture in Denmark – Facts and Figures 2004*. Copenhagen: Danish Agriculture and Danish Agricultural Council.

Landbrugsrådet (2006). *Agriculture in Denmark – Facts and Figures 2006*. Copenhagen: Danish Agriculture and Danish Agricultural Council.

Landskontoret for planteavl (1996). Håndbog for planteavl 1996. Aarhus: Landbrugets Rådgivningscenter.

Larrick, Richard P. (1993). 'Motivational factors in decision theories: The role of self-protection', *Psychological Bulletin*, 113 (3), 440–450.

Leibenstein, Harvey (1966). 'Allocative efficiency vs. X-efficiency', *The American Economic Review*, 56 (3), 392–415.

Levi, Margaret, Cook, Karen S., O'Brien, Jodie A. and Faye, Howard (1990). 'Introduction: the limits of rationality', in Karen Cook and M. Levi (eds), *The Limits of Rationality*. Chicago: University of Chicago Press.

Lomborg, Bjørn (2000). *Note 4. Forudsætninger for regression*. Aarhus: Institut for Statskundskab.

Lupia, Arthur, McCubbins, Mathew and Popkin, Samuel (2000). 'Beyond rationality: reason and the study of politics', in A. Lupia, M. McCubbins and S. Popkin (eds), *Elements of Reason. Cognition, Choice and the Bounds of Rationality*. Cambridge: Cambridge University Press.

Madsen, E. Kloppenborg and Ölander, F. (2001). 'Rationality deficits in behavioural intervention strategies', in Suzanne Beckmann and Erik Kloppenborg Madsen (eds) *Environmental Regulation and Rationality*. Aarhus: Aarhus University Press.

March, James G. (1994). *A Primer on Decision-making: How Decisions*

Happen. New York: The Free Press.

March, James G. and Olsen, Johan P. (1984). 'The new institutionalism: organizational factors in political life', *American Political Science Review*, 78 (3), 734–749.

March, James G. and Olsen, Johan P. (1989). *Rediscovering Institutions.* New York: Free Press.

March, James G. and Olsen, Johan P. (1995). *Democratic Governance.* New York: Free Press.

March, James G. and Simon, Herbert A. (1958). *Organizations.* New York: John Wiley.

Marcus, George E. and MacKuen, M. (1993). 'Anxiety, enthusiasm and the vote: the emotional underpinnings of learning and involvement during presidential campaigns', *American Political Science Review*, 87 (3), 672–685.

McFadden, Daniel (1999). 'Rationality for economists?', *Journal of Risk and Uncertainty* 19 (1–3), 73–105.

Mejeriforeningen (2009). *International Mælepriser. Årspriser i Danske Kroner.* Available at: www.mejeri.dk/Årspriser_i_danske_kroner .aspx?ID=1019 (accessed 3 May 2009).

Miljø- og energiministeriet (1998). *Aftale Vedrørende Vandmiljøplan* II. 17. februar 1998. Available at: www.mem.dk/publikationer/vandplan /aftale_2.htm (accessed 3 May 2009).

Miljøstyrelsen (1984). *NPO-redegørelsen.* København: Miljøministeriet.

Miljøstyrelsen (1990). *Landbrugets Gødnings- og Arealanvendelse i 1983 og 1989. NPO-forskning fra Miljøstyrelsen, Nr. A21.* København: Miljøministeriet.

Miljøstyrelsen (1998). *Drikkevandsudvalgets Betænkning.* Betænkning Nr.1 1998 fra Miljøstyrelsen. København: Miljø- og Energiministeriet.

Miljøstyrelsen (1999). *Kvælstofanvendelsen i Dansk Landbrug – Økonomi og Kvælstofudvaskning.* København: Miljø- og Energiministeriet.

Miljøstyrelsen (2003). *Grøn Markedsøkonomi – Mere Miljø for Pengene. Baggrund og Status.* Arbejdsrapport fra Miljøstyrelsen, Nr. 17, 2003. København: Miljøstyrelsen.

Miljøstyrelsen (2004). *Økonomiske Virkemidler på Natur- og Miljøområdet.* Miljøprojekt Nr. 887 2004: København: Miljøstyrelsen.

Ministeriet for Fødevarer, Landbrug og Fiskeri (1998). Landbrugets Strukturudvikling. Betænkning fra Udvalget vedrørende landbrugets strukturudvikling (1998). Betænkning Nr. 1351.

Moe, Terry M. (1979). 'On the scientific status of rational models', *American Journal of Political Science*, 23, (1), 215–243.

Monroe, Kristen Renwick (1991a). 'The theory of rational action: origins and usefulness for political science', in Monroe, K.R. (ed.), *The Economic Approaches to Politics: A Critical Reassessment of the Theory of Rational Action*. New York: HarperCollins.

Monroe, Kristen Renwick (ed.) (1991b). *The Economic Approach to Politics: A Critical Reassessment of the Theory of Rational Action*. New York: HarperCollins.

Monroe, Kristen Renwick, Barton, Michael C. and Klingemann, Ute (1991). 'Altruism and the theory of rational action. An analysis of rescuers of Jews in Nazi Europe', in Monroe, K.R. (ed.), *The Economic Approaches to Politics: A Critical Reassessment of the Theory of Rational Action*. New York: HarperCollins.

Mueller, Dennis C. (1997). 'Public choice in perspective', in Dennis C. Mueller (ed.), *Perspectives on Public Choice – A Handbook*. Cambridge: Cambridge University Press.

Mueller, Dennis C. (2003). *Public Choice III*. Cambridge: Cambridge University Press.

Mullainathan, Sendhil and Thaler, Richard H. (2000). *Behavioural Economics*. Working Paper 7948. Cambridge: National Bureau of Economic Research.

Nannestad, Peter (1991). 'Rational Choice Teori og Studiet af Økonomisk Politik – en Oversigt', *Politica*, 23 (4), 418–430.

Nardulli, Peter (1995). 'The concept of a critical re-alignment, electoral behaviors and political change', *American Political Science Review*, 89, 10–22.

National Agency of Environmental Protection (1984). *The NPO Report*. Copenhagen: National Agency of Environmental Protection.

Newell, Allan and Simon, Herbert A. (1972). *Human Problem Solving*. Englewood Cliffs, N.J.: Prentice-Hall.

Newell, Ben R., Weston, Nichola J. and Shanks, David R. (2003). 'Empirical tests of a fast-and-frugal heuristic: not everyone "takes-the-best"', *Organizational Behavior and Human Decision Processes*, 91, 82–96.

Niskanen, William (1971). 'Bureacracy and representative government', reprinted in Niskanen, William A. (1994), *Bureaucracy and Public Economics*. Cheltenham: Edward Elgar.

Noe, Egon (1998). *Værdier, rationalitet og landbrugsproduktion. Belyst ved en microsociologisk undersøgelse blandt danske økologiske og konventionelle kvægbrugere*. Kooperativ forskning: Notat 38/98. Esbjerg: Sydjysk Universitetscenter.

North, Douglass (1989). 'A transaction cost approach to the historical development of polities and economies', *Journals of Institutional and Theoretical Economics*, 145, 661–668.

North, Douglass (1990). *Institutions, Institutional Change and Economic Perfor-mance*. Cambridge: Cambridge University Press.

North, Douglass (1993). 'What do we mean by rationality?', *Public Choice*, 77, 159–162.

Næss, Arne (1980). *Vitenskapsfilosofi*. Oslo: Universitetsforlaget.

Nørgaard, Asbjørn Sonne (1996). 'Rediscovering reasonable rationality in institutional analysis', *European Journal of Political Research*, 29, 31–57.

Oatley, K. (2001). 'Emotion in cognition', *International Encyclopedia of the Social and Behavioral Sciences*. Elsevier Science Ltd. Available at: www.sciencedirect.com (accessed 3 May 2009).

OECD (1995). *Governance in Transition: Public Management Reforms in OECD Countries*. Paris: OECD.

OECD (2001). *Environmentally Related Taxes in OECD Countries – Issues and Strategies*. Paris: OECD.

OECD (2003). 'Public Sector Modernisation'. *OECD Policy Brief*, October 2003. Available at: www.oecd.org (accessed 3 May 2009).

OECD (2005). 'Paying for Performance: Policies for Government Employees', *OECD Policy Brief*, May 2005. Available at: www.oecd.org (accessed 3 May 2009).

Öhlmér, Bo, Olson, Kent and Brehmer, Berndt (1998). 'Understanding farmers' decision-making processes and improving managerial assistance', *Agricultural Economics*, 18, 273–290.

Olsen, Henning (2002). *Kvalitative kvaler. Kvalitative metoder og danske kvalitative undersøgelsers kvalitet*. København: Akademisk Forlag.

Olson, Mancur (1965). *The Logic of Collective Action*. Cambridge: Harvard University Press.

Opp, Karl-Dieter (1999). 'Contending conceptions of the theory of political action', *Journal of Theoretical Politics*, 11 (2), 171–202.

Ostrom, Elinor (1991). 'Rational choice theory and institutional analysis: toward complementarity', *American Political Science Review*, 85 (1), 237–243.

Ostrom, Elinor (1998). 'A behavioural approach to the rational choice theory of collective action', Presidential address, American Political Science Association 1997. Printed in *The American Political Science Review*, 92 (1), 1–22.

Padget, John F. (1980). 'Bounded rationality in budgetary research', *The American Political Science Review*, 74 (2), 354–372.

Pallant, Julie (2001). *SPSS Survival Manual, SPSS for Windows Up to Version 11*. Berkshire: Open University Press.

Pallesen, Thomas (1997). 'De Danske og Engelske sundhedsreformer: en test af New Public Management-bølgens indhold og betydning',

Politica, 29 (3), 279–294.

Payne, John W., Bettman, James R. and Johnson, Eric J. (1993). *The Adaptive Decision Maker*. New York: Cambridge University Press.

Payne, John W., Bettman, James R. and Johnson, Eric J. (1997). 'The adaptive decision maker: effort and accuracy in choice', in William M. Goldstein and Robin H. Hogarth (eds), *Research on Judgment and Decision Making: Currents, Connections and Controversies*. New York: Cambridge University Press.

Payne, John W., Schkade, D.A., Desvousges, W.H. and Aultman, C. (2000). 'Valuation of multiple environmental programs', *Journal of Risk and Uncertainty*, 21, 95–115.

Pellikaan, Huib and van der Veen, Robert (2002). *Environmental Dilemmas and Policy Design*. Cambridge: Cambridge University Press.

Peters, B. Guy (1996). 'Political institutions, old and new', in R. Goodin and Hans Peter Klingemann (eds), *A New Handbook of Political Science*. Oxford: Oxford University Press.

Peters, B. Guy (1999). *Institutional Theory in Political Science – The New 'Institutionalism'*. London: Pinter.

Picavet, E. (2001). 'Methodological individualism in sociology', in *International Encyclopedia of the Social and Behavioral Sciences*. Elsevier Science Ltd. Available at: www.sciencedirect.com (accessed 3 May 2009).

Porter, Michael E. and van der Linde, Claas (1995). 'Toward a new conception of the environment–competitiveness relationship', *The Journal of Economic Perspectives*, 9 (4), 97–118.

Redlawsk, D. and Humphrey, Jason (2002). 'What voters do: the implications of voter information search strategies', Paper presented at the Annual Meeting of the Midwest Political Science Association, Chicago, Illinois.

Redlawsk, David and Lau, Richard R. (2003). 'When rational choice works and when it doesn't', Paper presented at the Annual Meeting of the American Political Science Association.

Riker, William H. (1962). *The Theory of Political Coalitions*, cited in Mueller, Dennis C. (2003), *Public Choice III*. New York: Cambridge University Press.

Rothstein, B. (1996). 'Political institutions: an overview', in R. Goodin and Hans Peter Klingemann (eds) *A New Handbook of Political Science*. Oxford: Oxford University Press.

Rude, Søren and Frederiksen, Boie S. (1994). *National and EC Nitrate Policies – Agricultural Aspects for 7 EC Countries*. Statens Jordbrugsøkonomiske Institut Rapport Nr. 77. Copenhagen: Landbrugsministeriet.

Schwarz, N. and Bless, H. (1991). 'Happy and mindless, but sad and smart? The impact of affective states on analytic reasoning', cited in Oatley, K. (2001), 'Emotion in cognition'. *International Encyclopedia of the Social and Behavioral Sciences*. Elsevier Science Ltd. Available at: www.sciencedirect.com (accessed 3 May 2009).

Selten, R. (2001). 'What is bounded rationality?', in *Bounded Rationality: The Adaptive Toolbox*. Cambridge, MA: MIT Press.

Sen, Amartya (1977). 'Rational fools: a critique of the behavioural foundations of economic theory', *Philosophy and Public Affairs*, 6 (4), 317–344.

Sen, Amartya (1986). 'Behaviour and the concept of preference', in Jon Elster (ed.), *Rational Choice*. New York: New York University Press.

Sen, Amartya (1987). 'Rational behaviour', J. in Eatwell, M. Milgate, M., and P. Newman (eds), *The New Palgrave: Utility and Probability*. London: Macmillan.

Shafir, Eldar and LeBoeuf, Robyn A. (2002). 'Rationality', *Annual Review of Psychology*, 53, 491–517.

Shefrin, Hersh (2002). *Beyond Greed and Fear. Understanding Behavioural Finance and the Psychology of Investing*. New York: Oxford University Press.

Simon, Herbert A. (1955). 'A behavioural model of rational choice', *Quarterly Journal of Economics*, 69, 99–118.

Simon, Herbert A. (1976). *Administrative Behaviour. A Study of Decision-Making Processes in Administrative Organizations*. New York: The Free Press.

Simon, Herbert A. (1978). 'Rational decision-making in business organizations', *Nobel Memorial Lecture*, 8 December; reprinted in *Economic Sciences*, 344–371. Available at: http://nobelprize.org /nobel_prizes/economics/laureates/1978/simon-lecture.pdf (accessed 4December 2003).

Simon, Herbert A. (1985). 'Human nature in politics: the dialogue of psychology with political science', *The American Political Science Review*, 79 (2), 293–304.

Simon, Herbert A. (1990). 'Invariants of human behaviour', in M. Rosenzweig and L. Porter (eds), *Annual Review of Psychology*, 41, 1–19.

Simon, Herbert A. (1993a). 'Altruism and economics', *The American Economic Review*, 83 (2), 156–161. Papers and Proceedings of the Hundred and Fifth Annual Meeting of the American Economic Association.

Simon, Herbert A. (1993b). 'The state of American political science: Professor Lowi's view of our discipline', *PS: Political Science and Politics*, 26 (1), 49–51.

Simon, Herbert A. (1995). 'Rationality in political behaviour', *Political Psychology*, 16, 45–61.

Simon, Herbert A. (1997). *Models of Bounded Rationality: Empirically Grounded Economic Reason*. Cambridge: MIT Press.

Simon, Herbert A. (1997a). 'Rationality in psychology and economics', in *Models of Bounded Rationality: Volume 3: Empirically Grounded Economic Reason*. Cambridge: MIT Press.

Simon, Herbert A. (1997b). 'Methodological foundations of economics', in *Models of Bounded Rationality: Volume 3: Empirically Grounded Economic Reason*. Cambridge: MIT Press.

Simon, Herbert A. (2001). 'Rationality in society', *International Encyclopedia of the Social and Behavioral Sciences*. Elsevier Science Ltd. Available at: www.sciencedirect.com (accessed 3 May 2009).

Sivak, Michael (2002). 'How common sense fails us on the road: contribution of bounded rationality to the annual worldwide toll of one million traffic fatalities', *Transportation Research* Part F5, 259–269.

Smith, Vernon L. (1998). 'The two faces of Adam Smith', *Southern Economic Journal*, 65 (1), 1–19.

Smith, Vernon L. (2002). 'Constructivist and ecological rationality in economics', *Nobel Prize Lecture*, 8 December in Stockholm. Available at: www.nobel.se/economics/laureates/2002/smith-lecture.html (accessed 4 December 2003).

Speck, Stefan, Andersen, Mikael Skou, Nielsen, Helle Ørsted, Ryelund, Anders and Smith, Carey (2006). *The Use of Economic Instruments in Nordic and Baltic Environmental Policy 2001–2005. TemaNord 2006:525*. Copenhagen: Nordic Council of Ministers.

Sprenger, R.-U. (2000). 'Introduction', in M.S. Anderson and R.-U. Sprenger (eds), *Market-based Instruments for Environmental Management*. Cheltenham: Edward Elgar.

Steinmo, S. (2001). 'Institutionalism', in *International Encyclopedia of the Social and Behavioral Sciences*. Elsevier Science Ltd. Available at: www.sciencedirect.com (accessed 3 May 2009).

Strack, F. (2001). 'Heuristics in social cognition', in *International Encyclopedia of the Social and Behavioral Sciences*. Elsevier Science Ltd. Available at: www.sciencedirect.com (accessed 3 May 2009).

Thaler, Richard H. (1992). *The Winner's Curse. Paradoxes and Anomalies in Economic Life*. Princeton: Princeton University Press.

Thaler, Richard H., Kahneman, Daniel and Knetsch, Jack L. (1992). 'The endowment effect, loss aversion, and status quo bias', in Richard H. Thaler (ed.), *The Winner's Curse*. Princeton: Princeton University Press.

Thomsen, Søren Risbjerg (1997). *Om Anvendelse af Signifikanstest i Ikke-Stikprøve Situationer*. Institut for Statskundskab, Aarhus Universitet.

Thøgersen, John (1990). *A Behavioural Science Framework for Source Separation*. The Aarhus School of Business, Working Paper No. 20.

Thøgersen, John and Gärling, T. (2001). 'When choice of means undermines the goals: rationality from a psychological perspective', in Sizanne Beckmann and Erik K. Madsen (eds), *Environmental Regulation and Rationality*, Aarhus: University of Aarhus Press.

Tietenberg, T.H. (1990). 'Economic instruments for environmental regulation', *Oxford Review of Economic Policy*, 6 (1), 17–33.

Todd, Peter M. (2001): 'Heuristics for decision and choice', *International Encyclopedia of the Social and Behavioral Sciences*. Elsevier Science Ltd. Available at: www.sciencedirect.com (accessed 3 May 2009).

Todd, Peter M. and Gigerenzer, Gerd (2003). 'Bounding rationality to the world', *Journal of Economic Psychology*, 24, 143–165.

Trivers, Robert L. (1971). 'The evolution of reciprocal altruism', *The Quarterly Review of Biology* , 46, 35–57.

Tversky, Amos and Kahneman, Daniel (1974). 'Judgment under uncertainty: heuristics and biases', *Science*, 185, 1124–1131.

Tversky, Amos and Kahneman, Daniel (1986). 'Rational choice and the framing of decisions', *The Journal of Business*, 59 (4/2), S251–S278.

van den Bergh, Jeroen (2003). 'Bounded rationality and environmental policy', entry prepared for the *Internet Encyclopedia of Ecological Economics*. Amsterdam: Free University. Available at: www.ecoeco.org/publica/encyc/alttheories.pdf (accessed 3 May 2009).

van den Bergh, Jeroen C.J.M., Ferrer-i-Carbonell, Ada, and Munda, Guiseppe (2000). 'Alternative models of individual behaviour and implications for environmental policy', *Ecological Economics*, 32, 43–61.

von Weizsäcker, Ernst U. and Jesinghaus, J. (1992). *Ecological Tax Reform: A Policy Proposal for Sustainable Development*. London: Zed Books.

Walsh, Kieron (1995). *Public Services and Market Mechanisms: Competition, Contracting, and New Public Management*. New York: St Martin's Press.

Wengraf, Tom (2001). *Qualitative Research Interviewing*. London: Sage Publications.

Whitehead, Jaan W. (1991). 'The forgotten limits: reason and regulation in economic theory', in K.R. Monroe (ed.), *The Economic Approach to Politics*. New York: HarperCollins.

Wildawsky, Aaron (1994). 'Why self-interest means less outside of a social context. Cultural contributions to a theory of rational choices', *Journal of Theoretical Politics*, 6 (2), 131–159.

Wilson, James Q. (1989). *Bureaucracy: What Government Agencies Do and Why They Do It*. United States of America: Basic Books.

Williamson, Oliver E. (1997). 'Transaction cost economics and public administration', in Boorsma, P.B. *et al.* (eds), *Public Priority Setting: Rules and Costs*. Netherlands: Kluwer Academic Publishers.

Yee, Albert (1997). 'Thick rationality and the missing brute fact: the limits of rationalist incorporations of norms and ideas', *The Journal of Politics* , 59 (4), 1001–1039.

Yin, Robert K. (1989). *Case Study Research: Design and Methods*. Newbury Park, CA: Sage Publications.

Other references

Legislation

Bekendtgørelse nr. 469 af 3. august 1988 om sædskifte- og gødnings-planer samt grønne marker i jordbruget.

Bekendtgørelse nr. 1095 af 10/12/1992 om grønne marker, sædskifte- og gødningsplaner samt gødningsregnskaber i jordbruget.

Bekendtgørelse nr. 655 af 13/08/1993 om behov for tilførsel af kvælstof og indhold af kvælstof i husdyrgødning.

Bekendtgørelse nr. 662 af 12. juli, 1994 om behov for tilførsel af kvæl-stof og indhold af kvælstof i husdyrgødning.

Bekendtgørelse nr. 624 af 15. juli 1997 om jordbrugets anvendelse af gødning.

Bekendtgørelse nr. 523 af 8. juli 1998 om jordbrugets anvendelse af gødning og om plantedække.

Bekendtgørelse nr. 814 af 13. juli 2006 om erhvervsmæssigt dyrehold, husdyrgødning, ensilage m.v.

Council Directive 80/778/EEC of 15 July 1980 relating to the quality of water intended for human consumption.

Council Directive 91/676/EEC of 12 December 1991 concerning the protection of waters against pollution caused by nitrates from agri-cultural sources (Nitrate Directive).

Documents

DMU (2000/2001). Vejledning til interviewundersøgelsen.

DMU, Department of Freshwater Ecoology (FEVØ). Description of LOOP data, meeting document, 6 December, 2004.

Plantedirektoratet (2004). Vejledning og skemaer. Gødningsplan-lægning, gødningsregnskab, plantedække, harmoniregler, ændringer i ejer- og brugerforhold, 2004/2005.

Statistics

Danmarks Statistik (1971). 10–årsoversigten.

Danmarks Statistik (1989). 10–årsoversigten.

Danmarks Statistik (1990–91). Landbrugsstatistik.

Danmarks Statistik (2000). NYT fra Danmarks Statistik, landbrugs- og gartneritællingen 7. maj 1999, nr. 161 – 17.4.2000.

Danmarks Statistik (2002). Landbrug 2002.

Danmarks Statistik (2003a). 10–årsoversigten.

Danmarks Statistik (2003) NYT fra Danmarks Statistik, landbrugs- og gartneritællingen 3. maj 2002, nr. 80 21. februar 2003.

Danmarks Statistik (2003b). Landbrug 2003.

Danmarks Statistik (2004). Miljø 2004.

Danmarks Statistik (Documentation). Varedeklaration: Landbrugs- og gartneritællingen. Available at: www.dst.dk/Vejviser/dokumentation/varedeklarationer/emnegruppe/emne.aspx?sysrid=8/1 (accessed 3 May 2009).

Eurostat livestock density index, Eurofarm database. Available at: http://epp.eurostat.ec.eurorap.eu/portal (accessed 15 September 2007).

Knudsen, Leif (2000). 'Faktuelle tal til den aktuelle miljødebat'. Available at: www.lr.dk/planteavl/informationsserier/nyheder/lpnyhed24miljoedebat-bilag.htm, (accessed 3 May 2009).

Statistics Denmark. Statistikbanken. Landbrug. Available at: www.statistikbanken.dk/statbank5a/default.asp?w=1280 (accessed 3 May 2009).

Index